DISMANTLING DEMOCRACY

The Multilateral Agreement on Investment (MAI) and Its Impact

Edited by Andrew Jackson and Matthew Sanger

co-published by

Canadian Centre for Policy Alternatives, and
James Lorimer & Company Ltd.

1998

Canadian Cataloguing in Publication Data

Main entry under title:

Dismantling democracy

ISBN 1-55028-614-5
Co-published by The Canadian Centre for Policy Alternatives.
Includes bibliographical references.

1. Investments, Foreign -- Social aspects -- Canada. 2. Investments, Foreign -- Canada. 3. Investments, foreign -- Social aspects. 4. Investments, Foreign. I. Jackson, Andrew. II. Sanger, Matthew. III. Canadian Centre for Policy Alternatives.

HG4538.D57 1998 332.6'73'0971 C98-950087-X

Printed and bound in Canada

Co-published by

The Canadian Centre for Policy Alternatives
804-251 Laurier Avenue West
Ottawa, Ontario K1P 5J6

James Lorimer & Company Ltd., Publishers
35 Britain Street
Toronto, Ontario M5A 1R7

CAW 567 OTTAWA

DISMANTLING DEMOCRACY

Andrew Jackson and Matthew Sanger, editors

Table of Contents

IV. Political Economy of the MAI

Appendices

FOREWORD

by Bob White
President, Canadian Labour Congress

What the MAI Means for Canadians

The Multilateral Agreement on Investment (MAI) now being negotiated by Canada and the other wealthy industrial countries has accurately been described as a "charter of rights for transnational corporations" which will limit the role of democratic governments in important ways.

The MAI would make it difficult to maintain Medicare and not-for-profit public and social services. It would make it harder to review foreign takeovers and new foreign investments to make sure that they create jobs and economic activity here in Canada. It could limit the ability of our governments to give more support to Canadian-based business, or to favour Canadian artists and culture. It may make it impossible to keep natural resources, like our fisheries, in Canadian hands.

The MAI gives rights to investors and corporations but requires little or nothing in return. It puts few, if any, real obligations on corporations to create jobs, respect workers' rights or protect the environment. Corporations will have the right to launch expensive challenges, and demand compensation for government policies in front of international disputes panels. These panels will be non-elected and inaccessible; they will care only about narrow investment issues, not broader social goals.

The MAI does nothing about the real problems facing Canadians: loss in social benefits, unemployment, poverty, inequality.

The government promises we will all benefit from more investment here and overseas. But, after the FTA and NAFTA, there was an explosion of investment by Canadian businesses investing outside the country. That meant lost jobs, reduced collective bargaining gains, and a loss of social benefits. Those who stand to benefit from the MAI are companies who want to export investment and Canadian jobs.

Through the MAI, rich countries are making the rules for the developing world. Wealthy industrialized countries in the OECD are home to the corporations exporting investment capital to developing nations. They're writing the MAI to benefit themselves. The developing countries should have the power to put limits on foreign investment, to develop strong social programs, and environmental regulations. Canada was able to do this in the early years of our country—-and this still benefits us today. Developing nations should have the same chance to make sure investment leads to economic and social development.

Public and social services are threatened as well. Under the MAI, foreign corporations could claim that government grants to non-profit health or social services groups discriminate against U.S. health care and nursing home operators. Corporations will take complaints to trade panels and demand these fields be opened.

The Canadian government says "reservations" or "exemptions" like the ones under NAFTA will protect us. So far Canada has filed scores of reservations, but the NAFTA protections are very weak and there is no guarantee that reservations will not be traded-off or be subject to further reductions.

The MAI may tie the hands of governments in job creation. Many Canadian governments give subsidies, tax breaks and other support to Canadian companies to support jobs, training, research and development. The MAI calls this "discrimination" against foreign investors and would stop it. The MAI may even go further and prohibit government rules that say companies receiving public dollars must create jobs in return. Even NAFTA preserved our right to make corporations provide benefits in exchange for public dollars.

The MAI makes foreign takeovers easier. Even NAFTA allows the federal government to review large foreign corporate takeovers to make sure they benefit Canadians. The MAI could go beyond NAFTA, preventing governments from making sure takeovers or foreign investment create jobs. Foreign investors may no longer be required to source services in Canada.

The MAI threatens our control of resources. Foreign corporations could use the MAI to challenge the preferential access the governments give to Canadians in our fisheries, forests, and energy, and resource sectors. They could challenge programs like the B.C. Timber Accord, which requires corporations to process resources in Canada and create jobs here.

The MAI gives new rights to foreign corporations. The MAI makes Canadian governments liable to damages for actions which foreign investors see as "unreasonable and discriminatory" or as "expropriation" of expected profits. Corporations and investors could challenge government actions like toxic waste clean-up orders, new mining regulations, new programs like a national childcare program or a drug plan. It will cost governments money to defend their policies, and they could have to pay millions in damages to affected corporate interests.

The MAI undercuts Canadian culture. The basic MAI principle is that governments can't "discriminate" in favour of Canadians. This could rule out Canadian-content provisions and most other support for Canadian-based books publishing, film-making, writers and artists. The government promises that culture will be exempt, but the NAFTA exemption has proved to be little or no protection against challenge from U.S. corporations.

Even NAFTA could be abrogated. But, if the MAI is signed, we wouldn't be able to get out of the agreement for 20 years.

The Canadian Labour Congress has been working since last year at the national level, with both the NDP and with over 40 organizations in a Working Group on the MAI. Many members, like the Council of Canadians, are familiar allies from other struggles. Some are new partners, drawn in by the scope of this new investment deal. We are having an effect. Forty percent of Canadians are now aware of the MAI and oppose it.

The federal government has shifted its public stance, promising to protect Canadian culture, and public and social services, and to promote labour and environmental rights. Even the Liberal majority on a Parliamentary Committee was forced to recognize that the MAI posed many dangers. At the provincial level, the Yukon, B.C., and P.E.I. legislatures have all passed anti-MAI resolutions. Many municipalities are doing the same. Opposition to the MAI has also been growing rapidly in the U.S. and in Europe as information about these previously highly secretive negotiations has spread.

As of late March 1998, it looked as though the MAI would not be concluded quickly because of growing opposition, and because even the governments most closely involved have been forced to acknowledge key concerns. The MAI can be stopped. Even if it goes forward, it will likely be significantly changed.

Minister Sergio Marchi has called for an "informed" Canadian debate on the MAI, implying that many public criticisms are unfounded. The contributions to this book made it clear that there are very serious and legitimate concerns which will have to be addressed.

Progressive critics of the MAI know that we live in a "new global economy" which requires international rules if it is to work. But our starting point would be a very different one.

If we are to have an international investment agreement, it must be one which balances the interests of corporations with those of citizens and workers. We need international rules which require corporations to respect basic labour rights, and we need an international framework to stop corporations form playing one country off against another when it comes to taxation, and environmental and health and safety standards.

The CLC has strongly opposed the MAI, and we have worked with other labour movements around the world to expose this agreement. In the labour rights area, the Trade Union Advisory Committee to the OECD of which I am President has been pushing for an obligation on all MAI signatories to respect core labour rights and not to lower labour rights or environmental standards in order to attract an investment. We need to develop an alternative vision for the international system in other areas as well.

This book documents the case against the MAI, and explores some alternatives. It will be an essential tool for activists in the ongoing debate over how to govern the so-called "new global economy."

THE MAI. WHAT IS IT ?

by Andrew Jackson

THE NEGOTIATING PROCESS AND THE BASIC NATURE OF THE AGREEMENT

Over the past decade and more, foreign direct investment and short-term capital flows between countries have become the key driving force behind global economic integration, a more powerful force than even international trade. Total foreign production by affiliates of transnational corporations (TNCs) is now greater than total global exports, and foreign investment continues to grow faster than foreign trade.

Transnational corporations operate world-wide, even if they still largely remain headquartered and owned in one of the advanced industrial countries. The MAI is intended to create a set of rules to deal with this reality, a set of rules intended to complement the trade rules of the World Trade Organization (WTO). But the point of departure is very much designing rules to limit the power of governments to regulate, rather than designing rules to limit the power of TNCs and investors.

The Multilateral Agreement on Investment (MAI) has been under negotiation by the 29 member countries of the Organization for Economic Co-operation and Development (OECD) in Paris for the past three years. (The OECD includes all of the advanced industrial countries, and a handful of recent new members such as Mexico and South Korea.) It had been originally expected that the agreement would be concluded for ratification at the May, 1997 OECD Ministerial Council meeting, following two years of negotiations. However, the deadline was extended to May, 1998 and a final agreement will likely be further delayed. The long delay is due to the formidable technical as well as political obstacles which stand in the way of concluding this highly ambitious and profoundly far-reaching agreement.

Once concluded, the MAI would become a "free-standing" international agreement open to accession by non-OECD members. It would have a permanent institutional apparatus, run by a "parties' group" and would complement the WTO, the International Monetary Fund (IMF) and the World Bank as major governing bodies of the global economy.

The MAI, we are told by governments, is being negotiated to remedy the weaknesses of the WTO agreement with respect to investment issues. The basic intent is to prohibit all "discrimination" against foreign investors through the key principle of national treatment, and to make government decisions to regulate, control or "expropriate" foreign investment subject to binding appeals by foreign governments, as well as by foreign investors and companies.

Corporate lobby groups and the U.S. and the other major industrial countries where large TNCs are based have long pushed for GATT/WTO rules to limit the ability of governments receiving foreign investment to impose performance requirements, such as achieving a certain level of domestic content or export sales, or to transfer technology. They have also pushed for an opening of closed or regulated national markets to foreign investment.

Some of these objectives have been achieved through the "structural reform" programs imposed on heavily indebted developing countries by the IMF and the World Bank. The GATT system itself has only slowly and in a limited fashion begun to limit states' rights to regulate foreign investment.

The 1993 GATT/WTO agreement widened access in services to some degree (the GATS), and certain Trade-Related Investment Measures (TRIMS) were prohibited (e.g., requirements for local sourcing or export balancing). However, in the view of TNCs and many governments, this still leaves ample scope for restricting access to foreign investors and to negotiation of a wide series of performance requirements not directly related to trade.

Transnational corporations are also still concerned that governments can and do expropriate their assets, either directly or indirectly by regulatory changes. The proposed MAI builds on the North American Free Trade Agreement (NAFTA), and the treaties which have created the European Union, both of which are much more than "free trade" agreements and have extensive "WTO-plus" provisions regarding national treatment for investors and companies. It also builds on and is intended to replace the hundreds of investment treaties which have been negotiated between individual countries.

Notwithstanding its importance, it was only in 1997 that the MAI negotiations and the issues being considered by governments became public and subject to widespread and detailed scrutiny and criticism. Indeed, the draft MAI text was only made public in mid-1997 after it had been "leaked" and critically analyzed by non-governmental organizations (NGOs). It immediately became clear that the MAI, as drafted, could give TNCs and investors important new powers with which to challenge government policies and actions, and could significantly limit the ability of governments to regulate investment and corporate behaviour in the public interest. It was charged, with considerable reason, that the MAI draft amounted to nothing less than a charter for "global corporate rule" which would profoundly undercut democracy.

Major concerns over the thrust of the MAI have been raised by environmental organizations, trade unions, social justice organizations, and groups concerned with international development issues. Here in Canada, public criticism has been particularly intense, in large part because of Canadian experience with the Canada-U.S. Free Trade Agreement and NAFTA, which were the first major international agreements to address investment as opposed to narrow trade issues.

Due to mounting public pressure, a Parliamentary Committee held public hearings on the MAI in the fall of 1997, and the report of the Liberal majority validated many of the detailed criticisms, while unfortunately supporting continuing Canadian participation in the negotiations. Debate and criticism have been more muted in other countries, though international networks of NGOs and trade unions have been actively engaged in raising public awareness and concern around the world.

The most general grounds for concern over the MAI are that it establishes unnecessary and inappropriate barriers to achieving key social and economic objectives by ruling out various actions on the part of governments. The MAI limits the right of governments to act in a broad and still undefined range of policy areas, limiting our collective ability to define and reach goals which conflict with the narrow interests of corporations and investors. The MAI provides rights to investors and TNCs without providing appropriate counterbalances that would allow other parts of society to protect themselves against their decisions and actions.

Even if the MAI includes the labour and environmental clauses that have been proposed, it will still have the effect of freeing highly mobile capital from national legal constraints. Experience shows that it is too easy for "liberated" capital to pit governments and people against each other, thus undermining living standards and destabilizing communities at the national and local levels.

As the British Columbia government has argued:

> *"In the absence of effective and truly democratic international institutions, national governments must continue to play a central role in integrating the sometimes competing values of equity and economic efficiency, sustainability and growth... Canada should promote multilateral investment rules that clearly respect this central role of democratically elected governments...The proposed Agreement falls short. It tips the balance too far in favour of foreign investment protection. And it could significantly weaken the ability of governments to balance investor protection with other legitimate policy goals and interests, including protecting workers, consumers and the environment."*

The MAI is fundamentally unbalanced, intended to free capital from national restraints rather than to create new, positive rules which would make international capital accountable. However, the draft MAI does contain some—admittedly weak— provisions which are supposed to make it more balanced by speaking to the need to protect environmental and labour standards. The submissions to this volume by Roy Jones and Michelle Swenarchuk speak to these issues.

There is clearly a need to challenge the draft MAI on a number of fronts, but critics will also have to reflect on one of the thornier questions thrown up by the proposed agreement. Given the greatly increased investment flows between countries and the growing weight and influence of transnational corporations, is there a need for some agreed rules of the game? Clearly the MAI is overwhelmingly a "liberalizing" agreement, designed to dismantle regulations rather than to re-regulate at an international level.

There are some issues, however, which do need to be discussed—such as how to limit the ability of TNCs to play governments off against one another when it comes to seeking subsidies and tax breaks, and when it comes to demanding a relaxation of labour, environmental and other standards. A different kind of international agreement could address these issues. The debate over the MAI should spark off a broader debate about what kinds of international institutions are needed to regulate the "new global economy."

BASIC ELEMENTS OF THE MAI

The MAI, as proposed by the OECD Ministerial Council in 1995, would *"provide a broad multilateral framework for international investment with high standards for the liberalization of investment regimes and investment protection and with effective dispute settlement procedures."* The basic intent of the MAI is to prohibit all "discrimination" against foreign investors through the key principle of national treatment, and to make government decisions to regulate or control foreign investment subject to appeals by foreign governments and foreign investors and companies. The key principle of National Treatment is the philosophical and legal touchstone of the MAI:

> *"Each Contracting Party shall accord to investors of another Contracting Party and to their investments treatment no less favourable than the treatment it accords (in like circumstances) to its own investors and their investments with respect to the establishment, acquisition, expansion, operation, management, maintenance, use, enjoyment and sale or disposition of investments."*

The Most Favoured Nation (MFN) principle is also stated—meaning that all Contracting Parties shall be treated equally.

Consistent with the principle of national treatment, the MAI would prohibit governments from discriminating against foreign corporations when it comes to approving takeovers or the establishment of new businesses in a country, and with respect to the privatization of assets. Countries could not insist that foreign companies agree to "performance requirements," such as a requirement to export or import at a certain level, to purchase domestic goods and services, or a requirement to create jobs or invest in research and development. Further, if governments choose to subsidize businesses, they could not discriminate against foreign investors.

The MAI is a "top down" agreement—meaning that everything is included unless it is explicitly excluded. This contrasts with the WTO which is a "bottom up" agreement, applying only to specified areas. The nature of the agreement means that the central guiding principle of "non-discrimination" will apply and be binding, except where there is express limitation. This means that all government measures which "discriminate" against foreign corporations and investors—such as protection of Canada's cultural industries and subsidies for not-for-profit social service providers—will be vulnerable to challenge under the MAI unless the area is carved out of the agreement through a general exemption, or is excluded through a country-specific reservation.

Investment is defined very widely in the MAI to cover every stage of the investment cycle—pre-investment, operation and management, and repatriation of profits and dividends. An investment includes rights under contract, intellectual property rights, claims to money and performance, real estate, and government concessions and licences, including rights of access to natural resources and the right to contract to governments. Coverage of investment in its pre-establishment phase is far- reaching, going beyond existing agreements such as NAFTA.

This means that government policies and changes in policy could be challenged long before there has been any direct impact on a foreign investor or corporation. (The Canadian government has indicated that is shares the concern regarding the very broad definition of investment, but there has been no clear statement regarding the Canadian position on precisely which areas should be covered.)

To protect foreign investors, the MAI would prohibit and make open to challenge "unreasonable" and "discriminatory" measures against foreign investors. The MAI prohibits expropriation actions and "measures having equivalent effect," and requires that full compensation be paid without delay even if expropriation is non-discriminatory and is in the public interest. These provisions potentially threaten even regulations and policy changes which may not have an overt discriminatory intent, but simply reduce profitability, or reduce the market for an investor.

The Canadian Environmental Law Association and the B.C. government both argued to the Parliamentary Committee on NAFTA that the expropriation clauses of the MAI go far beyond the principle of non-discrimination. Under domestic law, expropriation is taken to mean the seizure of property by the state, not a change in a future stream of profits due to a regulatory or policy change. For example, the razoring of a property—a change in regulation—is not an expropriation. Property interests are weighed against other legitimate interests in determining fair compensation, and there would be only very limited compensation, at most, payable to a property owner in the event of a change in zoning or a change in the terms and conditions of a resource licence or permit.

The key problem with the expropriation clause in the MAI is that it raises the very real possibility of international arbitration and awards of compensation to investors who would not qualify for compensation under Canadian law. Indeed, foreign investors would have a clear advantage in that they could challenge a measure under the MAI, while domestic companies would have no case in Canadian courts and no recourse to the MAI. The B.C. government, to illustrate the problem of a clause which has a very broad and inclusive definition of expropriation, argues that such a clause could require payments of huge sums in compensation for the settlement of native land claims which would involve the transfer of resource permits from companies to Aboriginal bands.

Environmental experts have noted that many environmental regulations—including ones sanctioned under international environmental agreements—have been challenged before the World Trade Organization and struck down as unduly trade-restrictive. The provisions of NAFTA are already being used by the Ethyl Corporation to challenge a federal government regulation on the grounds that an import restriction could amount to "expropriation" which should be compensated. By casting its net very widely, the MAI could strike down legitimate regulation in the public interest in a wide range of activities.

A key intent of the MAI is to provide investors with a direct mechanism for seeking redress and compensation for violations of the agreement by governments. This element of the MAI builds on NAFTA, which opened up the normal state-to-state dispute resolution process to investors and corporations. The dispute settlement procedure will likely be available even before an investment is made—i.e., a company which wants to establish in Canada but is not allowed access will be allowed to challenge that decision. An investor can bring forward a dispute if there is an alleged breach *"which causes loss or damage to the investor."* Decisions can be made by domestic courts or by an international tribunal which can declare that a party was not complying with the agreement and can award pecuniary compensation or restitution.

Dispute settlement procedures under the MAI, like such procedures under the WTO and NAFTA, would be conducted in secret, without public scrutiny and accountability. As the Canadian Environmental Law Association has argued, dispute settlement under the WTO is argued on extremely narrow, technical grounds, and both citizens and non-trade experts are excluded. Unsurprisingly, panels have consistently struck down regulatory measures which interfere with the narrow principles of "non- discrimination". Indeed, not a single environmental measure has withstood a WTO challenge, notwithstanding the fact that Article XX of the GATT (now incorporated in the WTO) explicitly provides some protection for measures taken to protect the environment. The dispute settlement process thus raises major concerns even independent of the specific issues which could be raised under the MAI.

The MAI is an extremely onerous agreement in that, once signed, its provisions would apply for up to 20 years. The treaty could be abrogated only after five years' notice. And provisions would remain in place to cover existing investments for another 15 years.

The MAI is clearly a comprehensive and far-reaching set of rules restricting what governments can do to regulate foreign investment and corporate behaviour, and creating new rights for corporations to challenge government decisions. It is explicitly intended to go well beyond the rules which already exist in the WTO and even in the more far-reaching NAFTA and European Community (EC) agreements.

That said, the MAI does exempt some areas from the core principles of the agreement. There have been some important differences between OECD countries on the nature of the agreement. Some countries, and the OECD Secretariat, wanted a very "tight," legally binding agreement with very few exceptions and reservations. This implied a complex set of negotiations in which investment "barriers" in different countries would be traded off against each other. At the other end of the spectrum, some countries were prepared to sign on to certain key principles, provided that a wide range of non-conforming measures could be retained. France, for example, has sought a blanket exemption for cultural industries, and all countries have agreed to an exception or "carve-out" for national security measures.

While general exemptions are very limited, the MAI allows countries to file reservations if they want to preserve particular policies and measures which are threatened by the general principles of the agreement. A particularly large set of reservations has been filed by the Canadian government, defining areas in which the core principles of the MAI will not apply. Some of these reservations will be subject to "standstill" and "rollback," meaning that non-conforming measures cannot be made more restrictive and will be subject to removal in future negotiations. However, Canada has taken the position that some reservations must be open-ended or "unbound" —that is, future measures in the area can be undertaken and there is no commitment to further changes. The idea of an "unbound" reservation remains in dispute.

Both exemptions and reservations have to be carefully studied to see if they will withstand the scrutiny of dispute resolution panels and thus serve their intended purpose. But the point remains that the actual impact of the MAI will be blunted and conditioned to some extent by the exemptions and reservations which are agreed to. The contributors to this volume based their analyses on the draft agreement as known prior to February, 1998. At that time, the basic nature of the agreement was apparent, but specific details remained unresolved.

The MAI and Developing Countries

It is widely recognized that the central purpose of the MAI is to limit the role of the state in developing countries. The fact that the MAI talks are taking place at the OECD reflects the fact that many developing countries, particularly in Asia, were not prepared to participate in the negotiation of a major WTO round on investment issues. Many of these countries still maintain major restrictions and regulations on foreign investment, and are in no hurry to deregulate. For example, successful developing countries such as South Korea have closely regulated and controlled foreign direct investment and takeovers, and have maintained controls on even short-term indirect capital flows. It has been common for developing countries to place key sectors, such as banking, totally off- limits to foreign investment. Some countries, such as Chile, closely regulate short-term foreign capital inflows in order to insulate themselves from the potential economic damage caused by purely speculative capital flows.

The United Nations agency UNCTAD has stressed that foreign direct investment can play a positive role in national economic development, and it has certainly contributed to export-driven industrialization in the newly industrializing countries. However, UNCTAD has also stressed the need for retaining room for governments to regulate:

> *"The quality and quantity of investment can be improved by means of closer linkages with the world economy through trade and capital flows, including FDI. But these external linkages must be complementary to and not a substitute for the domestic forces of growth through capital accumulation and technological capacity building. This can be achieved only through a carefully managed and phased integration into the world economy, tailoring the process to the level of economic development in a country and the capacity of existing institutions and industries. Such a strategy contrasts sharply with the "big bang" liberalization adopted by some countries in recent years."*
> [UNCTAD Trade and Development Report 1997 p. vii.]

The MAI, without appropriate exemptions or reservations, would strike down the capacity of countries to limit destructive short-term capital inflows. As stressed by some developing countries at a recent forum on the MAI convened by the OECD in Mexico

City, short-term inflows can be highly destructive, driving up the exchange rate to unsustainable levels and fuelling unproductive, speculative booms. It was precisely these inflows which set the stage for the destructive meltdowns recently experienced by Mexico and a number of Asian countries.

With respect to long-term development, many developing countries have sought foreign direct investment, but have also sought to steer such investment to particular areas through a combination of regulations and tax measures. Foreign direct investment (FDI) has been used to build up domestic capacities, but regulation has been a central part of successful industrial development strategies. Left purely to their own devices, many export-oriented TNCs do not source local components, and do not invest in skills or research and development. They are concerned only with producing low value added items for global production chains, drawing upon pools of low-wage labour. The result can be a narrow export oriented manufacturing base, with limited positive linkages to the domestic economy. This is very much the reality of the TNC-dominated *maquiladora* sector in Mexico.

Compounding the damage, transnationals may squeeze out production, jobs and the development potential in domestic industries which are uncompetitive compared to large foreign firms. As even the World Bank recognized in a recent major report, successful development in countries like Korea involved some combination of support for domestic industries, regulated foreign direct and indirect investment, and managed trade. This is very much a model which could not survive under the rules of the MAI.

The advocates of the MAI in the industrialized countries—led by the U.S. government and transnational corporations—hope that a successful agreement among a smaller group of countries will eventually lead to wider participation. The MAI would not be just a treaty among OECD countries, but would be immediately open to any other country which wished to join. Already, some developing countries such as Brazil and Chile have joined the negotiations as observers, and have indicated some willingness to sign on.

If an MAI is concluded between an OECD-plus group of countries, it will be increasingly difficult for developing countries which want to attract foreign investment to remain outside. Unlike the original signatories, they may well be unable to reserve or grandfather non-conforming national policies. In short, a major, indeed absolutely central, purpose of the MAI is to do an "end run" around developing countries and to set out new rules which would compel these countries to allow foreign investors and corporations much greater access to their markets, and much greater room for manoeuvre.

The MAI and Canada

It is, broadly speaking, true to say that most OECD countries, including Canada, already largely abide by the core principles of the MAI. Certainly most OECD economies, including that of Canada, are highly open to foreign direct and indirect investment, "discrimination" against foreign companies is generally limited to a narrow set of sectors and issues, and outright expropriation of foreign assets is rarely, if ever, contemplated. That said, the MAI is supported by right-wing governments and businesses because it would lead to the erosion of important restrictions and regulations already in place, and because it would prevent any future "backsliding."

Canada greatly liberalized regulation of foreign investment under both the FTA and NAFTA, though some key reservations were maintained allowing for review of large foreign acquisitions and limited foreign ownership in some sectors. Nonetheless, the MAI does go beyond NAFTA in some key respects, and it is not certain that all of the reservations from NAFTA will be carried over into the MAI.

It is worth recalling that, as recently as a decade ago, Canada generally opposed U.S. attempts to limit the power of states to regulate foreign investment through the GATT system. Foreign investment review, regulated foreign access to natural resources, restricted foreign participation in industries such as transportation, communications and financial services, and domestic content requirements were centrepieces of Canadian economic policy well into the 1980s. The FTA and NAFTA reversed a lot of these policies. However, many "restrictions" remain in place. Large foreign investments are still reviewed and performance requirements can be imposed, and foreign investment and establishment are still limited in key sectors such as finance and culture. These are potentially challenged by the MAI.

In the case of Canada, the MAI would do three things. First, it would extend broadly the same rules which now apply to U.S. and Mexican investors under NAFTA to all other MAI signatories. Second, it would further entrench NAFTA limitations on our ability to shape investment by moving them into a multilateral context. Third, it would go beyond even NAFTA in terms of restricting the ability of governments to regulate, and in terms of expanding the rights of other countries and of TNCs and foreign investors to challenge government decisions.

The MAI, as drafted, will further undercut our ability to protect and create jobs, undermine our ability to maintain Canadian culture, and threaten our ability to maintain public and not-for-profit services like Medicare. It would further undermine the scope for implementing strong environmental and labour standards.

While the key question of the application of the MAI to provincial governments is not yet resolved, the provinces will be covered unless they are specifically excluded. In the past (under the FTA and NAFTA), the federal government has taken the position that it has the authority to limit provincial powers through trade agreements, though it has also been careful about limiting provincial powers. Ultimately, NAFTA reserved most non-conforming provincial measures and was not constitutionally challenged by any province. The federal government has indicated that it wants the provinces to be covered in a "good" MAI agreement, and that appropriate reservations for provincial policies would then be filed. But the implications of the agreement for a huge range of policies at the provincial level are largely unknown.

The MAI and Canadian Economic Development and Job Creation

The MAI makes no positive contribution to the real concerns of working people in Canada: unemployment, stagnating living standards, increasing inequality, and insecurity. Participation in the MAI negotiations is premised on the view that Canadians would benefit from still greater inflows and outflows of investment capital. But the explosion of national and international investment flows in recent years demonstrates that existing "barriers" are not significant, and that there are costs as well as benefits, from the perspective of workers and communities. The case for still greater openness, going even beyond NAFTA, is both dubious and unproven.

As detailed in the section on foreign direct investment (FDI), in recent years there has been significantly more Canadian investment outside Canada than there has been foreign investment in Canada. The total net outflow of capital from Canada (foreign direct investment and investment in portfolio equity combined) was $10.9 billion in 1995 and $11.2 billion in 1996, equivalent to 14% of total business investment in the Canadian economy in each of those years. Over the past two decades, Canadian investment outside Canada has grown much faster than foreign direct investment in Canada, with the result that the stock of Canadian direct investment abroad is now almost as large as foreign direct investment in Canada.

Some Canadian foreign direct investment outside the country may support job creation in Canada to a limited extent, but foreign direct investment and portfolio equity outflows in excess of inflows mean that Canadian capital is not being put to work creating jobs and raising living standards here at home. It is clear why Canadian businesses which are making large investments outside the country support an MAI. It is much less clear why Canadian workers and communities should support an agreement which would, in all likelihood, accelerate capital outflows and increase the bargaining power of transnational corporations vis à vis Canadian governments and Canadian workers.

There are a number of concerns regarding the potential impact of MAI on current and possible future policies which regulate foreign investment so as to create and sustain Canadian jobs. The key concerns relate to the ability of Canadian governments to extend financial support to Canadian-based businesses which create jobs, and our ability to review foreign investments to ensure that there are net employment and other benefits for Canadians.

New foreign direct investments and acquisitions may benefit Canadians; or they may lead to a loss of jobs, productive capacity and future productive potential in a particular sector. It is imperative that the federal government retain the right to review foreign direct investment to ensure that it benefits Canadians, and to impose conditions where appropriate.

The MAI provides that, in connection with the establishment, acquisition, expansion, management and operation of an investment, an investor *shall not* be required to: i) export a given level or percentage of goods and services; ii) achieve a given level of domestic content; iii) relate levels of exports to imports; iv) transfer technology, or v) locate its headquarters in the country. The addition of services to prohibited performance requirements is an addition to NAFTA and WTO limits, as is the addition of technology transfer.

Still bracketed clauses would further prohibit: i) achieving a given level of production, investment, sales, employment or research and development in its territory, ii) hiring a given level of nationals, and iii) achieving a minimum level of equity participation. The intent of the bracketed text is to move limits on performance requirements beyond trade-related areas, and to address all "distortions" created by government regulation of foreign investment. This goes beyond the principle of national treatment.

NAFTA maintains Canada's right to review foreign investments of more than $150 million, with such reviews not being subject to appeal by a potential investor or a foreign government, and allows Canada to turn down a foreign investment or takeover if there is no net benefit to Canada. The agreement also allows Canada to require a foreign investor to locate production, carry out R&D,

to employ workers, and to construct or expand facilities in Canada. Canada has much broader rights in this area under the WTO.

Reservations to the MAI tabled by Canada would retain some existing rights, but would weaken our ability to negotiate and enforce performance requirements for at least non-NAFTA countries, and with respect to the negotiation of Canadian equity participation.

Language on performance requirements has the clear potential to limit requirements to create or maintain jobs in return for access to resources, as envisaged, for example, in the B.C. Jobs and Timber Accord or in the Newfoundland—Inco agreement requiring that company to build a smelter in the province. Many provinces require that companies should, in return for access to forestry, mineral and fishery resources, maintain a certain level of local employment, often through a requirement that resources be processed to a certain degree. There is a very real concern that such performance requirements could run afoul of the MAI.

Clearly, requiring that jobs be maintained or created in Canada in cases of foreign establishment or takeover is potentially challenged by the MAI. It is important that the MAI should not dilute the current provisions of the Investment Canada Act and should ensure that Canadian governments retain the right to negotiate employment and other benefits from foreign direct investment.

The issue of access to resources is key for Canadians. Over many years, governments have regulated to ensure that Canadian enterprises have preferential access to some resources, and to ensure that more jobs are created in Canada through local content requirements and through processing as opposed to the export of raw resources. However, the principle of national treatment, combined with the inclusion of government regulations, licences, and concessions in the definition of investment under the MAI, means that TNCs could challenge as "discriminatory" any preferential access by Canadians to fishery, forest, energy, and other resources. One key area of concern is foreign access to the fishery and to Canadian commercial fishing licences, though a reservation has been filed, as under NAFTA, and may cover this issue in part.

NAFTA reserved petroleum and natural gas on federal lands for Canadian-owned companies, and reserved Canada's ability to require benefit plans (employment, domestic content) for developments on such lands. Hibernia and Nova Scotia offshore development benefit plans were specifically reserved. Again, reservations have been filed to respond to concerns that the ability to negotiate benefit plans may be undercut, but it remains to be seen if similar Canadian benefit plans could be negotiated in the future.

Subsidies

Some countries pushed for the MAI to prohibit a requirement that companies receiving subsidies create or maintain jobs in return for government support. Even Industry Minister John Manley expressed outrage at the idea that governments could ask for nothing in return for industrial and regional development subsidies. NAFTA preserved our right to make corporations maintain jobs, production and investment in research and development, and training in return for government support.

The MAI, however, will likely prohibit all "discrimination" in favour of Canadians and Canadian-based enterprises if governments extend subsidies for job creation, training, research and development, and regional development.

While it may well be appropriate to extend subsidies to foreign- owned enterprises in many commercial sectors, it is perverse that Canadian governments should not be allowed to direct taxpayer dollars only to Canadian enterprises. And it is absolutely vital that governments should retain the right to "discriminate" in the area of public and social services, and in the area of culture.

Public Enterprises and Privatization

While the MAI does allow for public enterprises, bracketed text provides that monopolies should not be allowed to cross- subsidize so as to artificially support services which compete with other providers, and should act solely in accordance with commercial considerations in the purchase or sale of a monopoly good or service. This language would provide foreign companies greater leverage in trying to break into areas of the market which have traditionally been served by state enterprises and state-designated monopolies. Regulation and public ownership in areas such as telecommunications and transportation are vulnerable to challenge.

The principles of National Treatment and Most Favoured Nation would explicitly apply to privatization and subsequent transactions involving privatized assets (i.e., share sales could not be restricted to nationals). Bracketed language would either prohibit special share-holding arrangements such as "golden shares" or privatization via a sale to employees—or, alternatively, would explicitly allow governments to ensure some continuing control of privatized assets. This is still an actively contested issue.

NAFTA reserved the right of Canadian governments to prohibit or limit foreign purchases of shares when a public enterprise is privatized, and to require that the boards of directors and senior management of privatized companies be Canadian citizens. Limits on foreign ownership of Air Canada and Petro-Canada shares (25%) and other privatized Crown corporations were grandfathered. Similar reservations have been filed for the MAI, though this could still greatly limit options in the case of future privatization. The MAI challenges the right of governments to determine the future ownership structure of privatized enterprises, and to bring such enterprises back under regulation or public ownership. If left intact, these provisions would mean that the CBC or TV Ontario, for example, could not be retained in Canadian hands if a decision to privatize were taken.

THE MAI AND PUBLIC AND SOCIAL SERVICES

The MAI has no general exclusion or "carve-out" for public and social services, opening up the very real possibility that TNCs could claim that public delivery of a service such as health care or government subsidies to not-for-profit providers are "discriminatory" practices. These concerns are greatest when public services are not delivered directly by governments, but rather through the mix of public, private and not-for-profit institutions which characterizes much of the Canadian health and social services sector.

While the federal government has indicated that a country-specific reservation for social services delivered for a public purpose identical to that to be found in NAFTA will be made to the MAI, the NAFTA provision is itself weak and inadequate. The MAI adds to these concerns already in existence because of NAFTA in that it provides that governments cannot "discriminate" if subsidies are given, meaning that foreign corporations could claim the same treatment given to not-for-profit organizations. Further, the MAI has a very broad definition of investment which includes government concessions and licences.

The defects of NAFTA and the additions of the MAI in combination pose a clear threat to the maintenance of not-for-profit public and social services. The MAI could give foreign investors such as large U.S. health care companies the right to establish for-profit enterprises in the social and health service area— particularly in areas of mixed public/private delivery. Further, the MAI could allow foreign investors to challenge government support of not-for-profit providers of social and public services.

Under NAFTA, there is a broad reservation for social services:

> *"Canada (the U.S., Mexico) reserves the right to adopt or maintain any measure with respect to the provision of public law enforcement and correctional services, and the following services to the extent that they are social services established or maintained for a public purpose: income security or insurance, social security or insurance, social welfare, public education, public training, health, and child care."*

The Government of Canada has filed a comparable reservation in the MAI.

In the debate over NAFTA and subsequently, fears have been expressed that NAFTA could lead to the undermining of Canada's system of public and mixed public/private delivery of health and social services. The context for that concern is the far greater extent of public and not-for-profit delivery of services —notably health care—in Canada compared to the U.S., and the fact that U.S. corporations delivering health and other social services have expressed interest in obtaining greater access to the Canadian market.

Canadian health services—physician and hospital care—are typically delivered by independent doctors and by non- governmental (but not-for-profit) hospitals, with the costs being covered by public health insurance (largely funded through general taxes). In short, the system is publicly financed (by the federal and provincial governments) and regulated (by provincial governments), but is not delivered directly by governments. Many significant areas (dental care, drugs outside hospitals) are largely delivered outside the framework of publicly-funded Medicare, and many elements of the health care delivery system are contracted out to private firms (e.g., diagnostic testing, some hospital operations).

Large U.S. health care corporations, such as insurance companies and health care management organizations, have occasionally expressed interest in entering the market, but have been generally excluded to this point and are confined to selling supplementary health insurance and some specialized and non-Medicare services to physicians, patients, and hospitals.

The pattern of mixed public/private delivery extends to social services such as elder care, child care, and home care. Often, government and public agencies contract for services from both commercial providers and not-for-profit agencies, and/or subsidize not-for-profit operations which compete with commercial providers.

The federal government long maintained that the general exclusion in NAFTA (which covers future as well as current measures) was sufficient to protect Medicare and social services from challenge by U.S. corporations and investors who are either excluded from the Canadian market or are denied subsidies and support on the same basis as Canadian not-for-profit or commercial providers of services. The issue has not been tested by NAFTA dispute settlement panels. However, it did arise in the context of the required listing of non-conforming provincial government measures.

Canadian provinces and U.S. states were given a grace period to reserve all existing non-conforming measures under Annex I through a process of detailed enumeration and listing, a process that was ultimately intended to lead to the application of NAFTA investment disciplines to lower levels of government and to further negotiations to roll back non-conforming measures. In the event, in April 1996, the NAFTA countries agreed to protect indefinitely from challenge all existing sub-federal investment (and trade in non-financial services) measures, meaning all non- conforming measures in place as of January 1, 1994. This general reservation under Annex I does not cover *future* provincial initiatives in the social services area.

This outcome arose largely because of growing Canadian concerns over the lack of adequacy of the general Annex II exclusion for social services, expressed particularly forcefully by the NDP government of British Columbia and by public interest groups and unions. While the federal government initially argued that the general exclusion in Annex II made it unnecessary to list non- conforming provincial measures in the social services and health area, critics argued that the general exclusion was vague, that it was interpreted differently by the U.S. government, and that it was vulnerable to challenge. Ultimately, the blanket exclusion of non-conforming provincial measures in Annex I reflected at least limited federal government acceptance of the case of the critics.

In the process of advising states on the listing of sub-national reservations, the U.S. trade representative expressed the view that the general exemption covered only services delivered *directly* by governments, and not services characterized by a mixture of public, private, and not-for-profit delivery. It was stated in a letter to the State of Oregon that a reservation could not cover government services "if supplied by a private firm, on a profit or *not-for-profit* basis." An extended legal opinion prepared by Dr. Bryan Schwartz of the University of Manitoba for the Canadian Union of Public Employees and the Canadian Health Coalition argued that the social services exclusion is ambiguous and rife with gray areas. In a context of government withdrawal from direct funding of at least some services, deregulation, and partial privatization, he argued that it is far from clear what a NAFTA dispute panel would find to be "a social service delivered for a public purpose."

While Schwartz thought the U.S. trade representative's view would likely be found extreme, he argued that the "for a public purpose" provision would be undercut by significant privatization, extra billing for services, and private delivery. He further argued that extending subsidies only to not-for-profit providers does not provide a shield from challenge. The key conclusions reached were that the vagueness of the general exclusion creates hazards, and that funding cuts and deregulation potentially undermine an exclusion on the basis of public purposes.

The reservation in NAFTA which has also been made in the draft MAI is not a good model because it is too vague and fails to take adequate account of the complexity of systems of delivery of public and social services. The fact that the MAI extends the principle of national treatment to subsidies and has left the area of government procurement of services unresolved creates significant additional grounds for concern that it could be a lever for privatization and commercialization of public and not-for-profit services. At a minimum, the MAI should contain a crystal-clear general exclusion or carve-out for public and social services.

The MAI and Culture

The fundamental principle of national treatment in the MAI and the inclusion of subsidies would rule out as "discriminatory" most existing forms of government support for Canadian culture, including Canadian content provisions and support for Canadian-based cultural industries and artists, as detailed in the contribution by Gary Neil. The Canadian Conference for the Arts has identified as vulnerable to challenge under the MAI a broad range of cultural policies, such as subsidies to Canadian publishers, the "net benefit" test applied to foreign acquisitions in the cultural sector, grants to artists, and even Public Lending Rights. Clearly, in the area of culture, "discrimination" in favour of Canadian artists is what public policy is all about.

The Writers Union of Canada has underlined "the fallacy of believing that every human activity must submit to the logic of the marketplace." Only a categorical, self-defined exemption for culture in the MAI could deal with this threat.

The Canadian government has said that a general exemption or reservation will be negotiated, and France has also pushed for a cultural sector exemption. However it is far from clear that this will be either possible or adequate.

Labour and Environmental Rights and Standards

The major thrust of the MAI is to prohibit or limit government regulation of foreign investment. The agreement as a whole is simply not intended to provide a basis for setting and enforcing standards in a world in which capital is highly mobile. That said, the need for a "positive" dimension has been recognized to a very limited degree in the draft MAI. The preamble speaks to positive goals with respect to labour and environmental issues. A draft clause provides that health, safety, environment and labour standards should not be lowered in order to attract an investment, and the (non-binding) OECD Guidelines for Multinational Enterprises are to be associated with the MAI. However, there is no unanimity on these issues, and there is disagreement on whether a commitment not to lower standards should be enforceable or should simply lead to "consultations."

The position of the Trade Union Advisory Committee to the OECD with respect to labour issues, as detailed in the contribution by Roy Jones, is that the preamble to the MAI—which is of some limited legal importance in terms of providing an interpretative context—should commit governments to protecting, enhancing and enforcing basic workers' rights as defined in the core conventions of the International Labour Organization. Such a declaration would commit governments to respecting a basic floor of internationally agreed-upon labour rights.

This key point should also be echoed in the "not lowering standards" clause—i.e., countries should not be able to attract foreign investment by violating core labour rights or by lowering domestic standards. It should be stressed that a commitment to respect workers' rights does not in any sense mean that wages or standards would or should be equalized between countries. Rather, countries would commit themselves to allowing free trade unions to exist and to collectively bargain with employers in order to negotiate wages and working conditions.

The text of the MAI should incorporate binding clauses which would prohibit governments from lowering domestic labour and environmental standards or violating internationally-agreed core labour rights in order to attract a foreign investment. This clause should cover health and safety and environmental standards, as well as domestic labour standards and core labour rights. It should provide that such standards should not be waived or derogated from in order to attract a foreign investment. The clause should be binding and subject to dispute settlement.

As noted above, at a minimum the MAI should also incorporate a wide "carve-out" for environmental laws and regulations, going beyond the language of Article XX of the GATT/WTO which has been interpreted very narrowly. Some environmental organizations have also suggested the incorporation of environmental rights. There is still a great deal of debate and discussion among environmental groups regarding the extent to which environmental goals can be promoted or even protected in international trade and investment agreements, while the international labour movement has campaigned strongly in favour of labour rights clauses in such agreements (while criticizing many other aspects).

Conclusions

The MAI is a fundamentally flawed and unbalanced agreement which would "dismantle democracy" by going beyond existing trade agreements to strike down legitimate public measures, and would give significant new rights and powers to transnational corporations. While the precise nature of the final agreement is still unclear, what is absolutely clear is that the MAI would make it much more difficult to regulate business in the public interest. The MAI goes well beyond even the sweeping principle of "non-discrimination" to challenge environment regulations and rules which secure jobs for Canadians.

Exemptions and reservations could blunt the impact of the MAI, and it is important that there be a clear carve-out for culture, for environmental regulation, and for public and social services, as well as reservations to protect existing "non- conforming" Canadian policies if Canada does decide to join the MAI. Positive labour and environmental provisions should also be incorporated. The better course, however, would be for Canada to stay out of a deal from which we have almost nothing to gain, and everything to lose.

FIGHTING THE MAI

by Elizabeth May

It must be a first—the industry gnashing of teeth, blame-laying columnists, a government embarrassed by its failure to sway public opinion. The fight against the MAI is the first time in my 30 years of activism that a citizen's movement has so effectively beaten the government to the punch. Media pundits have pointed to the "well-organized" efforts of the coalition of groups against the MAI. Government is being faulted for waiting so long to get its message out. It would be funny, if the MAI itself were not so dangerous.

Of course, the initial strategy for the MAI relied on stealth. International trade officials were hardly conducting a public awareness program when their goal was to avoid public awareness. No one was supposed to know much about the proposed investment treaty. Negotiations were far advanced when, in the spring of 1997, Tony Clarke's Polaris Institute came into possession of the draft text. When released to the media, it was clear that key Cabinet members, particularly Heritage Minister Sheila Copps, responsible for Canadian culture, had known nothing about it.

Recently, it has been amusing to watch officials, both within the Organization for Economic Cooperation and Development (OECD) and in the federal Department of International Trade, claim credit for their openness. Often noted is that the draft text is available on the Internet. Never noted is that it was first placed there by anti-MAI activists.

It didn't take long to explain to Canadians that the treaty proposed to turn democracy on its head, granting extravagant new rights to foreign corporations, while diminishing the legitimate role of governments to constrain corporate behaviour. As Michelle Swenarchuk of the Canadian Environmental Law Association so succinctly stated, "'Investment protection' actually means the removal of regulatory controls on corporate activity."

Public anxiety over the MAI grew despite the lack of a well-funded or well-orchestrated campaign. While there is no doubt that the Polaris Institute, particularly Tony Clarke, and the Council of Canadians, particularly Maude Barlow, have done a brilliant job in raising the issue and helping forge a broad coalition in opposition, there is equally no doubt that it was the essence of the agreement itself which spawned its own opposition. No amount of funding or organization could have prompted the virtually spontaneous uprising of public opposition to the MAI which has swept Canada in the last year.

Opposition to the MAI was swift. Following the first media leak of the text in early March 1997, an ad-hoc collection of groups concerned with trade and environment issues, called the Common Front on the WTO and including the Sierra Club of Canada, the Canadian Labour Congress, the Council of Canadians, the Polaris Institute and the Canadian Environmental Law Association, held a workshop for other non-governmental groups on the implications of the MAI. By the time of the federal election call in April 1997, word of the MAI was at least reaching the leadership of a wide spectrum of non-government organizations.

The Common Front held a press conference during the election focusing on the threat to democracy represented by globalization in general, and by the MAI in particular. The national radio news carried the news conference, and the Sierra Club and the Council of Canadians immediately felt the impact. People were calling in from all over the country, from the Maritimes to the Yukon, asking about the MAI.

Realizing that we were at a critical juncture, the Council of Canadians took the initiative to place a nearly full-page ad in the *Globe and Mail.* A number of groups, including the Sierra Club of Canada, co-funded the ad. It ran on May 29, 1997, proclaiming,

"Next Election, your vote may be irrelevant...The new Multilateral Agreement on Investment gives the corporations so much power, Parliament won't matter."

The text went on to highlight the threat posed by the MAI to Canadian jobs, environment, health care and culture. And, to make sure no one thought we were inventing this nightmare, we included the Council of Canadians' web site address so that anyone could read the entire text of the agreement.

The MAI surfaced as an election issue, to the surprise of the governing Liberals. Following our press conference, Alexa McDonough, leader of the federal New Democrats, issued a strong statement against the MAI. Her party's trade critic, Bill Blaikie, raised the issue forcefully in a nationally televised "town hall meeting." Candidates running for the Liberal party found themselves having to defend a deal of which some of them had never been aware. They were caught off-guard in all-candidates meetings. Standing MPs with senior responsibilities as Parliamentary Secretaries claimed the federal government did not support the MAI. Some MPs just answered in platitudes, hoping no one would realize they hadn't the faintest idea what the MAI was.

Then International Trade Minister Art Eggleton dismissed critics and claimed the deal would be good for Canada. But he had failed to brief members of his own party before the election.

It is one of my more speculative and unprovable hunches that the Cabinet shuffle of former Environment Minister Sergio Marchi into the International Trade portfolio was in response to the growing public opposition to the MAI and Eggleton's "top secret" approach to the deal. Treating it on a "need to know" basis had created a far more widespread need to know.

There was deep irony in the appointment of Marchi to the International Trade portfolio. As Minister of the Environment, Marchi had defied the threats of a U.S.-based manufacturer of the gasoline additive, MMT. Against advice from former International Trade Minister Art Eggleton, Marchi pushed through a bill to ban the importation of MMT. He was soon caught in the web of "investor protection."

The MMT Saga

The manganese-based gasoline additive MMT was originally introduced to Canada as a replacement for lead in gas in the late 1970s. At the time, a Health Canada study had noted that there were significant data gaps and that further studies should take place related to the low-dose chronic exposure of vulnerable groups, such as the elderly, pregnant women and children to MMT. Such studies were never done. The source of concern was that manganese itself was well-established as a neuro-toxin in occupational exposure. Manganese-exposed workers had suffered brain-poisoning, with Parkinson's-like tremors. Laboratory animals exposed to manganese had developed symptoms that in humans might have been diagnosed as Attention Deficit Disorder. No one knew what effect airborne manganese would have on the brains of children, exposed through MMT-contaminated exhaust. But we did know from the experience with lead-based additives that exhaust fumes were responsible for high levels of lead in the blood of children.

The manufacturer of lead-based gasoline, Ethyl Corporation, had argued for decades that its products were safe. But when leaded gas was finally banned in North America, the lead levels in the blood of children dropped dramatically. Thus, it is well-established that, if one wants to get a toxic metal into the blood and brains of children, a good delivery mechanism is to add it to gasoline.

Having ignored its responsibility to properly test or monitor for the effects of MMT, Health Canada was not the impetus of government action to get it banned. Rather, it was an unlikely coalition of environmental groups and automobile manufacturers who waged a war to get MMT out of Canadian gas. The car makers were worried when it became apparent that MMT interfered with the anti-pollution systems of cars. By gumming up the on-board diagnostic systems, MMT not only increased air pollution, but also threatened the bottom line of car makers. MMT was causing damage to the car, covered under warranties. And it was the warranties which created real exposure for the auto industry.

The Sierra Club of Canada was one of the leading groups working to ensure the banning of MMT, along with the Learning Disabilities Association and Pollution Probe. In our research, it was clear that the manganese-based additive was a probable neuro-toxin and that it was increasing air pollution.

Sheila Copps' first attempt at legislation had died on the Order Paper, and it was up to Sergio Marchi, with a deadline of Earth Day, 1996, to decide whether or not to reintroduce it. He was under intense pressure to drop the MMT file. Canadian refineries and a number of provinces rallied behind MMT's manufacturer to ridicule claims that it posed any risk. And once again, the manufacturer was none other than Ethyl Corp.—the same people who brought us leaded gas, higher levels of lead poisoning, and diminished intellectual capacities in an unquantifiable number of children.

At the same time Canada was debating whether or not to ban MMT, pressure was mounting south of the border to allow its introduction into the U.S. environment. The U.S. Environmental Protection Agency had been more cautious than Health Canada 17 years before. The EPA had ruled that MMT could not be used, while Health Canada gave it the go-ahead. Now, a U.S. court had, on a very narrow point of law, overturned the U.S. ban.

Ethyl Corp. was lobbying hard for U.S. registration of MMT. It was running advertisements in the U.S. press heralding the "17 years worth of Canadian experience" which had shown no problems with MMT. No one in the U.S. seemed to know that the Canadian Parliament was debating getting rid of the substance. Noted American physicians and toxicologists Dr. Philip Landrigan and Dr. Herbert Needleman characterized the issue in a New York Times op-ed piece as "deja vu all over again"—fighting Ethyl Corp. to get lead banned, and now fighting the same company to prevent the introduction of yet another neuro-toxin.

The administrator of the EPA, Carol Browner, announced that she was registering MMT under protest. Browner stated she did not want the population of the U.S. used as guinea pigs to establish the risks of MMT. Environmental groups pressured refineries. Most leading refineries, often the very same companies arguing to keep MMT in Canadian gas, pledged it would never be added to their products. If the U.S. public would not accept MMT, then, registered or not, it would not be getting into U.S. gas.

It was a high-stakes game for Ethyl. Not only was its market in Canada at risk, but it blew a hole in its public relations strategy if Canada, the happy country with 17 years experience with its wonderful product, banned MMT as an environmental risk. Ethyl pulled out all the stops. The lobbying was high-powered. But its strangest ally had to be the Minister for International Trade, Art Eggleton. In the midst of arguments about neuro-toxicity and anti-pollution devices, a NAFTA-based argument in defence of MMT was the last thing I expected to hear.

But former federal NAFTA negotiator Gordon Ritchie was suddenly a consultant working for Ethyl Corp. Banning MMT, he declared in the business press, would violate Chapter 11 of NAFTA. The Investment Chapter of NAFTA would make Canada's action to ban MMT trade-illegal.

I regarded this threat as far-fetched. The notion that a U.S.-based corporation could use NAFTA-enshrined rights to sue Canada for compensation struck me as absurd—until I looked at Chapter 11 of NAFTA. And, sure enough, investment protection would be available to Ethyl Corp. Never mind that it had never built a manufacturing facility in Canada. Selling neuro-toxic gasoline additives was an "investment." Ethyl Corp. was entitled to compensation if the government action in banning MMT could be seen as "discriminatory."

Since there were no Canadian makers of MMT, it seemed absurd. But banning it would probably be seen as discrimination against a U.S.-based company. This was the truth that dared not speak its name. We needed to get MMT banned. If investor protection was an issue, the groups working to get MMT out of our air were not going to admit it. And neither was our Environment Minister, Sergio Marchi.

In hindsight, it is nothing short of amazing that Marchi re-introduced the legislation to ban MMT. It was a hard fight through the Commons, and even harder in the Senate. But in the end, the bill was made law. MMT was banned. And Ethyl Corp. promptly sued Canada for $350 million in compensation. Ethyl claimed compensation not only for lost profits from the loss of its market, but also for damage to its reputation. One may well wonder what sort of reputation a company that kept lead in gasoline, long after knowing it stunted the mental growth of children, thought it had left to protect. But sue it did. The same minister who fought hard to get the substance banned, Sergio Marchi, was now Trade Minister, responsible for responding to Ethyl Corp.'s arguments. Ah, cruel fate.

THE MAI

Ethyl Corp. probably wouldn't want to take credit, but its law-suit over the banning of MMT probably did more than anything else to spur public opposition to expanded investor-protection rights as set out in the MAI. The idea that the maker of a toxic substance could sue any government that banned its use is so bizarre that hypothetical examples could have been dismissed as the ravings of the lunatic fringe. But Ethyl Corp. provided a real-life example. It illustrated the nature of "investment," of "expropriation" and of the kind of private dispute resolution that would shut out the Canadian public.

At the request of environmental groups, Marchi had asked for the Ethyl case to be held in open, so that the public and media could attend. However, under NAFTA Chapter 11, ditto in the MAI, this suggestion would have had to meet Ethyl Corp.'s approval. Needless to say, Ethyl did not want the hearing in public. It was conducted secretly in late February, 1998. No submissions were allowed from groups that supported the ban on MMT. The result is pending.

The Ethyl Corp. case is not the only example of Chapter 11 of NAFTA being used to retaliate against environmental protection. Another U.S.-based company, Metalclad, is suing a state government in Mexico, claiming compensation for the government's refusal to approve a waste disposal plant. The environmental assessment conducted for the state of San Luis Potosi revealed that the waste disposal plant was on an alluvial stream. A waste disposal facility could contaminate the local water supply for toxic chemicals. San Luis Potosi's Governor rejected the Metalclad plant and declared the area part of a 300,000 hectare ecological area.

Metalclad sued under the Investor Protection provisions of NAFTA for $90 million. As calculated by the Washington- based Preamble Collective, this amounts to more than the combined annual income of every family in the county where Metalclad's facility is located. (There is another Mexican case pending involving waste disposal.)

In fact, thus far, the investment protection provisions of NAFTA have only been used to retaliate against environmental regulations and decisions.

On one hand, pro-MAI spokesmen have argued that we are all in a flap over nothing. "After all," they point out, "everything that's in the MAI is already in NAFTA." In our hands, we argue that we have learned from bitter experience. We have learned that "expropriation" will be claimed when measures are taken for the good of public health or the environment (Metalclad, Ethyl Corp.). We have learned that companies will complain of "discrimination" if they are treated differently, even when no evidence of an intent to discriminate or of actual damage or loss due to "discrimination" has been alleged, much less proven (The Venezuelan refineries case before the WTO). We have learned that nice words in a preamble of a trade agreement don't protect the environment. We have learned that even specific language such as Article XX of the GATT, also part of the Canada-U.S. Free Trade Agreement, (which "permits" countries to maintain standards deemed necessary for the protection of "human, animal or plant life or health" and for "conservation of natural resources") have not worked. In fact, every time a country has argued that it be permitted to do so, it has lost.

If you weren't against NAFTA before, or if you'd never noticed the investment protection provisions, it's not too late to start noticing. No one, outside the business community, wants investor protection rights extended globally. And, unlike NAFTA, with its six months' notice requirements to exit the agreement, the MAI demands five years notice, but investments are "protected" for a further 15 years, creating an effective 20-year lock-in.

As opposition to the MAI spread around the world, the negotiators at the OECD felt the heat. In October 1997, the chair of negotiations invited representatives from environmental non-government organizations to come to Paris for "consultations" with the OECD. Without time to think about it, I agreed when Maude Barlow insisted I should head off to Paris with her. (Who could refuse?) In the end, three of us represented the concerns of Canadians: Maude, Michelle Swenarchuk from CELA, and me. We joined over 70 representatives of concerned groups from around the world. Over 30 countries were represented, including activists from the developing world. Developing countries are not part of the OECD, but it is the declared goal of the MAI drafters to take the finished product out of the OECD and straight into the World Trade Organization, where it would eventually become law virtually everywhere.

In our own strategy sessions in the offices of a Paris-based environmental group (found through the back of a parking garage and up three flights), we discovered a remarkable degree of consensus. One might assume that this is the norm when environmental groups get together. It is not. Especially not when the groups represent a broad cross-section from the large, well-heeled groups, like the World Wildlife Fund, to the U.S.-centric Washington-based groups, to Southern groups like the Third World Network. Jet-lagged anti-MAI campaigners from as far away as New Zealand and Hong Kong, India and Japan, joined a strong contingent of Europeans. In less than a day, we had an agreed declaration, and an agreed strategy. We would not argue for "improvements" to the MAI text. We would make demands. We agreed to argue for the suspension of negotiations and the abandonment of the April 1998 deadline for completion of negotiations, to allow time for the citizens of all countries to become fully informed.

We faced the cultured and cultivated diplomatic set of trade negotiators in the former Rothschild family palace, now headquarters of the OECD. In the ornate high-ceiled room, adorned with crystal chandeliers and gold leaf panelling, we were instructed that we were operating under "Chatham House Rules." No comment could be attributed to any particular speaker or delegation. But we could repeat what was said without attribution. Disciplining our participation was the brilliant and tireless trade campaigner from the WWF, Charles Arden Clarke.

After some to-ing and fro-ing about whether media could be allowed in the room (only for Canadian and OECD head Donald Johnston's opening statement), we began our assault on the MAI.

Our No. 1 weapon was the Ethyl Corp. case. To our amazement, many delegations claimed they had never heard of it. Many claimed that they had no intention of expanding the notion of expropriation from its usual meaning—the seizing and nationalizing of physical assets. (This was hard to swallow, as the language they had negotiated clearly had a big, broad, flexible meaning: "Expropriation includes direct expropriation, indirect expropriation, and any measures having the effect of direct or indirect expropriation.") The environmental community presented its arguments coherently—against the principle of national treatment, against the perversion of the principle of national treatment, against the removal of performance requirements, and against the secrecy of the binding dispute resolution process.

We kept asking delegations to give us specific responses to our demands. In the end, we were advised,"If you want to remove the April 1998 deadline, you'll have to go back to your capitols. The negotiators are merely following instructions from capitols." Clearer advice we didn't need. To kill the MAI deal, we had to increase the political heat at home.

That we did. Maude Barlow and Tony Clarke launched their book on the MAI. Maude kept up a hectic speaking schedule, criss-crossing the country in response to public hunger to learn more about the deal. It became clear that we had tapped into a deep level of concern about many aspects of globalization. We had been FTA'd and NAFTA'd, subjected to "GATT-zilla" and the World Trade Organization, downsized, deregulated and harmonized to death. Canadians were sick of seeing their elected officials parcel up their democratic rights and see them enmeshed in a new global economic order. The MAI offered a chance to say, "enough"—a chance to turn back what seemed an inexorable rush toward global corporate rule.

The House of Commons Standing Committee on Foreign Affairs and International Trade held hearings under its sub-committee on investment. With short notice and a rigid hearing schedule, few environmental groups were able to appear. But the message was strong: the problems with the MAI were fundamental. The Standing Committee's report advised the government to accept the MAI only if it "fully protects Canadian culture, the environment, labour standards, health, education and social services." Those of us familiar with the MAI text knew that any such agreement would not be possible if the fundamentals of the MAI remained in place.

Why the MAI is an environmental outrage

In essence, the MAI is the extension of a corporate coup in many U.S. states. The U.S. Constitution enshrines "property rights." Arguing that conservation measures to limit development, to protect shoreline from erosion, or wetlands, for example, constitutes a "taking" of that property right without due process of law, an anti-environmental backlash has pushed through laws requiring compensation at the state level across the U.S. The impact is predictable. If protecting a wetland means compensating a developer, the conservation movement is undone.

So far, these "takings" laws have not threatened Canada. Thankfully, our Charter of Rights and Freedoms does not contain protection of private property rights. But the corporate interests that have benefited from the concept of "expropriation" by conservation law found their opportunity to go global in the Multilateral Agreement on Investment. The initial drafts of the MAI came from the International Chamber of Commerce. The point of the effort is to hobble governments' ability to constrain corporate behaviour. If they succeed with the MAI, a U.S. investor can oppose "takings" anywhere around the world.

How will the MAI affect our environment? In ways too numerous to fully list. In any circumstance when a government—federal, provincial or municipal—makes a decision which reduces the profit of a foreign investor, that investor can sue for compensation. Nothing in the MAI discourages frivolous suits. Certainly, there is no disadvantage to threatening lawsuits when governments are considering regulatory action. It will become the least cost, highest impact strategy.

Prominent international trade lawyer Barry Appleton was requested by the Council of Canadians to provide his opinion on the environmental impacts of the MAI. His opinion listed the following measures as vulnerable under the MAI:

1. Remediation orders to prevent toxic seepage;
2. Changes to existing concession licences to protect fisheries, flora or fauna;
3. Changes to land use regulations that would reduce the value of property for a foreign investor;
4. Preventative measures taken to protect public safety that caused loss or harm to foreign investors;
5. Requirements that only environmentally-acceptable resource extraction techniques be used that would increase the cost of extraction.

While most environmental impacts of the MAI are indirect, the impact on fisheries regulation is as immediate as those protecting Canadian culture. Current law prohibits foreign fishing inside

Canada's 200-mile limit. Bearing in mind that our domestic over-fishing has fairly well eliminated our East Coast fishery, there are strong reasons to exclude foreign fleets. Canada is seeking a reservation to exclude the discriminatory fishing law from the effect of the MAI. Even if Canada is successful in negotiating such a reservation, the MAI operates under the principles of "stand-still" (i.e., no new "discriminatory measures") and "roll-back" (i.e., over time you will get rid of these temporarily grandfathered provisions.) So the 200-mile fishing exclusion will eventually be overturned if the MAI is adopted.

The indirect impacts are, as noted, numerous. There could well be significant impacts on Canada's forests. The Sierra Club is concerned that changes to lease agreements over Crown forested land with foreign investors would be MAI challenged. Currently, tenure reform is one of the central elements of efforts to stop the rate of overcutting and disastrous clear-cutting across Canada. Reforming lease agreements could be challenged by foreign, but not domestic logging companies.

Wilderness protection would also be at risk. As in the Metalclad example, if a government turned down a development application or rejected a proposed mine, and instead declared an area as a wilderness preserve, a foreign investor could sue. Endangered species legislation, still non-existent in most of Canada, could be argued by a foreign investor to have been applied in a discriminatory fashion if it hindered development.

As sensitive ecosystems and habitat for endangered species can be extremely site specific, an investor could point to similar developments in similar settings and claim discrimination. The last place I'd want to argue biological realities of species survival would be to a closed panel of trade experts. (But, after all, I'd never get to argue there, anyway!)

Clearly, the Ethyl case reveals the potential for governments to be sued when they regulate toxic chemicals. Just as site specific concerns in wilderness make them vulnerable to a discrimination argument, so too do individual cases against toxic chemicals. It has already been argued in Canadian regulatory hearings that toxic and cancer-causing chemicals should not be banned as a matter of fairness, if other competitors on the market are also potentially carcinogenic.

Right down to the level of municipal land use planning, if a foreign investor feels aggrieved, it can sue.

Beyond expropriation are other efforts for environmental progress that could be considered to violate national treatment provisions. Environmentalists have long argued for government procurement to favour environmentally sound choices. If those choices favour local products, under MAI an investor can sue.

The list of environmental impacts of the MAI is as long as the list of environmental impacts of corporate behaviour. While the MAI gives foreign investors new rights, it imposes no obligations on corporate behaviour. Shell's conduct in the Niger River delta would be untouchable, but changes to protect the Ogoni people or protect their environment could result in an MAI challenge.

Opposition to the MAI has been growing steadily, with environmental groups from around the world increasing their efforts and outreach. The joint NGO statement which we drafted in October 1997 in Paris continues to circulate. Before the ministerial meeting at the OECD, Feb. 16 and 17, the statement was re-submitted, by then endorsed by 565 organizations in 68 countries. As an indication of the level of Canadian concern, Canadian groups were the second largest national grouping, second only to the U.S. But the momentum has not flagged, and more groups and individuals are becoming involved each day.

The April deadline bites the dust...MAI down, but not out

On Friday, Feb. 13, Marchi spoke to a breakfast session of over 100 MAI-interested folks in Ottawa. It was the eve of the negotiation sessions in Paris and speculation was mounting that ministers would give up on the April deadline. Marchi gave no hints of that, but did set out the Canadian bottom line for the MAI. He said the government wanted a narrow definition of expropriation "that makes entirely clear that legislative and regulatory action by government in the public interest is not expropriation requiring compensation, even if it has adverse profitability consequences for companies and investors."

That would essentially mean a different agreement. He also said he wanted "ironclad" reservations to protect health, education, social programs, culture and Aboriginal peoples' programs, as well as measures to allow Canada to protect its natural resources.

It is clearly progress, although experience in the trade agreement area suggests that, if the thrust of the agreement is to undermine environmental protection whenever it could be tortuously construed as a trade barrier, nice language in a few clauses will not help. It is still our goal to prevent any MAI from being agreed upon. A true international investment treaty would regulate the behaviour of both investors and governments, and that is not on the table.

In the February negotiating sessions, ministers admitted there could be no agreement by the April 1998 deadline. Major sticking points were cultural protection issues, as advanced by France and Canada, as well as the U.S. Helms-Burton law, which discriminates against any investor doing business with Cuba. Helms-Burton had long been rumoured to be a "deal-breaker" for the MAI. (Is it time to start a Committee of Canadians for Helms-Burton?) But also mentioned in press reports was the pressure to include environment and labour protection. International business leaders have started to complain that the changes to the MAI, especially language to protect the environment, will no longer allow it to be a useful instrument.

The immovable obstacle of the April 1998 finish line has fallen. It is without a doubt a significant victory for everyone who has been working to stop the MAI. But the MAI is a long way from dead. Powerful interests still want a deal. Negotiations will no doubt continue through the fall.

New deadlines may emerge. Or the pro-MAI forces may shift to a different forum for negotiations. This deal started in the WTO, after all, and moved to the OECD once it was clear developing nations in the WTO did not want an investment treaty. It would be hard for the OECD, after its declarations of openness, to move back into the shadows. But another forum could provide the MAI with a new and more quiet home.

The one thing we should count on is that the fight to stop the MAI is not over. It has rekindled a sense of democratic outrage. It has empowered peoples around the world to reject yet another manacle of globalization in the name of corporate interests. History may well record the MAI fight as a turning point, when global governance ceased to be one-sided arrangements in the interests of transnational corporations and started to shift toward global governance in the interests of all.

It is not globalization that is inherently evil. It is globalization that precludes the protection of the weak in society and the voiceless creatures and ecosystems by domestic governments, while ignoring the need to ensure uniform global standards which protect the environment, human health, and labour and human rights. The MAI has probably rendered a service. The transparent greed of the instrument; the overreaching for corporate power and domination of every aspect of our lives went too far. The pendulum is beginning to swing back.

THE MAI AND DISPUTE SETTLEMENT

by Steven Shrybman

Introduction

Many of us take for granted the fact that our judicial system is open, democratic and accountable. After all, our legal systems are founded on English Common Law and Civil Code traditions that significantly predate Confederation. We no doubt share the conviction that the public administration of justice in a manner that is fair to all is so fundamental to a democratic society that it would be unassailable in the contemporary political context.

But under the MAI these principles of due and democratic process would be seriously undermined. While much has been written about the ways in which the substantive provisions of the MAI would undermine the democratic and sovereign prerogatives of the governments we elect, less attention has been paid to the likely impacts of the dispute resolution processes that would be established under this investment treaty. It is the impacts of the MAI's enforcement regime on our justice system that is the subject of this analysis.

Under the heading *Dispute Settlement,* a regime would be established for enforcing the investor rights created by the MAI which would supplant Canadian judicial processes by setting up an independent dispute resolution system, that would exist outside the confines of Canadian courts and Canadian law.

Under the investor-state procedures of this regime, all foreign investors would have an unqualified right to sue the Government of Canada for any alleged breach of the very expansive and broadly-worded investor rights that they would be granted by this investment treaty. Those disputes would then be decided, not by Canadian courts, but by international arbitration panels operating under the auspices of such institutions as the International Chamber of Commerce.

Moreover, panels would operate, not in accordance with Canadian legal principles and procedures, but under international law and according to procedures established for resolving international disputes arising under commercial contracts. These are procedures that are in many ways antithetical to the principles of open, participatory and democratic decision-making that are the hallmarks of our contemporary judicial system.

In creating this regime, the MAI represents a truly radical departure from the norms of international law in two key ways. The first has to do with providing individuals with the right to directly enforce an international treaty to which they are neither parties nor under which they have any obligations. The second concerns the extension of commercial arbitration regimes for resolving contractual disputes to investor claims that have no foundation in contract and which may only obliquely be considered commercial in character.

In broad terms, the investor-state suit provisions of the MAI extend the principles of international commercial dispute resolution to a vast new array of potential disputes that have very little to do with international legal commercial contractual relationships. In effect, the MAI would provide foreign investors with a large number of new substantive rights which can then be relied upon to challenge a broad diversity of government policies, programs and laws. In legal terms, these rights represent new "causes of action" or legal grounds upon which foreign investors would be able to directly proceed with claims against national governments.

This transposition of the principles of international commercial dispute resolution to the virtually unbounded domain of investor-state disputes engendered by the MAI appears to have been accomplished with very little analysis or consideration of the potential public policy consequences of such a transformation. It is not clear whether the promoters of the MAI fully understood the potential impacts of this new dispute resolution régime.

It is clear, however, that there has certainly been no informed public debate about the consequences of these, or any other, elements of this treaty. While the Canadian government offers the glib assurance that these developments are without adverse impacts, it seems determined to avoid any meaningful discussion or debate about these issues.

We suspect that its reluctance derives from a sense that any objective assessment of the investor-state procedures of the MAI would quickly reveal the enormity of the risks to the very democratic foundations of our legal system that we are being invited to take in order to secure investor rights that may prove to be of very dubious value.

Finally, by way of introduction, it is important to note that precedents for the investor-state suit procedures of the MAI can be found in NAFTA, and in certain bilateral investment treaties that Canada has very recently negotiated with a small number of developing countries. While the MAI would extend this regime in both substantive ways and to many more countries, much of the following critique applies equally to the MAI and these precedents.

1. ENFORCING INVESTOR RIGHTS UNDER THE MAI

Rarely is an agreement more effective than the enforcement mechanisms that may be enlisted to ensure that its terms are observed. For this reason, the most important provisions in the MAI are arguably the ones with teeth—i.e., those that will compel governments to comply with its dictates. These can be found in Part 5 of the MAI under the heading *Dispute Settlement*.

These provisions of the MAI would establish two distinct dispute resolution systems. The first, "State-State Procedures," would allow national governments ("contracting parties') to invoke binding arbitration when disputes arise with other parties concerning the investor rights created by the MAI. State-state dispute resolution under the MAI is analogous to procedures established under other treaties and international trade agreements, such as NAFTA and the World Trade Organization.

State-to-state dispute processes are not without controversy, largely because they exclude public access and participation. However, these concerns pale by comparison with those raised by the other dispute resolution system that would be established by the MAI under the heading *Investor-State Procedures.*

Because these rules represent such a departure from many of the norms of both international and domestic law, it is best to reproduce key portions of the text:

"D. DISPUTES BETWEEN AN INVESTMENT AND A CONTRACTING PARTY

1. Scope and Standing

This article applies to disputes between a Contracting Party, and an investor of another Contracting Party concerning an alleged breach of an obligation of the former under this Agreement which causes loss or damage to the investor or its investment.[……]

2. Means of Settlement

Such a dispute should, if possible, be settled by negotiation or consultation. If it is not so settled, *the investor may choose to submit it for resolution:*

a. to any competent courts or administrative tribunals of the Contracting Party to the dispute;

b. in accordance with any dispute settlement procedure agreed upon prior to the dispute arising; or

c. *by arbitration in accordance with this Article under:*

i. the Convention on the Settlement of Investment Disputes between States and Nationals of other States (the "ICSID Convention"), if the ICSID Convention is available;

ii. the Additional Facility Rules of the Centre for Settlement of Investment Disputes (the "ICSID Additional Facility"), if the ICSID Facility is available;
iii. the Arbitration Rules of the United Nations Commission on International Trade Law ("UNCITRAL"); or
iv. *the Rules of Arbitration of the International Chamber of Commerce ("ICC").*[1] [Emphasis added]

Thus, pursuant to these rules, anyone claiming the status of foreign investor has the unqualified right to invoke binding arbitration to enforce the investor rights established by the MAI. Arbitration would take place in accordance with the rules for adjudicating international commercial disputes under regimes set up by the International Chamber of Commerce, the World Bank, or the United Nations.

It is also important to appreciate that, under the MAI, arbitration panels would have formidable powers to ensure that all governments comply with the constraints imposed by the Agreement. Under Article 16, these powers include the authority to make damages awards and to order restitution.

As noted, these enforcement rights are virtually unprecedented and represent bold departures from the norms of international law. These are explored more fully under the following headings.

2. INVESTOR-STATE SUITS AND INTERNATIONAL LAW

Customarily, under international law, only nations have rights arising under the treaties they negotiate. With the exception of the International Convention on Human Rights, no international treaty has ever created rights that can be invoked directly by individuals, corporate or otherwise. Nor can the rights of individuals to basic human rights be seen as a legitimate precedent for founding the very broad investor rights that the MAI would establish.

Rather, the most appropriate comparison would be with the rules for dispute resolution under international trade agreements where, in keeping with this convention, only national governments have standing to invoke dispute resolution processes. Because individuals (read corporations), have no direct access to the enforcement machinery of these trade regimes, national governments have often acted to constrain their appetite to assail the policies and practices of other governments. But, under the MAI, a corporation need no longer persuade any government of the legitimacy of its complaint before seeking enforcement under an agreement to which it is not even a party.

It is also worth making this point to raise the prospect of investor-state suit regimes gradually acquiring larger and larger ambit. Consider, for instance, that the explicit goal of the OECD is to eventually negotiate the inclusion of an MAI-based regime under the WTO. Conversely, others have argued for the extension of investor-state suits to international trade disputes. It may not be unreasonable, given these ambitions, to regard this investment agreement as the Trojan horse that introduces these powerful and private enforcement rights to the much larger domain of international economic relationships.

3. INVESTOR-STATE SUITS AND INTERNATIONAL COMMERCIAL ARBITRATION

If the investor-state suit provisions of the MAI represent a fundamental departure from the norms of dispute resolution that apply under other international trade agreements, they represent an equally dramatic extension of the reach of international commercial arbitration regimes.

As noted, the dispute resolution rules of the MAI incorporate international arbitration processes established for the purpose of resolving disputes arising under international commercial contracts. Thus, under the provisions of the MAI reproduced above, foreign investors would be given the right to force Canada to binding international arbitration, notwithstanding the fact that they are neither parties to this investment agreement, nor do they have any other contractual relationship with or obligations to the Canadian government.

It is also important to note that paragraph 3(a) of Investor-State Procedures provides:

> *"Subject only to paragraph 3.b, each Contracting Party hereby gives its unconditional consent to the submission of a dispute to international arbitration in accordance with the provisions of this Article."*

Under this provision, Canada would concede to all foreign investors the right to invoke the dispute resolution machinery of the MAI without any constraint, and no matter how specious or ill-founded their claims may be. Should Canada decline to participate in the establishment of an arbitral panel, under paragraph 7(b) one would be established in its absence. While any particular claim may fail, the unqualified right to initiate dispute resolution is likely to be used as a harassing measure by corporations and business associations attempting to discourage government initiatives they oppose. Indeed, representatives of the Canadian business community have conceded as much.[2]

In effect, under these rules Canada would be extending a unilateral invitation to an unknown universe of foreign investors, both present and future, to initiate legal claims against it for any alleged violation of the investor rights created by the MAI. Moreover, the potential grounds upon which such claims might be asserted are often so broadly defined as to be virtually unbounded by any clear or precise parameters.

Now, the principle of encouraging the resolution of international commercial disputes in accordance with normative arbitration processes has sound public policy support when those disputes are essentially commercial in character, and founded on contractual relationships between parties of relatively equal bargaining power. However, when those regimes are applied, holus polus, to the resolution of disputes that concern the broadest sphere of public policies, which have no grounding in contract, and which may only in the most tangential way be considered commercial in character, the potential consequences create very real challenges for the democratic norms of Canadian society.

4. Investor-State Procedures

To fully assess the implications of these proposed dispute procedures, it is also important to understand how different the procedures of international commercial arbitration are from those that operate under Canada's legal system.

As we know, Canadian courts are first and foremost public institutions which operate under federal and provincial legislation firmly rooted in our Constitution. In contrast, arbitration tribunals established under the MAI would not be creatures of the Canadian state, but would rather operate under the auspices of the international institutions noted above. Nor would Canada maintain its constitutional authority under S.96 of the Constitution Act to appoint the judges who would otherwise preside over legal claims made against the government. Under the MAI, Canada would have the right to appoint only one of three members of an arbitral panel.

By removing disputes about Canadian policy and law to international fora, the MAI rules represent a direct challenge to Canadian constitutional authority, and probably represent an ouster of federal constitutional authority under S.96.

Supplanting Canadian Law

A second issue that arises here concerns the legal principles that will be relied upon to resolve disputes arising under the MAI. Article 14 of Investor-State Procedures provides in part as follows:

"14. Applicable law

a. Issues in dispute under paragraph 1.a. of this article shall be decided in accordance with this Agreement, interpreted and applied in accordance with the applicable rules of international law.

In other words, under this rule the standard against which Canadian policy and law will be measured may have no foundation in Canadian law and may not be compatible with the principles of law engendered in our Constitution. For example, under the MAI, as is the case under NAFTA, the term "expropriation" is not defined. Thus, when a dispute panel attempts to interpret the meaning of this term, it must have recourse to its meaning as defined under international law. However, international law on the subject of expropriation has been greatly influenced by the U.S. position, which reflects the fact that private property rights have been accorded constitutional protection in that country. In Canada, they have not. Finally, on this point, we would under the MAI be agreeing to submit our legislative prerogatives to the test of international law, not only as that law now exists, but as it may evolve in the future.

Abrogating the Rules of Natural Justice

Another critical element of these investor-state dispute rules are embodied in paragraph 17 of Part D, which provides as follows:

> *"Parties and other participants in proceedings shall protect any confidential or proprietary information which may be revealed in the course of the proceedings and which is designated as such by the party providing the information. They shall not reveal such information without written authorisation from the party which provided it."*

Because this rule allows arbitration proceedings to be entirely shrouded in secrecy, it is simply antithetical to the principles of natural justice and norms of accountability, openness and democratic process that represent the bedrock of all Canadian adjudicative processes. Perhaps the best way to expose these contradictions is to contrast the procedures that are being applied in the two different legal proceedings against the Government of Canada that have been initiated by Ethyl Corporation, a U.S.-based transnational.

Both cases concern federal government regulations banning the importation and trade of a toxic fuel additive that is manufactured and distributed by this corporation. One of these cases has been brought in the Supreme Court of Ontario, the other, seeking compensation in excess of $300 million, has been brought under the investor-state procedures of NAFTA, which have provided the prototype for the MAI. The substantive grounds upon which these claims are being made are quite different, and under the investor rights of NAFTA Ethyl has been able to assert claims that would simply not be tenable under Canadian law. For present purposes, however, it is the very different character of these adjudicative processes that is of concern here.

Ethyl's case in the Supreme Court of Ontario is obviously taking place in an open courtroom, with full public access both to the proceedings and to all of the documents and evidence. Under NAFTA's rules, Ethyl's claim is proceeding in an international forum that is entirely closed to public scrutiny, and where there is no right to access the record of proceedings.

The Supreme Court of Ontario may direct that notice be given to others with a potential interest in the case, and in whatever terms it considers appropriate. It may give others standing to participate in the proceedings, either as full parties or as friends of the court (amicus curiae)—the latter where the participant has abroad policy interest in the case. Under NAFTA's rules, there are no provisions for notice, and there is no opportunity for third party or amicus interventions. The arbitration panel does have the authority under Article 9 to consolidate similar claims by other foreign investors, creating a right analogous to a class action, to their benefit.

The first fundamental problem engendered by these elements of the MAI derives from the apparent assumption that a regime designed for resolving contractual commercial disputes could be applied, without modification, to public policy disputes between foreign investors and national governments. However, even were one to concede this highly dubious proposition, this would still leave the question: what conceivable rationale is there for adopting a model for dispute resolution that so entirely abandons the rules of natural justice, and the norms of democratic adjudicative process?

5. Canada and International Commercial Dispute Arbitration

Having considered the derivation and character of Investor-State procedures, the following analysis describes the domestic laws that have been established to make this international legal regime a part of Canadian law.

Adherence to the norms of international commercial dispute arbitration is a relatively recent development in Canadian law. Under Canada's constitutional division of powers, arbitration agreements and awards are purely a head of provincial legislative competence. The reluctance of provincial governments, and uncertainty about the competence of the federal government to enact legislation on the topic of arbitration, stalled efforts to join or implement international commercial dispute resolution agreements for many years.[3] Thus, until relatively recently, Canada had not yet incorporated international conventions concerning commercial dispute resolution into its domestic law.

In fact, it was not until 1985 that agreement was finally reached among the provinces and the federal government to adhere to the United Nations Convention on the Recognition and Enforcement of Foreign Arbitration Awards (the New York Convention), which had been signed nearly 30 years earlier. Following that agreement, Canada enacted the *United Nations Foreign Arbitral Awards Convention Act* [R.S.C. 1985, c.16 (2nd supp.)] declaring the Convention to have the force of law in Canada. Federal legislation concerning the UNICTRAL Model Law was also enacted in that year as *The Commercial Arbitrations Act* [R.S.C. 1985, c.17 (2nd supp.)].

At the same time, the provinces and the federal territories proceeded to enact their own provincial legislative regimes to implement either, or both, the New York Convention and the UNICTRAL Model Law. In this endeavour, various provinces and territories adopted somewhat different approaches, but in all cases to the same end, which was to provide for the enforcement of international arbitration awards as if they were orders of a Canadian court.

At this juncture, two key points should be noted. The first is that Canadian legislation implementing international conventions for the resolution of commercial disputes is a very recent phenomenon in this country. These are not regimes that have been a feature of the Canadian legislative landscape, nor do we have very much experience with them. Nor has the constitutional authority of the federal government in this sphere ever been determined.

The second and more important point is that the enactment of these provincial and federal statutes preceded by several years the provisions of NAFTA, and bilateral investment agreements that have so dramatically extended their application. In this way, the investor-state provisions of the MAI attempt to build on a foundation of domestic Canadian law that was never established for that purpose. Nor is there any indication that the framers of these statutes had any notion that they might serve one day to give effect to an international arbitration regime of such radically different character than one based on resolving legal disputes between parties to commercial contracts.

Recognition and Enforcement of Arbitration Awards

Paragraph 16(c) of the MAI provides as follows:

> *"An arbitration award shall be final and binding between the parties to the dispute and shall be carried out without delay by the party against whom it is issued, subject to its post-award rights under the arbitral systems utilized."*

Canadian laws which implement the international arbitration conventions provide for the efficacious enforcement of international arbitration awards. For example, under the *United Nations Convention on the Recognition and Enforcement of Foreign Arbitration Awards Convention Act* (the *New York Convention Act*), a party seeking enforcement can apply to the Federal Court or to any superior, district or county court. Under Article III:

> *"Each Contracting State shall recognize arbitral awards as binding and enforce them in accordance with the rules of procedure of the territory where the award is relied upon, under the conditions laid down in the following articles. There shall not be imposed substantially more onerous conditions or higher fees or charges on the recognition or enforcement of arbitral awards to which this Convention applies than are imposed on the recognition or enforcement of domestic arbitral awards."*

While no right of appeal or other review is provided for under MAI rules, Canadian implementing legislation does provide for judicial oversight. The most broadly worded provisions in this regard can be found under s.2 of Article V of the *New York Convention Act*:

"Recognition and enforcement of an arbitral award may also be refused if the competent authority in the country where recognition and enforcement is sought finds that:
(a) The subject matter of the difference is not capable of settlement by arbitration under the law of that country; or
(b) The recognition or enforcement of the award would be contrary to the public policy of that country."

While the terms of this provision are broadly put, there is little guidance as to how this language might be interpreted by Canadian courts. We are aware of no case that has arisen under the investment rules of NAFTA that has tested this language. A review of the case authority that has addressed issues relating to international commercial dispute arbitration demonstrates a strong deference in favour of supporting the autonomy of the arbitration process. For example, in *Quinette Coal Limited v. Nippon Steel Corp* (1990), 50 B.C.L.R. (2d) 207 (C.A.), Mr. Justice Gibbs stated:

> *"It is appropriate for the court to adopt, as a matter of policy, a standard which seeks to preserve the autonomy of the forum selected by the parties and to minimize judicial intervention when reviewing international commercial arbitration awards."*

But, given the commercial and contractual nature of the dispute at issue in this particular case, it is impossible to know whether the same approach would be taken in a dispute such as the one currently under way between Ethyl Corporation and the government of Canada. Neither can we gauge how the courts would deal with the issues of notice or standing under these statutory regimes. Nor can we know in a case where neither party to the dispute invokes the court's jurisdiction, whether a court would grant an application by a third party to do so.

While the possibility of invoking judicial oversight of arbitration awards provides some hope that these dispute procedures will be required to respect some of the norms of Canadian law, it provides no answer to either the substantive or procedural complaints that we have raised here.

Summary

I have attempted to address one particular dimension of this proposed investment treaty: the investor-state procedures that it would establish. The Department of Foreign Affairs and International Trade has taken the position that there is nothing unique or untoward about these dispute resolution rules, and points to a number of precedential agreements. However, it is very clear that the advent of these investor rights is a very recent phenomenon in Canadian law.

In fact, it was only in 1985 that Canadian governments even decided to adhere to the norms of international commercial dispute arbitration. Moreover, the advent of investor-state suit procedures under multilateral investment agreements are of even more recent vintage, dating only from the implementation of NAFTA.

We have discovered in the years since NAFTA that foreign corporations will make ready use of the new rights they have acquired under these investment regimes. In Canada, U.S.- based corporations have enlisted NAFTA's investment rules in support of claims and lobbying efforts intended to frustrate or challenge Canadian initiatives on issues as diverse as restricting the trade of a toxic fuel additive, mandating plain packaging for cigarettes, terminating leases to the terminals at the Toronto International Airport, and establishing a public auto insurance system.

While much has been made of Ethyl Corporation's claim for compensation under the expropriation rules of NAFTA, often overlooked is the fact that it is also claiming breaches by Canada of the national treatment and performance requirement rules of NAFTA. Indeed, its claims on these grounds may be stronger than the one it has founded on the expropriation rule.

What has made the arguments of these investors so potent is the direct recourse that each enjoys to the dispute resolution apparatus of international arbitration. Simply, the resource demands that such claims impose on scarce government resources will often be sufficient to discourage government initiative in the face of such complaints, no matter how compelling the public policy rationale for proceeding may be.

Ultimately, however, the real challenge presented by these new and powerful enforcement mechanisms is to the very democratic foundations of our judicial system. In many ways it would be difficult to devise a dispute resolution system that was less compatible with the conventions of either international or domestic laws. It is absolutely essential that the implications of these new regimes be fully considered and debated before irrevocable commitments to them are made.

ENDNOTES

1 Organization for Economic Co-operation and Development, Directorate for Financial, Fiscal and Enterprise Affairs, *Multilateral Agreement on Investment: Consolidated Text and Commentary* (Paris: OECD, 1997) at 62.

2 According to a trade lawyer, who represents large corporations, Canadians should regard the Ethyl suit as a harbinger of things to come, as corporations make more frequent use of investment treaties to "harass" governments contemplating regulatory initiatives those corporations oppose - see "Ethyl sues Canada over MMT law," Globe and Mail, April 15, 1997.

3 John E.C. Brierly, *Canadian Acceptance of International Commercial Arbitration,* in Maine Law Review, Vol. 40:263 (1988) at 287.

THE MAI AND THE FIRST NATIONS

by Ovide Mercredi

The powerful corporate movement to establish a world-wide investment regime is advancing without the knowledge or in-put of citizens of those countries involved in a major strategy to make the world freer for investors. Canada is one of those countries that is secretly negotiating this global treaty about money, a treaty that will impact negatively on Canada's sovereignty and its ability to protect the public interest and promote the common good.

In a country that hides this development from its own Canadian citizens, it is not surprising that First Nations governments, leaders and citizens have not been alerted to this new world initiative being co-ordinated by the Organization for Economic Cooperation and Development (OECD) and the World Trade Organization (WTO).

In this age of growing interdependence, any diminishment of Canadian sovereignty will result in a corresponding reduction in the power and capacity of First Nations to govern for the common good of their citizens. Today, as in the past, Canadian governments routinely deny First Nations their inherent and traditional rights to lands, resources and government. Undoubtedly this proposed international treaty, which creates "special status" and "special rights" for foreign investors, will entrench the political excuses or legal grounds for Canada to continue its policies of deliberate assimilation of First Nations peoples and governments into the national legal and political structures without regard for the unique constitutional rights of First Nations. With the MAI, Canada could use international law to achieve this policy.

Without a doubt, this strategy of employing international standards and commitments for investors and transnationals is a new assault, not just on the political rights and freedoms of First Nations, but also on the capacity of First Nations to govern their lands and resources. Equally important will be the impairment of the legal and political capacity of Canada to uphold and perform its constitutional and treaty obligations to the First Peoples of this country.

The MAI vs. Aboriginal Beliefs

The belief systems of First Nations have always been in conflict with the world view of the colonizer. Many great orators of our past have inspired countless generations of First Peoples to resist full assimilation and to continue the sacred mission of ensuring the survival of our peoples and cultures. Perhaps it is the concept and role of money that has provided the greatest contrast between us and Canada, as is evidenced by this statement of Chief Crowfoot of the Blackfoot Nation:

> *Our land is more valuable than your money. It will last forever. It will not even perish by the flames of fire. As long as the sun shines and the waters flow, this land will be here to give life to men and animals. We cannot sell the lives of men and animals. It was put here for us by the Great Spirit and we cannot sell it because it does not belong to us.*[1]

A century and a few decades after this statement was delivered by Chief Crowfoot to the Treaty Commissioners for Queen Victoria, it still resonates in our relationship with Canada. Yes, we are still fighting to retain our lands and we continue to resist the efforts of governments to use their money to entice our people to surrender their Aboriginal title. Now we are faced with another use for money--investing—that gives contemporary significance to the words spoken on our behalf: "Our land is more valuable than your money."

The relationship between us, the land and the Creator continues to guide our behaviour on issues such as economic development, resource exploration and environmental management. For our people, it sounds foolish to hear that money should have special status when we see all around our country the ongoing resistance to the recognition and protection of our special status to the land.

What is particularly disturbing is that much of the "money looking for non-discrimination" has its origins in the massive theft and expropriation of indigenous lands and resources all over Mother Earth. When we view the ongoing struggles with national and provincial governments and corporations here in Canada, we can see the double standard. Our country is willing to recognize special rights and "non-discrimination of treatment" for transnational corporations and the rest of the privileged class of people with money, while denying the First Nations their rights to generate a livelihood or wealth from their land and resources.

In fact, the theft of our land, now called "development" of natural resources, continues to position Aboriginal people against the rest of Canada. For instance, the preferential treatment given to transnational corporations in Voisey's Bay and the Lubicon territory presents a violation of human rights of the Innu in Labrador and the Cree in northern Alberta. But for most citizens in those provinces, the issues are jobs and economic development.

In spite of the constitutional provisions that recognize and affirm treaty and Aboriginal rights in Canada's Constitution, we still see throughout this country Canadian governments taking issue with our rights and siding with already powerful corporate interests to fight against and to attempt to defeat our treaty and aboriginal rights.

We know, too well, based upon hard history, that our treaty and aboriginal rights have been and remain threatened by the laws, policies and decisions for development made by federal and provincial governments that have showed their propensity to further empower already powerful economic interests in Canadian society.

Be forewarned that the MAI will dwarf the grave injustices already committed by nation states against indigenous peoples and nations all over the world. The manifest destiny of a White society in North America that resulted in the dislocation of our sovereignty and territories as First Nations was a violation of human rights that has not yet been given a fair hearing in Canada or the United Nations. This latest version of manifest destiny uses different code words such as "liberalization," "global economy," "free movement of capital," and "non-discriminatory treatment of investors," but to seasoned citizens of the First Nations these are synonyms for "discovery," "settlement," "development," "civilization," "Christianity," "pagan," and more recent weasel words like *sui generis*, that seek to maintain the dominance of Canadian society over indigenous cultures and societies.

No doubt our land will outlast all the money, past, present and future, but if we ignore the potential import of the MAI on our future as First Nations, we will certainly imperil our sovereignty, territory and culture. We are not one with the transnationals, who represent the new wave of indifference towards the perpetuation and survival of indigenous peoples and societies.

For the many elders of our indigenous Nations across Canada, the place and role of money in contemporary life has been viewed as a mixed blessing. As the traditional lifeways give way to a money economy, more and more of our people see the generation of wealth as the only alternative to overcoming current conditions of poverty and poor standards of life.

On the other hand, the introduction of money has unfortunately helped to break down traditional values, and has served to accelerate our assimilation into the mainstream society. But we have become accustomed to using money to survive, for food, clothing and shelter, while we have not fully understood the impact of investors' money on our rights and our quality of life. As poor people, First Nations do not have much money for investments. On the other hand, we should be rich in land and resources. However, we have barely hung on to our reservations, much less our traditional territories.

While White governments in the past have been the primary opponents to our capacity to rule our lands, resources and people, the transnational corporations have also become a source of anxiety in the past several decades. Now the MAI will grant special rights to investors without any protection for treaty and aboriginal rights, and further impair the capacity of all governments, including First Nations governments, to pass laws or undertake economic measures that regulate the economy even for the interests of Canadians, not just for us.

Canadian economic initiatives always place our people at the bottom of the ladder. The MAI will restrict the ability of Canada to act in the best interests of its own citizens. It does not take much imagination to see that our rights and interests will be, for Canada, the ground of least resistance in the new investment regime.

For the indigenous elders, who have often expressed deep regrets about money becoming a new god for humanity, the hopes for a more just society, based on traditional values, have just been given another major setback as we enter the new millennium.

NATIONAL TREATMENT/MOST FAVOURED NATION: THE TWO PRINCIPLES FOR THE NON-DISCRIMINATION OF INVESTORS AND INVESTMENTS

The MAI will definitely impair the obligation of countries to plan for long-term stewardship of the environment. This restriction on all governments will arise due to the MAI principle of National Treatment, a principle of treating all investors the same (non-discrimination) which will prohibit governments from favouring "community land tenure or resource management rights, citizenship requirements for seeking fishing or woodlot licences, or subsidies to support community economic development".[2]

This same concern about the undue limits placed on Canadian sovereignty was elaborated by the Government of British Columbia in its submission to the Sub-Committee on International Trade, Trade Disputes and Investments on Nov. 26, 1997:

"British Columbia is concerned, for example, that the extension of National Treatment could lead to challenges that public expenditures targeted to small businesses and/or to community-based or non-profit health, social service and education providers should be extended on a "non-discriminatory" basis to large foreign-affiliated investors and service providers. Similarly, subsidies directed preferentially to non-profit enterprises (such as subsidies available only to non-profit child care providers) would also be exposed to challenge."[3]

Other concrete examples are provided by the Western Governors' Association, which has studied the potential effects of the MAI on state and local governments. In their report dated April, 1997, the Governors state:

"Many states restrict in some way the ownership or sale of real estate, the use of public lands, and business licenses based on residency or citizenship. These restrictions would be inconsistent with the proposed MAI anti-discrimination provision for national treatment."

"State restrictions in commercial fishing could violate proposed MAI standards for national treatment, either because they explicitly favour state residents or because they have the effect of excluding new market entrants to the disadvantage of foreign contracts."

"Many states seek to balance economic development with sound resource management of state lands. They do this by placing limitations and controls on the sale of public lands and the use of its resources. One of the mechanisms used is to limit beneficial use to state residents. Many of these measures could violate anti-discrimination and MFN [most-favoured nation] protections for investors under the MAI." [4]

To First Nations, the MAI adds just another layer in our fight to govern ourselves and our lands consistent with our traditions and values, including the attachment and deference of our culture to the land and all of creation. In the future, any measure undertaken to protect our land and resources or even to limit its exploitation by other citizens will run afoul of the MAI.

As the Indian Act restricts our self-rule over our lands, the MAI will become the Kitchi (Cree for "Great" or "Big") Indian Act to restrict our ability to make laws for investors and investments in our lands and resources in our territories. Whatever concerns the provincial governments and the American governors have about the MAI also apply to us, only our situation is weaker by virtue of the fact that these same governments (provincial and state), while expressing concern for their own sovereignty, have no qualms whatsoever in ignoring ours. This, of course, does not lessen the threat that the MAI presents to the capacity of First Nations governments to exercise within their jurisdiction the principle of most-favoured treatment for their own people and cultures and not for investors. In short, the MAI is the new threat to our self-rule.

What is particularly galling about the federal government negotiating for all Canadians is that, in so doing, it has forgotten its constitutional obligation and duty to consult with First Nations before proceeding with negotiations that will ultimately infringe upon our Treaty and Aboriginal rights. Indeed, its duty from our point of view is not just for "mere consultation" but to demonstrate respect for our people as distinct peoples and nations who have the inherent right to represent themselves in any negotiations that may impact on our rights to land, resources and self-rule. And one can be confident that, if the MAI affects provincial and federal powers on matters such as the environment, the economy, health care services and the rights of workers, then First Nations will once more become unwitting victims.

Another issue for First Nations is the assumption by Canada that it can bind our peoples and governments to international standards of any kind without our involvement or consent. Our people and nations have never surrendered their political sovereignty to the colonizer. An aspect of inherent self-determination is the historical convention that sees and treats us as nations of peoples. While we may not be nation-states in the same sense as Canada, we are no less determined to maintain our political freedom. We have no desire to be reduced to sub-national local governments within the Canadian nation-state.

Canada's negotiations for a new international regime for investors and investments cannot be deemed to have our approval. Nor can any such deal assume our eventual compliance. Indeed, it is not likely that our people and First Nations governments will allow the MAI to extend deep into their culture or territory. Non-compliance to measures of assimilation--Canadian laws against our spirituality provide an historic example--will more likely prevail, rather than our people eventually acquiescing to the MAI.

Indeed, we find it less than amusing to see the Canadian government argue for a most-favoured treatment to foreign investors when in our own backyard it has yet to clean up its most-**un**favoured treatment of Aboriginal peoples. At the same time that Canada has been helping to delay and prolong the international Declaration of Indigenous Rights, it has been supporting the hasty establishment of a money treaty that, unlike a declaration, is binding on all countries which sign it. Why was not a treaty made between nation-states to recognize the special status and position of indigenous peoples, rather than one that will create new rights for people with money to spare for investments?

Prohibition Against Performance Requirements: Padlocking the Public Interest and Good Government

The so-called Performance Requirements of the proposed MAI should be more accurately called "non-performance" requirements, since they severely restrict the ability of nation-states to better provide for the redistribution of wealth and social benefits in society.

Some of the practices in Canada that could become the basis of legal challenges under the MAI are the "buy domestic" programs and the small business set-asides. Just at a time when the federal government finally sets up an aboriginal procurement policy, the MAI rears its ugly head against such domestic procurement preferences. Indeed, any existing or future affirmative action measures would be deemed not to comply with the non-discrimination requirements of the MAI, leading to costly litigation that could result in taxpayers compensating aggrieved investors.

First Nations governments that are ready for or already engaged in mainstream economic development on their lands need to understand that doing business under the MAI will definitely entail the loss rather than the retention of First Nations sovereignty. We will be unable to initiate our own procurement preferences that promote local business development, preferential hiring for women or people with disabilities, local buying and hiring measures, or undertake anything that appears to be an advantage, even for our people on our land.

That the MAI can be so far-reaching as to create a Bill of Rights for investors shows how threatened the public interest has become under the new global economy. While we are denied our Treaty and Aboriginal rights to land, resources and cultures by the Canadian governments on domestic soil, it is clear that Canadian negotiators are seeking completely inadequate "reservations" or "exceptions" to the MAI as a way of shielding our people, lands, resources and self-rule from the operators of this international treaty. Investors come first, First Nations come last.

Imagine the complicity of the federal government that continues to deny us our Treaty rights to education, for example, while keenly helping to establish Treaty rights for investors and protections for their investments. If Canada would only show the same esteem for Aboriginal people as it does for people with money, we most definitely would not be sharing one common experience—poverty in the land of plenty.

How the federal government can be so willing to forgo the "performance requirements" as a tool to hold investors accountable for jobs and local economic development is difficult to comprehend and accept. But for them to do so and affect the power of provincial governments, local governments and First Nations governments without their knowledge and consent is not just underhanded but downright irresponsible. In particular, when the federal government purports to bind the First Nations governments to all the MAI provisions, it is rewriting its own constitutional obligations to all Aboriginal peoples. For First Nations, this unilateral rewriting of our Treaties without our consent, like the Migratory Bird Convention of 1919 with the U.S. and Mexico, is another assault on our nation-to-nation relationship with the Crown and another means of assimilating our Treaties into Canadian law and economics.

In its submission to the House of Commons Standing Committee, the Government of British Columbia reminded the federal government that "performance requirements are used by governments to hold investors accountable to job creation and other economic benefit pledges; for example, when companies receive government financial assistance or permits to exploit publicly-owned resources" [5]. The B.C. submission goes on to lament that the "MAI would prohibit governments from linking approval of investments, or providing a subsidy or other 'advantage' to investors or investments, with certain types of performance requirements"[6].

While the Government of British Columbia stated its position in strong language for foreign or domestic companies that are "granted the right to develop publicly-owned natural resources,"[7] it hardly bears repeating that all of those so-called publicly-owned natural resources are lodged in the homelands of First Nations Aboriginal titles. Of course, the issue of ownership and title is very much the heart of the matter whenever Aboriginal title is negotiated anywhere in Canada, including beautiful British Columbia.

I suppose some satisfaction can be felt by First Nations in British Columbia to learn that its government is eager to assert its jurisdiction in a responsible manner that holds investors accountable to the people in the province. One cannot help wondering, however, if that government or, for that matter, any Canadian government can empathize with the First Nations peoples in both the displacement of their lands and the dismissal of their sovereignty over traditional territories. On the other hand, two wrongs do not make a right. While we can sympathize with the loss of capacity to protect one's lands, resources and peoples, we don't have to accept the loss as inevitable.

THE COST OF DOING BUSINESS IS COMPENSATION

Most of the analyses done on the MAI correctly identify the broad definition of "an investment" and its linkage to "expropriation" as the most offensive aspect of the MAI. This part of the treaty is nothing less than a bald measure to protect investors and their investments with a big stick ...the right to compensation in the event of a breach of the treaty. Those with money to invest want to do business and to be guaranteed full compensation by any offending countries; namely, taxpayers. In the language of the global market it is called "liberalization of trade," but the consequences for countries which fail to "liberalize" are far from egalitarian; it is, pure and simple, opportunism. In any indigenous language, including Cree, Dene, Micmac or Coast Salish, "liberalization of trade" means simply to remain "open or receptive to trade with others." For investors and their investments, the new, expanded definitions carry the meaning "fair and equitable treatment and full and constant protection and security."[8]

Being open to trade should not carry any liability by trading countries for "states of emergency," revolutions, civil disturbances, or armed conflicts. Yet the MAI may result in the creation of new rights for investors to restitution or compensation. On the other hand, if Canada wants to pay out taxpayers' dollars for "civil disturbances" related to conflicts about treaties or land claims and thereby provide "protection from strife" to all investors and their investments, it may open up an entirely new political strategy for First Nations people. Time will tell if we will take advantage of these provisions to force Canada to comply with our rights.

It does seem rather odd, however, to see Canada so eager to create these new rights for investors and protections for their investments, especially in light of the fact that "restitution, indemnification, compensation or any other settlement" are the very issues that remain outstanding to First Nations and other Aboriginal peoples who have suffered losses under the domination of Canada in the past century and more. Perhaps we should redefine ourselves as First Nations Investors in order for Canada to take notice and become our champion for the "fair and equitable treatment and full and constant protection and security."

"Because I Am Special I Shall Have My Own Tribunal"

Under Part V of the MAI, "Dispute Settlement," investors would be given the right to have their own investor-state dispute mechanisms. The arbitration tribunal would be obligated to give full meaning and effect to the MAI. The concern expressed here is that disputes between an investor and a country would routinely bypass domestic laws and courts, thereby "increasing the uncertainty for policy-makers and expos[ing] the Canadian taxpayer to additional financial liability" [9].

Apart from the issue of whether investors should have their own tribunal, the other uncertainty is *what* conflicts, under the broad protection given investors, would allow them to allege expropriation.

For the First Nations in British Columbia, this should serve as a warning that action be taken to protect the land claims process and negotiations, which are already viewed as threats by investors. Indeed, the Government of B.C.uses the following example of what potentially qualifies as a valid claim by an investor for full compensation:

> *"To take a current, complex and highly sensitive issue —if the settlement of an Aboriginal land claim involves depriving third parties of property interests covered under the broad MAI definition, then, if that third party is a foreign-affiliated investor, it could seek full compensation under the investor-state provisions of the MAI. (This recourse would not be available to domestic Canadian investors.) An arbitration panel ruling would be binding and monetary damage awards would be enforceable through the Canadian courts. Consequently, the MAI could expose governments to increased costs and, by providing for-*

eign-affiliated investors with a unilateral option to go to binding international arbitration, could adversely change the dynamics of land claim settlement negotiations."[10]

The danger identified is the "increased costs" to governments, but of course the real damage to First Nations will be the adverse impact on settlement negotiations that result from the new rights to compensation bestowed on investors. Public opinion would be hostile to the possibility of paying twice for the same settlements.

The question that immediately jumps to mind is: Who is minding the store? Where is the federal fiduciary responsibility to protect Aboriginal peoples, their lands and their resources? Why is the federal government ignoring its responsibilities to Aboriginal peoples, while at the same time bowing to the wishes of transnational corporations and big-time investors? For that matter, who is protecting the public purse against investors who see an opportunity to recover bad investments?

Another approach that we can take as First Nations is to demand from the federal government our own international tribunal for the resolution of our disputes on treaties and Aboriginal rights and title. The idea of being able to nominate our own representative on a tribunal has been for decades an expressed alternative to domestic courts, many of which have shown a complete disregard of our inherent rights. But the likelihood of Canada championing an independent international tribunal for First Nations is indeed remote. In fact, it isn't hard to prophesy that, if another country were to seek the establishment of an independent tribunal at the UN to resolve our Treaty and Aboriginal title disputes, Canada would oppose it in the strongest language, including arguing for preservation of its sovereignty. That Canada is perfectly willing to give up its sovereignty for the sake of investors and their investments, and to pay the additional costs (compensation) of doing business in the future, is incomprehensible and irresponsible.

Preserving First Nations' Jurisdiction and Territories

One of the biggest grounds for suspicion of the MAI has been the secrecy of the negotiations. The Government of Canada has not reached out to Canadian citizens, and even the provincial governments are outside the loop of negotiations, although they are being briefed on developments.

In the recent decision on *Delgamuukw*, the Supreme Court of Canada went to great lengths to define the fiduciary duty of government to talk to Aboriginal people whenever the governments are considering measures that may or will impact on Aboriginal title. The duty has been described as ranging from consultation to the involvement of Aboriginal people in the decisions to even requiring "the full consent of an Aboriginal nation." In describing when "full consent" may be required, the Supreme Court cited the example of when provinces enact hunting and fishing regulations in relation to Aboriginal lands:

> *"In most cases, it will be significantly deeper than mere consultation. Some cases may even require the full consent of an Aboriginal nation, particularly when provinces enact hunting and fishing regulations in relation to aboriginal lands."*

The MAI has been hidden from Canadians, and were it not for the Council of Canadians, many of us would still be in the dark. Yet, Canada has been told by its Supreme Court that it has a fiduciary duty not just to disclose information to First Nations, but, more importantly, in measures that are likely to infringe on Aboriginal title, to go beyond "mere consultation". The MAI is a measure in which that duty can only be satisfied if First Nations consent to its provisions. To date, no First Nation government or organization has been approached for a "heads up," much less consultation or consent.

First Nations can and will use their lands in ways that are good for the nation and the environment. In so doing, First Nations will develop laws that will represent their character as a people and not as ordained by the MAI. Reserve lands are only a small piece of the Aboriginal title, not all of it. The Treaties, as understood by our people, do not surrender title to the Crown. In sum, Aboriginal title exists in all parts of Canada and that title has not been extinguished. But the MAI, which would apply everywhere in Canada, would infringe upon how we use our lands and what laws we may make in the future to protect our lands and to provide benefits to our citizens as other governmental jurisdictions have done in the past, unfettered by the MAI.

Even though the federal government has a battery of lawyers at its disposal, it is not inconceivable that the issues of Treaty rights and Aboriginal rights have not been broached in relation to the MAI. What is more likely and consistent with First Nations-government relations is that the federal government has once again chosen to ignore the constitutional rights of First Nations and its fiduciary responsibility towards them.

A STRATEGY FOR FIRST NATIONS: SECURING RESPECT

First Nations, in compliance with their nation-to-nation status and their constitutional rights, should be automatically granted immunity from the MAI, through the use of exceptions and/or reservations.

Exceptions are used in international agreements to blanket certain areas from the provisions of the agreement. In the MAI, the general exceptions that would apply across the board are: national security, public order, and international peace and security.[11] There are no proposals for exceptions to protect the rights and freedoms of indigenous peoples. Canada has not yet proposed any exceptions on their behalf. It is not likely to do so unless pushed hard.

Reservations are a lower form of exception that are used to deal with country-specific "carve-outs" to an agreement. In a legal opinion prepared for the Council of Canadians, international lawyer Barry Appleton advised that "Reservations are a form of exception to international treaty commitments and are interpreted narrowly by international courts and tribunals. Great care must be taken in the making of reservations, as they will be interpreted strictly by international tribunals."[12]

Canada's role in the negotiations has been criticized, and rightly so, for placing investors and their investments over its constitutional and good government obligations and its responsibility to Canadians. Issues have been raised about the absence of protection in the MAI for "matters that go to the heart of being a Canadian," such as health and child care, education services, environmental conservation and protection, culture and cultural industries. If the Government of Canada will not fight for Canadian identity, it will certainly not fight for those values and matters that are at the heart of being First Nations peoples. In other words, a country-specific reservation for First Nations and their inherent rights has not been proposed or even contemplated by the Government of Canada.

First Nations are not given the same kind of respect that Scandinavian countries have shown to the Sami people, an indigenous nation. These countries have proposed a country-specific reservation to protect the Sami people and their traditions. Why was this done? Because these countries are "committed to preserving and developing the means of livelihood, language, culture and way of life of the Sami people".[13] This proposed reservation for the Sami is attached at the end of this section.

What is interesting about this reservation is that it seeks to protect the exclusive rights to reindeer husbandry and their "traditional Sami areas." Instead of conforming with the ideas of "rollback" and "standstill," this reservation may allow for future amendments "to take account of further developments of exclusive Sami rights linked to their traditional means of livelihood." Unfortunately for the Sami, this reservation is permissive and not mandatory.

In Canada, First Nations can negotiate for a stronger reservation, taking into account the recent decision of the Supreme Court that Aboriginal title entails the use and occupancy of land that transcends "traditional only" activities. In that decision, the Supreme Court defined Aboriginal title to include "more than the right to engage in specific activities which may be themselves Aboriginal rights." In other words, First Nations in Canada must take immediate measures to negotiate with Canada a country-specific reservation that will entail an exception to the MAI for First Nations peoples, their lands and resources, and their sovereignty. A non-derogation clause, as in the Meech Lake Accord, will not suffice.

CONCLUSION AND RECOMMENDATIONS: THE POWER OF ALL

First Nations leaders have power whenever they move as one political force to fight government and to protect their rights, lands and people. In the past, whenever we have chosen to do so, we have also formed powerful coalitions and alliances with churches, human rights groups, environmental groups, labour, women's groups and others to collectively take on governments that have in some way violated the public trust.

THIS IS SUCH A TIME!

In essence, we have two choices: to oppose the MAI or to change it. Neither choice will be easy since complete opposition will entail international dimensions and any changes we seek will be resisted by a federal government that has shown no desire to involve the provinces or its citizens in the negotiations, much less Aboriginal peoples.

However, in terms of power to challenge the unilateral actions of the federal government, no collective in Canada except the First Nations has the legal muscle (fiduciary duty) to challenge and halt Canada's involvement in these ongoing negotiations in the domestic courts.

The following recommendations to the First Nations are made as direct measures that will help to advance and protect our rights and interests in relation to the future impacts of the MAI:

1. Make the MAI a priority issue for your First Nation and organization by placing it as a regular agenda item for information and action.

2. First Nations with Treaty-based organization and First Nations involved in land negotiations should seek legal advice from their respective legal counsels on the impact of MAI on existing treaties and on current negotiations for new treaties.
3. The First Nations can mandate the Assembly of First Nations to intervene on their behalf with direction to the National Chief and Executive to take all measures, including political action, to protect Treaty and Aboriginal rights.
4. All First Nations can write to the Prime Minister condemning his government's role to date on the MAI and demanding that the Government of Canada seek exemptions to the MAI on health, culture, environmental, labour and on the Treaty and Aboriginal rights of First Nations, including the inherent right of self-government and Aboriginal title.
5. First Nations can insist that the nation-to-nation relationship be respected by Canada and that First Nations representatives be involved in the negotiations, assuming First Nations opt to be guided by the second choice stated above.
6. A legal strategy must be devised by First Nations that will include an injunction to all negotiations in the event the Government of Canada continues to ignore First Nations interest or refuses to involve First Nations in the negotiations.
7. First Nations can take steps to form coalitions and alliances with national organizations such as the Council of Canadians and invite their representatives to speak on the MAI at Chiefs' gatherings and conferences.
8. First Nations can organize a Special National Conference dedicated to the issue of the MAI or, alternatively, organize this national conference together with leaders of the labour, women's and environmental organizations, churches and human rights organizations and the Council of Canadians.
9. First Nations can make contacts and establish joint strategies with other indigenous peoples and organizations: for example, the Maori of New Zealand, the Sami of Scandinavia, the Abo-

rigines of Australia, and the indigenous peoples of Central and South America.

10. First Nations need to designate representatives with mandates to participate in international lobbies to protect their rights and interests in subsequent negotiations on developments surrounding the MAI.
11. Most important of all the recommendations: do not dismiss the MAI and its import in the future of First Nations peoples, land, resources and sovereignty.

The principal purpose of this analysis is to alert First Nations governments and people to the impact of the MAI on our lands, resources, people and sovereignty. The recommendations are designed to further the goal of understanding the impacts of the MAI and developing a strategy that would result in protecting First Nations rights and interests.

ENDNOTES

[1] p.18 Native American Wisdom, Dovetail Books, ed. Kristen Maree Cleary

[2] West Coast Environmental Law, paper entitled "Multilateral Agreement on Investment"

[3] Submission by the Government of British Columbia to the House of Commons Sub-Committee on International Trade, Trade Disputes and Investment of the Standing Committee on Foreign Affairs and International Trade, entitled "The Proposed Multilateral Agreement on Investment", November 26 1997.

[4] Paper by the Western Governors' Association entitled "Multilateral Agreement on Investment: Potential Effect on State and Local Government", April 1997.

[5] Government of British Columbia submission to Sub-Committee, November 26, 1997

[6] Ibid

[7] Ibid

[8] DAFFE/MAI/NM (97)2, Multilateral Agreement on Investment, Consolidated Text and Commentary (iv. Investment Protection 1.1 General Treatment), p. 52

[9] Government of British Columbia submission to Sub-Committee, November 26 1997

[10] Submission by the Government of British Columbia to the Sub-Committee, November 26 1997

[11] Western Governors' Association paper entitled Multilateral Agreement on Investment: Potential Effects on State and Local Government, April 1997
[12] Legal opinion dated November 14, 1997 by Appleton and Associates.
[13] Draft MAI, p. 176

APPENDIX

PROPOSED MAI ANNEX ON THE SAMI PEOPLE

THE CONTRACTING PARTIES,

RECOGNIZING the obligations and commitments of these countries with regard to the Sami people under national and international law,

NOTING, in particular, that these countries are committed to preserving and developing the means of livelihood, language, culture and way of life of the Sami people,

CONSIDERING the dependence of traditional Sami culture and livelihood on primary economic activities, such as reindeer husbandry in the traditional areas of Sami settlement,

HAVE AGREED on the following provisions.

ARTICLE 1

Notwithstanding the provisions of this Agreement, exclusive rights to reindeer husbandry within traditional Sami areas may be granted to the Sami people.

ARTICLE 2

This Annex may be extended to take account of any further development of exclusive Sami rights linked to their traditional means of livelihood. The Parties Group may adopt the necessary amendments to this Annex.

THE MAI AND LABOUR RIGHTS

The Role and Significance of the OECD Guidelines for Multinational Enterprises and Prospects for a Binding Labour Clause

by Roy Jones

INTRODUCTION

The trade union campaign to get meaningful and enforceable labour rights and standards in the MAI has been a long one[2]. The MAI Negotiating Group now talks of the "three anchors" approach to labour standards in the Agreement: a preambular reference to core labour standards, the annexation of the OECD Guidelines for Multinational Enterprises to the MAI itself, and the inclusion of a clause committing governments not to lower labour standards to attract investment. The first two measures have for the most part been resolved. As to the third "anchor", the so-called labour clause, governments have yet to resolve this to the satisfaction of the trade union movement.

The issues surrounding the MAI and labour standards will be discussed later. First, however, a brief historical digression is required to discuss previous trade union campaigns to regulate the activities of multinational enterprises (MNEs).[3] An overview of the OECD Guidelines for Multinational Enterprises will follow, including the reasons why TUAC has not completely written them off. The chapter will then cover the way in which the debate has evolved as regards the MAI and labour standards, including the proposal for a binding labour clause. The concluding remarks will draw the threads of the arguments together.

Regulating Multinationals: A Historical Perspective

Far from being a post-Second World War phenomenon, the activities of MNEs have been traced back as far as the 14th century[4]: estimates suggest that by the end of that century as many as 150 Italian banks were operating internationally, along with international commerce based in Germany and the UK. Colonialism and the industrial revolution gave a further boost to Foreign Direct Investment (FDI), and by the 1920s international business activity had evolved sufficiently to give rise to truly diversified and integrated MNEs. FDI activity slowed during the 1930s and war years, and then began to expand in the 1950s before truly accelerating in the mid-1980s[5].

Governance issues related to multinationals were first debated around trade-related matters in the 1940s (though in an indirect manner). The linkage of the trade and labour standards (TLS) debate to multinationals would surprise some, but given the prominence today of MNEs in international trade—witness, for example, that around one-third of trade is intra-MNE, and that a further one-third is between them—then the real world linkage is there, even if some policy-makers and theorists have yet to connect it.[6]

Over and above the debates around fair trade in the late 19th century, and at the inception of the ILO, the first substantive attempt at introducing a social dimension into trade relations came in 1947. Then, the United Nations Conference on Trade and Employment held in Havana sought to establish an institutional framework for encouraging the growth of trade and investment and avoid a return to the "beggar-my-neighbour" trade wars of the 1930s.

The founding Charter of the International Trade Organization (ITO) approved by governments at Havana included a social clause committing ITO members to observe fair labour standards. Article 7 stated, among other things that "The members recognize that unfair labour conditions, particularly in product for export, create difficulties in international trade..." However, the international institution whose creation was agreed by governments at

Havana—the International Trade Organization (ITO) —never saw the light of day. In 1950, the United States Congress failed to ratify the Charter and the ITO was never created.

Had the ITO come into being, along with its social clause, then the debates around regulating multinationals would undoubtedly have taken a different route. In concrete terms, the ability of governments in developing countries to create export processing zones that deliberately suppress workers' rights to attract foreign investment would have been undermined.

From that time until the 1970s, outside of the trade union movement and some developing countries little attention was paid to linking labour standards to international trade and investment. The 1970s changed all that as events forced policy- makers to focus their attention on the activities of MNEs. Events in Latin America prompted the International Labour Organiation (ILO) to start looking into the social impact of MNEs in 1972, but the catalyst for change was the role played by U.S. multinationals in the 1973 coup that toppled the democratically elected President of Chile, Salvador Allende.

The events in Chile led to a chain reaction. In parallel moves the United Nations, following the report of a Group of Eminent Persons, set up in 1975 a Commission and Centre on Transnational Corporations. The Commission then started work on a UN Code of Conduct for Transnational Corporations. In 1976, the OECD adopted its voluntary Guidelines for Multinational Enterprises, to be followed in 1977 by the equally voluntary ILO Tripartite Declaration on Multinational Enterprises and Social Policy.

The implementation of voluntary regulations covering multinationals and social issues was as far as things got. An attempt was made by the then EEC to adopt a Directive[7] covering the activities of MNEs (the "Vredeling Directive"). But it too ran into the ground for the same reasons that the 1980s and early 1990s became a lost period for any attempt to implement social regulations on foreign investors, namely the changing political economy, including that related to international investment. The rise of Thatcher and Reagan coincided with the monetarist revolution that overturned the post-war Keynsian consensus, giving rise to a political underpinning for the resurrection of the neo-classical concept of supply side labour market policies, including the hegemony of the "managerial prerogative' in terms of industrial relations.

As regards international investment, the implementation of rules to control multinationals gave way to the development of mechanisms and institutions to promote foreign investment and investors. Because of this, the UN Code of Conduct for Transnational Corporations was finally killed off in the early 1990s by the combined efforts of the then U.S. government, the International OrganiZation of Employers, and the International Chamber of Commerce. In 1994, the UN Commission On Transnational Corporations was scaled down and reorganized as the Commission on International Investment and Transnational Corporations, while the Secretariat serving it was reorganized as an UNCTAD Division *for* Transnational Corporations and Investment. It has been said that one of the main achievements of the UN Centre was in giving assistance to China for the establishment of their Special Economic Zones.[8]

Turning to the ILO, while the Workers' Group managed to block an attempt to abolish the Multinational Enterprises Branch, the resources devoted to this work were substantially reduced in 1993. As regards the ILO Tripartite Declaration on Multinationals, the Employers' Group, with the support of some governments, successfully blocked throughout the 1980s and early 1990s any meaningful interpretations of the Declaration. This was in the face of incontrovertible evidence presented by the International Confederation of Free Trade Unions (ICFTU) of abuses of workers' and trade union rights. In fact, throughout this time, it was mainly due to the efforts of the ICFTU that the Declaration remained alive.

The OECD Guidelines For Multinationals

Throughout this period, the political fate of the OECD Guidelines was broadly similar to that of the ILO Declaration. Outside of a few governments and TUAC, most OECD Members paid lip service to their implementation. On the basis of this, some critics dismissed the Guidelines as worthless. TUAC has not shared that view.

Although voluntary, the Guidelines which date from 1976 have moral weight as they express OECD governments' collective expectations concerning the behaviour and activities of multinational enterprises. The Guidelines are much broader than the ILO Declaration in that they cover the full range of MNEs' activities, with chapters covering: General Policies, Information Disclosure, Competition, Financing, Taxation, Employment and Industrial Relations, Environmental Protection, and Science and Technology. They also differ from the ILO Declaration in that all OECD Members are obliged to set up National Contact Points (NCPs) in government to promote and implement the Guidelines, and to help solve problems as they arise. The OECD also holds periodic reviews of the Guidelines, which have in the past led to revisions and clarifications. The next review (discussed below) will be held in 1998.

The chapter in the Guidelines on Employment and Industrial Relations represents a clear statement of good industrial relations practice which is of relevance today[9]. In particular, multinationals are expected to:

- respect the rights of workers to be represented by trade unions and other *bona fide* organizations, and engage in constructive negotiations with them;
- provide the necessary facilities and information to employee representatives to allow the development of effective collective agreements;
- provide information to employee representatives for a true and fair view of the performance of the enterprise;
- observe standards of employment and industrial relations not less favourable than those observed by comparable employers in the host country;
- in cooperation with employee representatives and relevant government authorities utilize, train and prepare for upgrading their

local labour force;

- provide employee representatives with reasonable prior notice of changes in operations, in particular on intended closure and collective layoffs or dismissals, and cooperate with employee representatives and government authorities so as to mitigate their adverse effects;
- refrain from discriminatory practice in their employment policies;
- in the context of negotiations with employee representatives not to threaten to transfer production nor workers in an attempt to influence the outcome of negotiations or to hinder the right to organize; and
- enable employee representatives to conduct collective bargaining or labour management relations with the level of management authorized to take decisions on the matters in hand.

TUAC's main criticism of the Guidelines has been the lack of attention paid over the years by governments and business to their implementation. Around 30 cases have been brought to the attention of the OECD Committee on International investment and Multinational Enterprises (CIME) that deals with Guidelines- related issues. Most were initiated by TUAC, but also by the Belgian, Danish, Netherlands, and French governments.

During the 1980s and early 1990s, the CIME discussions on cases brought forward under the Guidelines would be akin to a dialogue with the deaf, with most government representatives remaining silent. In one particular case brought forward in 1993, one of the governments involved complained that TUAC should not be allowed to name the company during the discussions. That case is still unresolved, some five years later. In a similar vein, an updated handbook on the Guidelines that was agreed by the 1992 Review was finally published in 1994, while the report of an OECD Symposium on the Guidelines took over two years to publish.

Outside of a few countries (notably Belgium, Finland, Sweden and Switzerland), the National Contact Points became moribund. Trade union requests for information on the Guidelines were and still are often ignored. The OECD itself reviewed the NCPs in 1996. On this it is worth recalling the NCPs' terms of reference, which are: to promote the Guidelines; collect information on the experiences with the Guidelines; handle enquiries; discuss matters related to the Guidelines; assist in solving problems between business and labour, or between NCPs, in matters covered by the Guidelines. The results of the Review came as no surprise to TUAC.

Six countries engaged in promotional activities, with five saying that they had disseminated the Guidelines and provided a forum for exchanges of views with trade unions. Four countries collected information on experiences in applying the Guidelines, while two said that they prepared regular reports on national level observance and experiences. Five countries circulated the CIME clarifications to the social partners, and the same number said that they helped to find solutions when issues arose under the Guidelines. These disappointing results are all the more so given that the OECD observed that "considerable caution" was required in interpreting the results, in that some respondents had in their response to the Review stated that they had undertaken all possible activities. The OECD concluded:

> *"The main impression left by the replies (and the absence of replies from over half of the delegations) is that, with some exceptions, the modus operandi of the NCPs is reactive rather than initiating and that the activities undertaken by many NCPs have been modest, at least in the past years."*[10]

These results were confirmed by a TUAC survey[11] of its affiliates as part of the OECD Review. Several TUAC affiliates reported that their NCP had all but ceased to exist, and as such could not respond to the survey. As regards those that were aware of their NCP, the responses confirmed the OECD's view that the NCPs had inflated the number of activities that they engaged in. Moreover, trade unions in those countries that had recently joined the OECD (Czech Republic, Hungary, Mexico and Poland) reported that no attempt had been made by their NCP to contact them.

Our criticisms of the Guidelines and the NCPs were recognized by the OECD itself when it noted in 1996[12]: "To-date, no formal evaluation of these criticisms has been made. In particular, further study is needed in order to assess whether the Guidelines have had any impact on the observance of core labour standards by MNEs in developing countries." (Another TUAC criticism.)

From this section it is clear that the OECD Guidelines do have a role to play in governing the activities of multinationals, but that government inaction is the major stumbling block to achieving this, along with the negative attitudes of many multinationals. At present, there is a conjunction of two events that have the potential to shift governments into a more pro-active stance on multinationals: the Asian crisis, and the MAI. The former is beyond the scope of this chapter, and the next section will discuss the latter.

THE MAI: AN OPPORTUNITY TO REINFORCE AND STRENGTHEN LABOUR STANDARDS

The MAI will become the focal point and benchmark for all issues related to international investment, and within this the way that multinationals operate. Given the way that non-OECD governments are queuing up to negotiate their membership, the MAI has the potential to become a global treaty.[13] The MAI is therefore a challenge to governments and the way in which they themselves adhere to labour standards, as well as how they expect multinationals to adhere to high standards of industrial relations practice. How governments respond to this challenge will be gauged by their response to the TUAC demands for the inclusion of the following in the MAI:

1. a forceful reference in the Preamble of the MAI in which governments affirm their support for both core labour standards and the OECD Guidelines for Multinational Enterprises;
2. the annexing of the full Guidelines to the MAI itself, and not the Final Act;

3. the establishment of National Contact Points to enforce the Guidelines, which should be a legally binding element of the Agreement for all Parties without exception;
4. the wording of the text so that non-Members acceding to the MAI would automatically adopt the Guidelines;
5. the inclusion of a binding clause in the MAI, subject to dispute settlement, such that governments "shall" not seek to attract investment by the suppression or non-enforcement of domestic labour standards or by violating internationally recognized core workers' rights. This clause would also encompass environmental standards.

At this time, points one through four appear to have been accepted by the Negotiating Group. This should send a powerful signal that governments intend that the Guidelines take on the nature of a universal code of conduct for multinationals, not least because of the accession to the Agreement of many non-OECD countries. Making the Decision on National Contact Points part of the MAI should reinforce their role as a monitoring and enforcement mechanism of the Guidelines, and a monitoring body on international investment more generally. This is recognized by the OECD itself in its Report on Trade, Employment and Labour Standards,[14] which stated:

> "*The OECD Guidelines on Multinational Enterprises have a role to play as a voluntary instrument to promote reasonable behaviour by MNEs. This role would be enhanced if home and host countries make it known that they expect foreign investors to follow the Guidelines world-wide and if non-Member countries were encouraged to endorse the Guidelines...This would send a clear message of the importance OECD governments attach to the respect of these standards.*"

Two interrelated elements could also add weight to the implementation of the Guidelines. First, it is TUAC's intention that the NCPs should play an active role in the settlement of any disputes concerning labour standards arising through the implementation of a binding "labour clause" (discussed below). This would bring the Guidelines closer still to the every-day application of the MAI. Secondly, the OECD will shortly begin a review of the Guidelines. TUAC has argued that the review should agree, *inter-alia*, on the inclusion in the Guidelines of references to relevant core labour standards, other textual revisions to take account of the outcome of the 1997 Renault case brought forward under the Guidelines, and the strengthening of the Environment Chapter. However, the main focus of the review should be on strengthening the implementation mechanism and promotional measures for the Guidelines.

At the same time, the incorporation into the MAI text of a binding "labour clause" would add a new dimension to the regulatory regime for multinationals. As proposed by TUAC, the clause would bind signatories to observe internationally recognized core labour rights and not to reduce or offer to lower domestic labour standards to attract foreign investment[15].

We recognize that the inclusion of such a clause raises technical questions around the definition of domestic and "core" labour standards, and the implementation mechanisms. However, these would not be more difficult to resolve than technical questions posed by other aspects of the Agreement[16]. At the end of the day, the inclusion of such a clause is a political question as to whether governments are prepared to balance legally-binding rights for investors with those for workers.

We understand that there is little dispute about the definition of domestic labour *standards* as preferred to the word *measures*. In our view, a clause on not lowering domestic labour standards is intended to guarantee the implementation and enforcement of labour standards on a non-discriminatory basis for both domestic and foreign investors, reflecting in the labour field the principle of National Treatment which is fundamental to the MAI.

As regards core workers' rights, there is now an international consensus regarding the special significance of fundamental workers' rights in the present global context, and the need for their universal application. They are enabling rights for workers rather than quantitative labour standards. The World Summit for Social Development held in Copenhagen in March 1995 made several authoritative statements of relevance. In particular, commitment 3(1)(i) of the Summit, to which the 117 Heads of State and Government subscribed, read as follows:

> *"... (we will) freely promote respect for relevant International Labour Organization conventions, including those on the prohibition of forced and child labour, the freedom of association, the right to organize and bargain collectively, and the principle of non-discrimination..."*

These core labour standards were also identified in the 1996 OECD Report on Trade, Employment and Labour Standards, and currently form the basis of the elaboration in the ILO of a declaration concerning the promotion of fundamental principles and rights within the mandate of the ILO. MAI signatories should be in a position to commit themselves in a binding way to observe these fundamental principles which are embodied in the relevant ILO conventions, namely:

(i) to ensuring freedom of association and the effective recognition of the right to collective bargaining;
(ii) to suppressing all forms of forced or compulsory labour;
(iii) to ensure the effective abolition of child labour; and
(iv) to combatting discrimination in employment and occupation in all its forms, including differences in remuneration for work of equal value.

The signatory states should be the bodies involved in any eventual dispute settlement. Our intention is the avoidance of conflicts and the promotion of settlements initially through consultation or conciliation. In this sense, the binding obligation of parties to the Agreement to set up National Contact Points would play a vital role. A dispute settlement tribunal would be envisaged only as a last resort. In the event of a dispute going to a tribunal, we envisage a leading role for the ILO in determining the outcome. Regarding the outcome itself, in the first instance, any offending party should bring its labour standards into conformity with its obligations under the Agreement, with a pecuniary compensation as a last resort.

The clause on not lowering labour standards, alongside the parallel issue of environmental standards, has become one of the key issues standing in the way of the conclusion of the MAI negotiations. On the one hand, a majority of governments favour the inclusion of a binding clause covering domestic labour standards. On the other hand, a small minority (Australia, Korea, Mexico and New Zealand) remain opposed to the majority view[17]. Mexico has raised the stakes by signalling its opposition to joining the Agreement should it include a binding clause. At the same time, several governments favour the inclusion of a non-binding "best efforts" clause, where disputes would be handled through a consultation process with no binding outcome. The U.S., Germany and Japan are believed to be in the latter camp. Governments are also aware that, without a binding clause covering domestic and internationally agreed labour standards, then trade union opposition to the MAI in several key countries would make ratification increasingly unlikely.

The solution to this issue is said to rest in the hands of the U.S. It is widely felt that, if the administration were to swing behind a binding clause, then the majority position for a binding clause would prevail, in that Germany and Japan would also switch sides and isolate the hard-liners. As to the situation now, following President Clinton's inability to gain Congressional authority for the renewal of presidential fast track authority, a broad debate has now opened up across the government departments with an interest in this issue. The AFL-CIO is lobbying hard on this issue, and the administration is acutely aware of the important role that the trade unions played in shaping the outcome of the fast track debate. At this time, it is too early to say what the outcome will be, and most negotiators expect this matter to go to the wire in the negotiations.

CONCLUDING REMARKS ON THE MAI AND LABOUR STANDARDS

This chapter has sought to highlight the past and present trade union campaigns to regulate the activities of multinationals, especially in the social sphere. In this sense, the campaign around the MAI is the latest of many that have arisen in a number of forums. However, the situation today is especially acute, given that the MAI would become the benchmark for all future issues related to foreign investment, going beyond the OECD area itself to encompass many developing countries. Once agreed, the opportunity to revise upwards labour standards in the MAI would be difficult. The outcome of the OECD negotiations would also shape the debate on investment-related issues in the WTO. At some point, negotiations to agree on an MAI-type treaty will begin there.

It is crucial, therefore, that the trade union demands on the MAI and labour issues, as highlighted above, are met by governments. The importance should not be underestimated. Incorporating the OECD Guidelines into the MAI, as demanded by TUAC, could revitalize them as a universal code of conduct for multinationals, especially if the NCPs' role as an agent to implement and enforce them were to be strengthened.

The inclusion of a binding labour clause would be a major advance: for the first time ever, a multilateral investment treaty would include a mechanism to enforce internationally agreed labour standards. This would have an undoubted effect on the wider campaign to get enforceable labour standards into international trade agreements.

Trade unions and other progressive groups have little time left to drive home the message to their government representatives that the inclusion of meaningful labour standards in the MAI is a threshold issue to begin the debate at home on the ratification of the Agreement. Governments, for their part, have to signal their unwillingness to tolerate the abuse of workers' rights to attract investment in a globalizing world. The acceptance by OECD governments of the TUAC package in this area would be a first step.

Endnotes

1 TUAC is the Trade Union Advisory Committee to the OECD. It has consultative status with the OECD and represents 70 million workers in 55 affiliated trade union national centres in the 29 OECD countries. Further information on TUAC and its work, including the MAI can be found by visiting its website at "http:/www.tuac.org".

2 The chapter will focus solely on the campaign by TUAC and its affiliates to get meaningful labour standards in the MAI.As to the trade union strategy on the MAI in general, successive TUAC Plenary Sessions (where policy is set) have mandated the Secretariat to pursue the MAI/labour linkage, while affiliates themselves pursue this at the national-level, alongside the adoption of their own positions *vis-a-vis* their governments and the Agreement as a whole.

3 The parallel trade union campaign for a social clause in international trade agreements at the World Trade Organisation (WTO) will not be discussed in this chapter. It should be said however that a binding labour clause in the MAI would greatly help the campaign at the WTO, in that around one-third of world trade is intra-MNE based, with around a further third between MNEs.

4 See for example P. Hirst and G. Thompson (1996): "Globalisation in Question", Polity Press or J. H. Dunning (1993) Multinational Enterprises and the Global Economy Wokingham: Addison-Wesley.

5 ibid, P. Hurst and G. Thompson.

6 This insight appears to have been overlooked by the majority of trade specialists who continue to base their trade related policy prescriptions, especially in relation to employment and labour standards, on the axioms of perfect competition.In reality, the starting point should be imperfect competition, and then extended to a sectoral analysis based on monopsonic or monopolistic competition. The outcomes would then be radically different.

7 Eventually this was resurrected into the 1996 European Works Council Directive that gives workers rights to information and consultation with multinationals operating in Europe that meet a certain threshold. Attempts are currently being made to develop a European Company statute that European trade unions would hope to include co-determination rights.

8 Kari Tapiola, International Affairs Director, Central Organisation of Finnish Trade Unions. Speech to a TUC Conference on European Works Councils, UK, March 1995.

9 This paper will focus solely on the provisions of the Guidelines chapter on Employment and Industrial Relations. Those readers interested in other elements of the OECD Guidelines for Multinational Enterprises should request a copy from TUAC. As to their relevance today the Chair of the OECD Committee on International Investment and Multinational Enterprises stated at

the 15 January 1998 consultations between the MAI Negotiating Group and a group of employers that: "if the Guidelines did not exist today then we would have to invent them."

10 CIME note on the 1996 OECD review of the National Contact Points.

11 TUAC Survey of the National Contact Points, November 1996. The survey also included questions on the implementation of the Guidelines, and the experience of trade unions with them. The responses pointed to a growing trend of trade union rights abuses in several countries.

12 OECD Report on Trade, Employment and Labour Standards.

13 At the time of writing the following non-OECD countries have signalled their intention to join the MAI: Argentina, Brazil, Chile, Hong Kong, and the three Baltic states, Estonia, Latvia and Lithuania. Others are said to be awaiting the outcome of the negotiations before committing themselves.

14 OECD Report on Trade, Employment and Labour Studies. Paris 1996.

15 TUAC has also demanded the inclusion of a similar clause in the MAI to cover environmental standards.

16 TUAC has disseminated a paper that shows in an illustrative way potential approaches to the questions that have arisen concerning definitions of domestic labour standards and core workers' rights, and their implementation mechanisms, notably the binding dispute settlement mechanism.

17 The situation within the hard-line group of countries is however very fluid. For example, the election of Kim Dae-Jung as President of Korea has led to strengthened trade union rights, and may lead to a softening of the government posit°ion *vis a vis* labour rights in the MAI. Furthermore, the MAI is now becoming a big issue in Australia and New Zealand, and pressure will increase on these governments to take a less hard-line approach.

THE MAI AND HUMAN RIGHTS

by John W. Foster

Introduction

The MAI presents a fundamental challenge to human rights. The challenge is so broad that it may lead citizens to forget 50 years of progress in the definition, enhancement of respect for, and increasing legal force of a wide range of fundamental rights. The Canadian government, which has played a significant role in the development of international human rights frameworks, does not appear to have examined seriously the implications of the proposed MAI for the standards and rights which have taken decades to negotiate.

Furthermore, while the government exerts considerable energy and applies significant resources and political capital to the negotiation of new agreements to protect the rights of investors and corporations, it is not taking adequate leadership to strengthen the implementation and enforcement of the social, economic and cultural rights to which it is already committed.

The promise of human rights

> *"Not only are all human rights universal, indivisible, interrelated and interdependent, they are inherent in human nature and pertain to the individual."*
>
> *—Mary Robinson, UN High Commissioner for Human Rights, November, 1997.*[1]

This year, 1998, ought to be a good year for human rights. We are celebrating the 50th Anniversary of the Universal Declaration of Human Rights, the keystone of what is now known as the International Bill of Human Rights, signed Dec. 10, 1948. Canadians were instrumental in the development of this visionary document.

The Universal Declaration sets out a broad horizon for civil, political, economic, social and cultural rights. To cite just a few examples: the right to social security, the right to free choice of employment, equal pay for equal work, the right to form and join trade unions, the right to a standard of living adequate for health and well-being, the right to education.

The Universal Declaration built on the commitments of the Charter of the United Nations, which included the promotion of "social progress and better standards of life in larger freedom" and of *"the economic and social advancement of all peoples"*.[2]

International covenants

While the Universal Declaration was a statement of intentions, two *international covenants* were negotiated in the following years to give the legal force of treaties to the rights outlined in 1948. By 1966, an International Covenant on Civil and Political Rights (ICCPR) and the International Covenant on Economic, Social and Cultural Rights (ICESCR) were negotiated, coming into force 10 years later. Canada ratified both more than 20 years ago.

These treaties added a range of rights to those already embodied in the agreements founding the International Labour Organization (ILO) in 1919 and the many conventions agreed on through that body in the intervening years. In addition to the Covenants, the United Nations developed a series of further agreements which elaborate and make much more specific the covenant rights, including the Convention on the Elimination of All Forms of Discrimination Against Women (CEDAW), the Convention on the Rights of the Child (CRD), and the International Convention on the Elimination of All Forms of Racial Discrimination (CERD).

Many Canadians, whether as officials or as representatives of social and non-governmental organizations (NGOs), have taken part in the development of these international agreements and the standards they embody.

In the last decade, the United Nations attempted to push beyond the social vision in these agreements with a series of world conferences and summits, from the Earth Summit in Rio and the Vienna Human Rights Conference, through the Copenhagen Summit on Social Development and the Beijing Women's Conferences. The expanding field of environmental regulation and rights, the right to food and food security, and a variety of other urgent issues were confronted and plans of action set in motion which were aimed to enhance and expand respect for and implementation of human rights for all humanity.[3]

The results of these world encounters provided raw material for new norms and standards which might ultimately find legal force in new treaties and agreements in such areas as wide-ranging as climate change and the rights of indigenous people.

When citizens' groups met at any of these world conferences, one had the sense that they were working toward a series of human rights, environmental protections and workers' rights which would govern economic and social development around the world—a framework of norms which would transcend the interests of particular states or economic interests, and offer both standards of behavior and avenues for protection for all the globe's citizens.

INSTITUTIONS AND RIGHTS

The United Nations is not a fully democratic body; it represents states and not universal direct suffrage. However, it embodies the desire for global governance, albeit incomplete in fulfillment. As Canadian UN advisor Maurice Strong has declared:

> *"The establishment of an effective world order must be based essentially on the extension into international life of the rule of law, together with reliable mechanisms for accountability and*

enforcement, that provide the basis for the effective functioning of national societies."[4]

As he points out, the need for the United Nations is even greater now than when it was created. It must provide a global framework for actions taken at national, regional, sectoral, and other levels.

Compared to the multilateral economic institutions--the International Monetary Fund (IMF) or the World Trade Organization (WTO)--the UN is quite transparent and accessible. It currently recognizes more than 13,000 non-governmental bodies which have a variety of rights of access and in many cases of participation in debates and deliberations, including women's, environmental, indigenous and human rights groups, bodies as diverse as the National Anti-Poverty Organization, OXFAM, and the International Confederation of Free Trade Unions.

We face a situation in which the power of citizens, through their governments represented in the United Nations, is being marginalized by a concentration of power and resources in parallel global organizations set up to manage and enhance trade and investment, monetary security, and the funding of development -- namely, the WTO, the IMF, and the World Bank. Regional trade and investment agreements like NAFTA and the proposed MAI are part of this development. These bodies also represent governments, principally their trade and finance ministries. They tend to operate on a one-dollar/one-vote principle, and they are either opaque or marginally transparent.[5]

These global economic institutions (GEIs) are dominated by rich states. Their agendas, priorities and points of view are conditioned by clubs of rich states and large corporations, including the G-7 or G-8, the Organization for Economic Cooperation and Development (OECD)--the nursery in which the MAI has been developed--and annual gatherings like the "World Economic Forum" in Davos, Switzerland, which brings together 1,000 top business leaders with 250 political leaders and as many academics and media leaders. The latter Forum proudly proclaims its "leading role in the economic globalization process," including such products as the Uruguay Round of Trade Liberalization (and the WTO) and the current round of financial services liberalization agreements.

Neither the WTO nor the proposed structures for the MAI recognize the transcendance of UN authority. They may consult from time to time, as the heads of the World Bank and IMF do, with the UN Secretary General. But they are effectively out from under the global guidelines and standards developed through the UN since 1945. While the IMF and World Bank are official "specialized agencies" of the UN, the UN per se has little ability to supervise them in exercising governance of the global economy.

The MAI draft refers only to one other regime, the Articles of Agreement of the IMF. (Section X of the May, 1997 Draft MAI.)

The result of this behaviour by governments is that, while the UN has been quite successful in developing norms and standards for rights and obligations, states have encouraged the growth of economic institutions which can ignore them virtually at will. Governments like our own have encouraged this relative anarchy to develop, with the effect of marginalizing the very treaties which protect universal democratic and social economic rights. The current effort to enhance and protect property rights dramatizes the situation.

The rationale for agreements like the MAI is often that they would "extend the rule of law" or make rules which make the world safer and more predictable. This in itself is not objectionable, but it is extremely partial. The laws or rules would affect only one highly prioritized area of international life, at the expense of others. Further, they are being made by and would be administered by undemocratic, closed and inaccessible institutions, whose agendas, as British academic Susan Strange has pointed out, are dominated by large global private firms and cartels. Our governments are ceding sovereignty, and with it the potential for democratic decision-making about the shape of our economies, environments and societies, to non-state or supra-state authorities, none of which is democratically governed.[6]

Howard McConnell, a Canadian constitutional law professor, notes that, rather than extending the rule of law and constitutional norms, the MAI would "create a zone of immunity from local control by member states that make large international corporations *above the law* of signatory powers"[7]

North-South Institute President Roy Culpeper points out that global governance, including economic elements, was part of the original vision of the UN. Western governments have been quite happy to get by with "piecemeal solutions to problems as they crop up". But the challenges of a world economy characterized by enormous daily currency transactions, periodic and sudden crises, the operations of rogue currency traders, and the polarizing effects of many development interventions urgently require the creation of "a new, competent international authority to oversee and manage global economic cooperation," and with a reformed United Nations as the host of such an authority.[8]

Such a reform would offer the possibility to relate standards and international agreements more directly to the evaluation of global economic policy. In a recent address in Oxford, U.K., UN High Commission for Human Rights and former President of Ireland Mary Robinson pointed out that the interventions of the IMF or the World Bank ought to be evaluated as to whether or not they contribute to the realization of a number of human rights.[9] A system of global regulations governing investor and corporate behavior, integrated into and subject to the global human rights, labour and environmental agreements might then take shape.

Human rights law puts the individual at the centre and erects a series of protections and procedures to enhance the rights of that individual, particularly with reference to negative action by the state. It seeks to ensure the right of individuals to participate in political decisions that affect the exercise and enjoyment of their rights.

Thus the fundamental human rights challenge of the MAI and of similar agreements is to our *democratic rights*—our rights, whether expressed through our national governments or our representatives in the UN, to affect the shape of the global society and the rules by which we will relate to one another around the world. As the Harvard project points out, "The MAI impairs the right of individuals to participate in decisions impacting implementation of social, cultural and economic rights, and it excludes the individual from the adjudication of disputes regarding disposition of resources and investment."[10]

The Canadian government, in embracing the MAI, has apparently undertaken no assessment of its potential implications for human rights, and the Parliamentary Sub-Committee which reviewed the draft MAI in the late fall of 1997 paid scant attention to these implications, as well.[11]

There is some basis in international law for assuming that fundamental norms, such as those relating to human rights, prevent states from agreeing to "contract out" of their commitments. As the Vienna Convention on the Law of Treaties states, in the "jus cogens" principle: "A treaty is void if, at the time of its conclusion, it conflicts with a peremtory norm of general international law;" and further, if a new peremptory norm of general international law emerges, any existing treaty which is in conflict with the norm becomes void and terminates."

Does this mean that the commitments in the Universal Declaration and the Covenants to an adequate standard of living, or to freedom to organize trade unions, would transcend MAI commitments if they came into conflict? In what jurisdiction or body would such a conflict be worked out? Why should such far-reaching matters be left vague or exempt from study and consideration prior to confirming an agreement? The apparent absence of review on the part of a government firmly committed to an MAI is disturbing.[12]

The MAI challenge goes beyond rights to the constitutional means by which rights are embodied in law or protected and enforced. In the context of the Canadian federal state, where many social, economic and environmental protections depend on the action of provincial governments, the MAI represents, in the words of B.C. Cabinet member Michael Farnsworth, "an unprecedented rollback of provincial constitutional powers."[13] Prof. McConnell notes that, as provincial governments have often been the initiators of progressive social legislation and innovations that embody international human rights principles in Canadian practice, the MAI treaty could inhibit the potential for future innovation. "Viewed in such a fashion, the proposed restriction on provincial jurisdiction amounts to a constitutional amendment without the necessary formal agreement of seven provinces, as required in Section 38 of the Constitution Act 1982."[14]

THE MEANS

> *"Human rights are integral to the promotion of peace and security, economic prosperity and social equity."*
>
> *—UN Secretary-General Kofi Annan.*[15]

The interrelationship between the enjoyment of human rights and the ability of a society to put its resources to work to that end has been clear from the inception of the International Bill of Human Rights.

Both International Covenants, right after an initial commitment to self-determination, declare that: "All peoples may, for their own ends, *freely dispose of their natural wealth and resources* without prejudice to any obligations arising out of international economic cooperation, based upon the principle of mutual benefit, and international law. *In no case may a people be deprived of its own means of subsistence."* (ICCPR Article 1(2), ICESCR, Article 1(2).)

Both also declare that nothing in the present "Covenant shall be interpreted as impairing the inherent right of all peoples to enjoy and utilize fully and freely their natural wealth and resources." (ICCPR, Article 47, ICESCR, Article 25.)

This commitment is related, particularly in the Covenant on Economic, Social and Cultural Rights, to the obligation of the state to achieve "progressively the full realization of the rights recognized in the present Covenant," including the equal right of men and women to enjoy these rights and "the continuous improvement of living conditions." (Articles 3 and 11.)

If states take on these obligations, they must have the tools with which to assure their fulfillment. The recent imposition by the IMF of stringent neo-liberal "reform" regimes on a number of Asian economies in crisis gives evidence of how quickly global economic institutions can remove these tools, and even threaten the deprivation of means of subsistence from whole populations.[16]

Behind these orienting commitments in the Covenants stands a fundamental assumption that democratic and self-determining governments would define their economic and social pathways in accord with universal standards aimed at the emancipation of all human beings. Effective control over the resources to do so is instrumental to the vision.

The states ratifying the Covenants make many more commitments. In the case of Economic, Social and Cultural Rights, they recognize:

- the right to form trade unions,
- the right to the enjoyment of just and favourable conditions of work, including fair wages, a decent living, and safe and health working conditions,
- the right to social security, including social insurance,
- the right to care, education and protection of children,
- the right to an adequate standard of living, including adequate food, clothing and housing, and to the continuous improvement of living conditions,
- the right to freedom from hunger and equitable distribution of food, and
- the right to the highest attainable standard of health.

Virtually all member states of the OECD, like most of the members of the United Nations, have ratified both Covenants. The United States is a notable truant in the case of the Covenant on Economic, Social and Cultural Rights, and Turkey has signed and ratified neither.[17]

If states lack the ability to marshal the resources of a nation, including taxation, rents on natural resources, and potentially the use of monopolies or state enterprises to achieve their ends, their ability to respect, protect and fulfill the Covenant rights and those embodied in other similar agreements is likely to be frustrated. As the Harvard project declares: "The MAI limits the ability of states to formulate policy independently, and impairs the rights of peoples to enjoy the benefits of their natural resources."[18]

CONTRAST: PROPERTY DOING WELL, THE PEOPLE NOT SO WELL

The question of *enforcement* of rights is key: what can an aggrieved party bring about in terms of recourse, action and compensation?

Compare what the MAI seeks to create in this regard with what has been happening in the enforcement of internationally recognized economic and social rights for Canadians. The MAI proposals on dispute resolution provide more choice to corporations than to states, as to which forum to use to settle disputes.

The composition and authority of dispute tribunals under the MAI have raised urgent concern. The variety of issues which might arise could comprise matters of environmental, health, cultural and human rights complexity. Those concerned with such matters argue that those who sit in judgement over them should have competency and sensitivity in these areas, rather than being primarily experts in trade or investment.

Others, including the Harvard MAI Clinical Project and Canadian social activists Tony Clarke and Maude Barlow, question the potential for judicial competence, impariality or independence of the proposed panels.[19]

Still others are profoundly opposed to the secretive procedures proposed, particularly as the resulting decisions would be binding and unappealable.

In short, as the Harvard Law School study points out, the MAI would contravene Article 14(1) of the Covenant on Civil and Political Rights, which assures judicial impartiality and transparency, and would contravene--in its secrecy and unappealability--

the guarantees of the Covenant to ensure that individuals whose rights might be injured by dispute resolution decisions have access to effective remedies, determined by competent judicial authorities. (Article 2(3).)

As the Harvard group point out, a state's "laws designed to guarantee the fundamental rights of its people can be challenged by foreign investors under the MAI. The MAI increases investors' power and rights, yet creates no comparable protections for human rights."[20]

Critics of the MAI point to the current suit against Canada by the Ethyl corporation under NAFTA provisions to give one example of what could be a chilling multitude of corporate actions under MAI affecting people's health, nutrition, education, and right to information, among others.

Canadians have a right to expect that Canada will honour and implement its commitments under the international human rights treaties and agreements it has signed. To take the Covenant on Economic, Social and Cultural Rights as a case in point, Canada has ratified the agreement and has obligations to *respect, protect and fulfill* all the rights elaborated in the agreement.

ENFORCEMENT

The issue of enforcement is crucial, both internationally and domestically. At the moment, the Covenant's implementation is supervised by a Covenant Committee which meets periodically to review country reports. States submit reports and are questioned and evaluated by the Committee. At the moment, there is no formal channel for individuals or groups to bring actions to the Committee, although they do provide information. There is a proposal that an additional protocol be signed which would permit individuals and groups formal recourse to the Committee, somewhat similar to that which exists within the European Community's human rights and social charter system.[21]

The Committee will hear a report from Canada in 1998. In the past it has been very critical of Canada, telling the government to pull up its socks on homelessness, hunger, and income discrimination in Canada. But if Canada is found lacking in fulfilling its Covenant commitments, what power does the Committee have? Essentially, just moral suasion, and perhaps a bit of publicity or embarassment. In some cases, the Supreme Court or other judicial bodies in Canada may bring the Covenant or the Covenant Committee's assessments into a judgment in Canadian courts.

The Committee has indicated that we need to do much more to educate our judges about our obligations. Tragically, and unlike such other jurisdictions as South Africa, Canada's Constitution and the Charter of Rights and Freedoms do not specifically link our international treaty commitments to our domestic laws and guarantees.[22]

Within Canada, our implementation of Covenant Commitments was, for example, understood to be embodied in the Canada Assistance Plan. National standards were outlined and individuals seeking recourse had the right to an appeal procedure. These guarantees were enforced in part by the federal spending power. The Budget Implementation Act of 1995 and the Canadian Health and Social Transfer essentially destroyed these national commitments. As Canadian anti-poverty and equity groups put it, "On April 1, 1996, Canada transformed from a country in which the right to adequate financial assistance for persons in need was a legal requirement, enforceable in court by individuals affected, to one in which there is no federal legislation recognizing this right or providing means of enforcing it."[23]

When Canada comes up before the Covenant Committee in November, 1998, an association of anti-poverty and equality rights groups will charge Canada with failing to meet its treaty obligations. The Committee may agree. But its power to enforce a restoration of national standards, the right to an appeal procedure, or the right to challenge rollbacks in support levels or eligibility is very limited.

The Canadian courts have shied away from utilizing provisions within the Charter of Rights and Freedoms which might be brought into play on behalf of the economic rights and interests of disfranchised Canadians. They have not enforced the implication and understanding embodied in the Covenant on Economic, Social and Cultural Rights that an individual's security of person involves respect and fulfillment of basic standards in health, education, nutrition, etc. Canadians seeking to press the case for national standards confront a relatively informal meeting of federal and provincial ministers, whose performance to date has been characterized by human rights expert Shelagh Day as "feeble, weak and frankly silly."[24]

The Martin/Chretien retreat has led Canada to break its international commitments in a way that neither "collaborative federalism" nor recent initiatives on child poverty can offset. Queen's University Law Professor Christine Elwell cautions that we are moving toward further balkanization of Canadian social and environmental policy, creating a "vacuum of state responsibility" which threatens the effective rule of law with respect to human rights, particularly economic, social and cultural rights.[25]

The contrast is sharp. The internationally agreed system of rights guarantees for all citizens is left with inadequate international enforcement mechanisms, while federal commitment to the treaties Canada has ratified is being subverted by the government itself. Individuals find standards and rights to appeal removed, while corporations have access to secretive procedures that result in compulsory enforcement, with significant monetary damages or restitution.

The trend regarding social and economic commitments and the Covenant affects Canada's respect for its ILO commitments and implications for international Conventions on racial and gender discrimination and the rights of the child, as well as emerging agreements on the rights of indigenous peoples which could be reviewed in a longer treatment of the issues.

The contest between the protection of the rights of citizens and the aggressive extension of private property rights and privileges revolves as well around the Canadian Constitution. It is argued that the corporations, through the MAI, will win rights and recognition which were denied in the Constitution and in judicial decisions affecting corporate rights based on the Constitution. When proponents of the MAI call it a new global economic constitution, they are right. While Canadians remain fixated with the domestic constitutional spats of the past, democracy and our constitutional guarantees are subverted by extra-constitutional challenges on behalf of corporate property in which our current government is complicit.

Faced with this government sleight-of-hand in corporate favour, it is important to re-assert the responsibility of democratically-accountable states. In 1997, a group of distinguished jurists were brought together in Maastricht, the Netherlands, and asked how violations of economic, social and cultural rights in the Covenant should be dealt with. They stated that "a violation of economic, social and cultural rights occurs when a state pursues, by action or omission, a policy or practice which deliberately contravenes or ignores obligations of the [Charter]."

Further, "the obligation to protect includes the state's responsibility to ensure that private entities or individuals, including transnational corporations over which they exercise jurisdiction, do not deprive individuals of their economic, social and cultural rights. States are responsible for violations of economic, social and cultural rights that result from their failure to exercise due diligence in controlling the behaviour of such non-state actors."[26]

These Maastricht guidelines are very clear about the obligations of states. The implication is that states should create domestic and international regulations which would regulate corporate behaviour in such a way that it would not deprive individuals of their rights. The MAI, however, places corporate rights in a transcendent position. Instead of states holding corporations accountable for their behaviour, the MAI would grant legal standing to private investors to sue states, holding states and their citizens or voters accountable to corporate priorities and interests.

EQUAL OPPORTUNITY, THE MARGINALIZED AND THE LOCAL

Citizens and regional governments seeking to address persistent problems of marginalization, underdevelopment and unemployment would find many of the tools they might use in addressing these challenges frustrated or removed by the MAI, particularly in its restrictions regarding performance requirements on investment.

To enhance the participation of the local work-force, to facilitate and guarantee the participation in equity of local or regional players, to require enhanced investment in a particular region for a particular time, and to offer incentives—these are all instruments which local and regional governments have utilized in seeking to enhance economic development and equity. Further, with a view to promoting the advancement of particular groups, often the marginalized, in accord with human rights commitments, many jurisdictions have implemented affirmative action and other incentive policies.

The restrictions on performance requirements on investors in the MAI would inhibit the power of states and sub-state jurisdictions to apply investment policies which might seek to advance the economic and social situation of women, minorities and children in accord with such international agreements as the Convention on the Elimination of All Forms of Discrimination Against Women, that on the Rights of the Child, and that on the Elimination of Racial Discrimination.[27]

As is noted elsewhere in this volume, the MAI "standstill" and "rollback" provisions not only threaten existing social programs, but could prevent future innovations and improvements.

CORPORATE RIGHTS AND THE BATTLE FOR INTERNATIONAL HUMAN RIGHTS

An aspect of the MAI which has received perhaps too little attention is the extent to which it would prevent either citizen- or state-mandated conditionality on outgoing foreign investment directed to countries characterized by gross violations of human rights. Religious and civic groups who pressed for regulation of investment in South Africa during the apartheid era, those who seek municipal, corporate-specific or national boycotts aimed at offending corporations or regimes like those in Myanmar or Nigeria, might find the MAI an effective block to action.

It is conceivable that, in a case where a UN General Assembly authorized boycott-mandated domestic action to forbid or regulate the purpose of outgoing investment, the investor-protective provisions of the MAI might be transcended. But, if the resolution was simply that of the UN Human Rights Commission or a similar body, would it supersede the MAI's provisions? Nor is it clear just where and how a conflict between the MAI and such UN decisions might be resolved.

The use of boycotts and sanctions has often been an initiative of publicly spirited community, labour or religious groups. The anti-Apartheid movement which sustained 30 years of international activity is perhaps the most remarkable example of the range and effectiveness of this form of citizen action, in the end resulting in concerted state pressure. The contemporary movement against child labour and the use of boycotts and/or compulsory labelling, could be frustrated by MAI provisions on secondary boycotts. Human rights activists who frequently are the creative originators of such initiatives should be alerted to the potential for "chill" or, perhaps more appropriately, a "deep-freeze" implied in the MAI.

As the Harvard project points out: *"The MAI would render investment considerations independent of all human rights concerns and would undermine concerted international action to address such abuses."*[28]

The right to development

In 1986, the UN General Assembly passed a Declaration on the Right to Development (GA Res. 41/128 (1986)), which recognized "development" as a "comprehensive economic, social, cultural and political process, which aims at the constant improvement of the well-being of the entire population and of all individuals on the basis of the active, free and meaningful participation in development and in the fair distribution of benefits resulting therefrom."[29]

This declaration grew out of work in the Commission on Human Rights and remains both controversial and incomplete in terms of the broadness of the concept and the institutional arrangements needed to implement its objectives.

The Declaration emerged from the idealism of the new international economic order in the 1970s and the vision of the UN Charter of Economic Rights and Duties of States in 1974.[30] It was motivated by such concepts as "fair price" for commodities and the potential for using the "common heritage of mankind"— embodied in such resources as found in the sea-bed or in space—for the benefit of all.

It embodied a desire to put an end to inequality in development and to provide a justifying framework for the demands of poorer states for resources and resource control which would enable them to fulfill the full promise of economic, social and cultural rights for their peoples.[31]

UN Under-Secretary-General Nitin Desai, speaking at the opening of the UN Commission on Social Development in February 1998, underscored the links between development and human rights. "These rights make no sense unless we have development which allows people to exercise these rights...Human rights cannot be realized unless you have development which is people-centred, equitable, and just."[32]

It should be clear from the arguments outlined above, as from other essays in this volume, that the MAI would essentially strip states (and their citizens) of the essential tools to implement *the right to development.* This would strip most meaning from the right.

As the World Development Movement in the United Kingdom put it, "The MAI's powers would redefine the role of governments, taking away one of their central functions: to ensure that markets work for the public good."[33]

Toward a program of action

The overall issue raised in this article is that of the relationship between democratic governance and the management of the world economy for the benefit of all its citizens. Clearly, our structures of democratic accountability are in deficit. The attempt to extend corporate and investor rights is partial and dangerous, and not an adequate form of rule-making for the globe.

The overall challenge is to develop democratically accountable structures of global economic governance which are effectively conditioned by the normative standards of the key international human rights, labour protection and environmental agreements. While daunting, this challenge comes with a considerable wealth of reform proposals, particularly accompanying the 50th anniversary of the UN system. In such documents as "Our Global Neighbourhood," world leaders have sketched the sort of steps which might bring us to a more accessible, transparent and accountable framework of governance.[34]

Because the MAI would essentially move us in the wrong direction, it should not be approved in its present form. This does not remove the necessity, in fact the urgency, of global corporate and investor regulation.

We need a different locus--preferably within the UN system– and a different range of participants in the development of that regulatory framework. Returning to the draft standards in the original proposed UN Code of Conduct for Transnationals, moving from the sort of voluntary standards in the OECD Guidelines for Multinational Enterprises to mandatory rules, facilitating and supporting evaluations under environmental, human rights and labour standards frameworks are all elements of a new regime.

Under such a regime, legal processes would be open and accessible, with equity-building intervenor financing for the less privileged actors, with appeal procedures subject to review by an elected international body.

In addition to a regulatory regime, the development of an effective global tax regime on capital exchanges, along the lines of the Tobin Tax or related proposals, should be brought to the top of the agenda.[35]

Government representatives, focused on the practicalities of the current texts and the current negoations, are reluctant to lift their eyes to this horizon and to reorient the project. But they must meet several of the challenges raised in this article if they are to adequately defend the rights and interests of all their citizens.

Firstly, they must avoid a legal regime which places corporate interests above the democratic sovereignty of their citizens as expressed in their own constitution.

Secondly, they must place the regime of investor regulation within the context of international human rights, labour and environmental treaties and law. To be blunt, an agreement on regulation of investment should refer not only to the constitution of the IMF, but should express a consensus of the parties that nothing in the agreement shall negate fundamental international human rights covenants and conventions, ILO conventions, and environmental treaties.

Thirdly, governments must assure that legal processes related to dispute resolution and clarification of the agreement are open, accessible, and with an appeal to a body which expresses international democratic sovereignty. The implication of the second provision is that, where such issues touch on relevant human rights, environment or labour subject matter, the body which treats them should represent the highest international level of expertise and authority in those areas.

But, as important as the regulation of investment may be, even more so is the need to strengthen the existing mechanisms for the implementation and enforcement of agreed international rights. A permanent supervisory committee for the International Covenant on Economic, Social and Cultural Rights, together with an agreed channel for individual and group actions under the Covenant, would be a first step. The development of more effective penalties for failure to comply and incentives for compliance should accompany the structural reforms.[36]

The basic fulfillment of fundamental economic, social and cultural rights is feasible. Initiatives like the "20/20" proposal at the World Summit on Social Development are a small step along the way, but donor countries need to energetically renew their commitment to development assistance with an overwhelming priority given to social development and human rights.

Canadians need to pay special attention to strengthening the relationship between Canada's international human rights and labour standards commitments and the interpretation and application of the law by governments and courts within Canada in order to renew national standards, effective rights of appeal, and commitment to the enjoyment of equity for all Canadians.

ENDNOTES:

1 Mary Robinson, "Shame of failure on Human Rights", *The World Today,* (February, 1998) 54:2 London, RIIA, 1998.

2 The Charter of the United Nations.

3 see Peggy Teagle and John W. Foster, "U.N. Futures, U.N. Reforms and the Social Agenda", The Sarlos Papers, Ottawa, United Nations Association of Canada, 1997, see also Christine Elwell, "World Social Policy Conferences as Rule-Making and a Decentralized Canadian Federation", *Canadian Foreign Policy*, (Winter, 1997) 4:3, Ottawa, Norman Patterson School of International Affairs, 1997.

4 Maurice Strong, "The United Nations at Fifty: Issues and Opportunities", *The Sarlos Papers* Ottawa, United Nations Association of Canada, 1997.

5 The procedures of bodies like the World Trade Organization are intentionally obscure to non-governmental and individual actors. Agendas are released

only after meetings are held, and many documents are unavailable to the public. The World Bank in recent years has undertaken energetic efforts to build bridges with non-governmental and civil society actors and is increasingly an exception to the opaque and closed behavior of the WTO, the IMF and the proposed MAI.

6 Susan Strange, *The Retreat of the States. The Diffusion of Power in the World Economy.*, Cambridge, Cambridge University Press, 1996. p. 197

7 Howard McConnell, Memorandum. March 16, 1998.

8 Roy Culpepper, "The United Nations and the World Economy", *The Sarlos Papers*, Ottawa, United Nations Association of Canada, 1997.

9 M. Robinson, op.cit., p. 48

10 MAI Clinical Project, *The Multilateral Agreement on Investment: A Step Backward in International Human Rights*, Cambridge, Harvard Law School, 1997.

11 Repeated inquiries to the Ministry of International Trade have elicited no reply at time of publication. The Saskatchewan Minister of Intergovernmental Affairs writes: "I am not aware of any studies that have specifically examined the effect of the MAI on Canada's ability to implement and comply with the Covenant and other treaties you mention. In this regard, your suggestion that any federal impact analysis study this question is a good one." B.H. Wiens/J.W. Foster March 16, 1998.

12 McConnell, *op.cit.*

13 Michael Farnsworth in the *Vancouver Sun* (March 10, 1998) as quoted by McConnell, *Ibid.*

14 McConnell, *Ibid.*

15 Secretary-General Kofi A. Annan., *Renewing the United Nations: A Programme for Reform*, New York, United Nations, 1997.

16 See the essay by Martin Khor elsewhere in this volume.

17 MAI Clinical Project. The project has compiled a useful chart of the OECD members and the key human rights agreements they have ratified (or not).

18 MAI Clinical Project.

19 *Ibid.*, and Tony Clarke and Maude Barlow, *MAI: The Multilateral Agreement on Investment and the Threat to Canadian Sovereignty*, Toronto, Stoddard, 1997. pp. 40-42.

20 *Ibid.*

21 See Manfred Nowak, "The Need for an Optional Protocol to the International Covenant on Economic, Social and Cultural Rights", in *The Review,* (December, 1995) 55, Geneva, International Commission of Jurists, 1995. On the functioning of the European social charter see OXFAM-UKI.

22 The Covenant Committee on Economic, Social and Cultural Rights, at its most recent examination of the Canadian record, expressed concern about the education of judges in this regard.

23 Letter from Bruce Porter (on behalf of the National Anti-Poverty Organization, the Charter Committee on Poverty Issues, the National Action Committee on the Status of Women and the Canadian Association of Foodbanks) to Philip Alston (Chairperson, the Committee on Economic, Social and Cultural Rights), November 27, 1996.

[24] Shelagh Day, "The Politics of Debt, Deference and Devolution", Address at the College of Law, University of Saskatchewan, October, 1997. [unpublished]

[25] Elwell, *op.cit.*

[26] Human Rights Library, University of Minnesota, *Maastricht Guidelines on Vilations of Economic, Social and Cultural Rights*, Maastricht, ICJ, January 22-26, 1997.

[27] MAI Clinical project. P. 3

[28] See Clarke & Barlow (p. 13-15, 68-9, 95) on the issue of secondary boycotts. The author is grateful to suggestions made by Peter Rosenblum of the Harvard Human Rights Program with regard to the implications for citizen's action.

[29] Henry J. Steiner and Philip Alston, *International Human Rights in Context: Law, Politics, Morals.* Oxford, Clarendon Press, 1996. p. 1124

[30] See commentaries by the editors and by Abi-Saab and Bedaoui in Steiner and Alston, *op.cit.* pp. 1110 ff.

[31] *Ibid.*

[32] Nitin Desai, "Address to the Commission on Social Development, February 10, 1998." New York, United Nations, 1998.

[33] World Development Movement, *Pulling Up the Drawbridge: The Multilateral Agreement on Investment*, London, WDM, 1997.

[34] See *Our Global Neighborhood: The Report of the Commission on Global Governance*, New York and Oxford, Oxford University Press, 1995, also the Sarlos Papers on UN reform published by the United Nations Association of Canada.

[35] See Alex C. Michalos, *Good Taxes: the case for taxing foreign currency exchange and other financial transactions.* Toronto and Oxford, Dundurn Press, 1997.

[36] On the European examples, see OXFAM-UKI, *Securing Social Rights in Europe.* Oxford, OXFAM-UKI, 1997, and various authors in "Economic, Social and Cultural Rights and the Role of Lawyers", *The Review*, (December, 1995) 55, Geneva, International Commission of Jurists, 1995.

Note:

The author wishes to acknowledge the critical support of colleagues Christine Elwell, Howard McConnell, Ken Norman, Bruce Porter, Tim Quigley and Steven Shrybman, in the preparation of this article.

THE MAI AND THE ENVIRONMENT

by Michelle Swenarchuk

INTRODUCTION

The international discussions of the MAI have raised questions of whether it will have impacts on the environment. After nearly 10 years of free trade regimes in Canada, we are in a position to conclude that it will. It is intended to have impacts on various areas of public policy, including environmental policy.

The MAI is the latest in a network of international agreements being used to undermine local, national, provincial and international initiatives for various public policy goals, through the creation of a legal regime of deregulated trade and investment. The goal is achieved by regulating national governments, through the agreements, preventing them from exercising powers available to them in their national constitutions.

Domestic regulations, including environmental ones, are precisely the targets of investor-rights documents like the MAI, since regulations do affect the capacity of corporations to engage in profit-generating activities. "Investment protection" actually means the removal of regulatory controls on corporate activity. The MAI is therefore the latest in the international deregulation initiatives.

In the environmental field, there has been a progressive undermining of domestic environmental regulation over the past 10 years through the Canada-U.S. Free Trade Agreement, NAFTA, and the 1994 GATT. This has occurred despite consistent public opinion polls showing very high levels of public support for strong environmental laws, including in areas where Canadian governments refuse to regulate, such as climate change issues.[1]

From the perspective of Canada and many Southern countries, it is important to recall that resource management is a fundamental element of both environmental protection and community stability.

International agreements which reduce the powers of governments to lessen reliance on raw resource exports, for example, by limiting such strategies as increased local processing, are antithetical to principles of sustainable resource management and conservation.

ENVIRONMENTAL ELEMENTS OF THE MAI

The MAI undoubtedly further constrains Canadian governments from exercising powers to benefit Canadian communities and the environment.

NATIONAL TREATMENT

The MAI draft includes very broad definitions of "investor" and "investment" and extends national treatment and most favoured nation treatment to foreign investors.[2] These provisions not only eliminate arbitrary interference with foreign investors' rights, but, in the view of the B.C. government, also restrict "transparent and non-discriminatory efforts to negotiate and enforce local and national economic benefits."[3] The requirement for national treatment for investment incentives (subsidies) appears to require payment of the same subsidies to large foreign corporations as may now be provided to small, local or non-profit community-based health, social service, and education organizations, and the health and Medicare sectors overall.

PERFORMANCE REQUIREMENTS

The MAI includes extensive prohibitions against performance requirements for linking approvals or providing subsidies or other advantages to investors regardlessof whether investors are foreign or domestic. It exceeds the NAFTA provisions in the types that are prohibited and the breadth of scope and application. Prohibitions extend to requirements of specific export levels, domestic content, local purchasing, hiring, or investment levels, technology transfer, or prescribed levels of production.[4]

These provisions will particularly affect provincial (and federal) rights to require job creation, local processing, and other benefits for local communities from foreign investors' exploitation of natural resources. Requirements for "best available" green technologies, including for pollution prevention purposes, may also be affected.

"EXPROPRIATION" RIGHTS

A most dangerous provision in the MAI is the NAFTA-style "expropriation" clause which provides to investors an unconditional right to compensation for expropriation of an investment, "directly or indirectly," or for "measures having equivalent effect." The clause requires that no "expropriation " occur unless it is "for a purpose which is in the public interest; is non-discriminatory; is in accordance with due process of law; *and is accompanied by payment of prompt, adequate and effective compensation."*[5] (Emphasis added.)

This wording extends beyond the principle of national treatment, since even measures applied to both foreign and domestic investors could give rise to a claim for compensation by the foreign one. It extends "expropriation" claims beyond what is compensable in Canadian domestic law, with no balancing of the public interest in resource conservation, human health and safety, or any other purpose, in determining whether compensation is payable and to what extent. This use of the term "expropriation" is a departure from Canadian law to date, since it appears to encompass *any* governmental action which reduces the potential returns on an investment.

In Canada, the issue of expropriation generally arises in relation to real estate, and not other forms of property. The MAI permits an "expropriation" claim for loss or diminution of a wide range of investment opportunities (e.g., loss of contract, licences, permits, etc.), unlike domestic Canadian law, which provides expropriation compensation only when government claims land to which clear title rests in the landholder.

Land use zoning, however, although it may substantially change a landowner's profits from a piece of land, is not at law compensable expropriation. As CELA has written:[6]

> *...the term "expropriation" traditionally refers to a landowner's loss of use, title or benefit of property <u>and</u> a transfer of the value of use, title or benefit to a public authority. Thus, an aggrieved landowner must be able to demonstrate that not only has property been taken, but that the taking has also benefitted the expropriating authority.*

However, Canadian courts have long recognized that land use regulation is not "expropriation," primarily because zoning by-laws or other planning instruments do not generally involve a taking or transfer of the full use, title or benefit of property. Therefore, if a landowner's ability to use or develop his or her property is constrained by a properly enacted zoning by-law, the landowner is not entitled to compensation, even if the zoning by-law causes a diminution in property value.

The distinction between expropriation and land use regulation has been noted by the Supreme Court of Canada on several occasions. For example in *Soo Mill & Lumber Co. Ltd.* v. *City of Sault Ste. Marie*, the Supreme Court of Canada rejected arguments that a municipal by-law was invalid because its effect was to prohibit any practical use of the appellant's land. In this case, Chief Justice Laskin went on to state that it is open to a municipality to freeze development in accordance with the purposes of official plans and zoning by-laws, provided the municipality has not acted in bad faith. This principle was also expressed by Chief Justice Laskin in *Sanbay Developments Ltd.* v. *City of London,* where a municipal development freeze was again upheld by the court.

Similarly, in *Hartel Holdings Co. Ltd.* v. *Council of the City of Calgary*, the Supreme Court of Canada refused to grant an order directing a municipality to expropriate land which had been designated as a proposed park:

> "The appellant's case in a nutshell is that by freezing its land with a view to its subsequent acquisition as a park, the respondent has deprived the appellant of the potential value of its land for residential development. No doubt, this is true. *The difficulty the appellant faces, however, is that in the absence of bad faith on the part of the respondent, this seems to be exactly what the statute contemplates. The crucial rider is that the City's actions must have been taken pursuant to a legitimate and valid planning purpose. If they were, then the resulting detriment to the appellant is one that must be endured in the public interest."* (Emphasis added).

In addition, the Supreme Court of Canada has clearly rejected the suggestion that municipalities must compensate landowners who are subject to land use restrictions such as "downsizing":

> *"Ordinarily, in this country, the United States and the United Kingdom, compensation does not follow zoning either up or down."*.....

CELA concluded:

> The important principle which emerges from these cases may be stated as follows: *planning authorities may regulate, restrict or prohibit land use or development without triggering the remedy of compensation for affected landowners, provided that such*

measures are undertaken in good faith for a proper planning purpose.

Thus, Canadian law maintains the principle that legislatures may legitimately regulate property use in the public interest, without having to pay compensation, if the measures are undertaken in good faith and do not involve a change in title.

In contrast, the NAFTA Investment Chapter[7] and the MAI extend the concept of expropriation, with a requirement of compensation, so broadly that virtually any governmental regulatory action which reduces the potential for generating profits may generate a claim for compensation.

Public attention in Canada has been drawn to the Ethyl Corporation claim against the Canadian government for $350 million compensation for enacting an effective ban on the use of MMT, a neuro-toxin, in gasoline. It is indeed unprecedented and sobering that the right of the Parliament of Canada to pass an environmental and health protection measure can now give rise to a claim from the polluter for a huge amount of compensation.

It is less well known that other claims are currently being processed under the NAFTA chapter, including one by Metalclad Corporation against Mexico.

In January 1997, the U.S.-based waste disposal company Metalclad Corporation filed a grievance with ICSID, alleging that the Mexican state of San Luis Potosi violated a number of provisions of NAFTA when it prevented the company from opening its waste disposal plant. On the basis of a geological audit performed by environmental impact analysts at the University of San Luis Potosi, the Governor deemed the plant an environmental hazard to surrounding communities, and ordered it closed down. The study had found that the facility is located on an alluvial stream and therefore could contaminate the local water supply. Eventually, the Governor declared the site part of a 600,000 acre ecological zone. Metalclad seeks compensation of some $90 million for expropriation and for violations of national treatment, most favoured nation treatment and prohibitions on performance requirements. This figure is larger than the combined annual income of every family in the county where Metalclad's facility is located...

The Metalclad case raises other alarming questions. Metalclad claims the Mexican federal government is (unofficially) encouraging the company's NAFTA lawsuit so that it can deflect the political fall-out of forcing the state to open the facility. If Metalclad's claims are indeed accurate, this case raises the disturbing possibility that investors can use their rights to collude with governments to force unwanted or even dangerous investments on unwilling populations.[8]

There is at least one other current case, *Robert Azinian et al v. Mexico,* which also relates to waste disposal.[9]

The true purpose and likely result of the "expropriation" chapter of the MAI is evident in these cases. Canadian law would not treat these legitimate governmental regulatory actions to protect the environment and human health as expropriation giving rise to compensation. Indeed, the Supreme Court of Canada has recently emphasized the importance of environmental protection as a value in Canada, in upholding the constitutionality of the *Canadian Environmental Protection Act.*[10]

However, the MAI does not include any exception in its presumption of compensation for "legitimate objectives" undertaken by governments.

The combination of the NAFTA "expropriation" claims and those possible under the MAI may well constitute the most effective anti-environmental strategy yet devised by corporations and their government allies. No government will take lightly the prospect of a huge financial claim against it for legislation, however high the public support for the measure. This is especially true in this historical moment. The "chilling effect" of the Ethyl case and potential claims under the MAI after its completion, will make effective environmental protection in this country even more difficult.

In developing countries, many of which do not yet have environmental law frameworks in place, this corporate strategy will be even more effective in preventing public interest legislation. This will undoubtedly smoothe the path for such Canadian interests as mining companies operating abroad. Unfortunately, given significant examples of environmental and community damage caused by certain Canadian mining corporations in developing nations, this is not a positive result.

The B.C. government identified the issue of native land claim settlements which may require return of land or other resources (fish, forest) now subject to non-native use (investment). Foreign investors could claim full compensation, no matter how tenuous or preliminary their "investment."

This provides an excellent example of the problems of international harmonization without regard to historical, social, or environmental differences. Aboriginal rights are not issues for public policy decisions in European OECD countries, but raise many live and pressing issues in Canada, and other countries with extant Aboriginal populations. The federal government has proposed a partial exemption of its Aboriginal obligations from the purview of the MAI, but whether the exemption will survive the negotiation process is unknown.

REVERSION TO SECRET DISPUTE PROCESSES

Like NAFTA, the MAI provides for expropriation through private tribunals without public scrutiny, appeals, or interventions. That confidential dispute resolution through arbitration is widely used in private commercial disputes is not a justification for its use in trade and investment processes. The secrecy and broad powers of trade and investment dispute panels are fundamentally antidemocratic, since they provide that the capacity of governments to legislate can be squelched.

In these cases, what is at stake is the authority of governments to use their constitutional powers to enact laws for public protection. The accountability of governments to the electorate for these actions is a cornerstone of democratic society. A legal system with open, visible processes is the corresponding dispute resolution process for democracies. The rights of citizens and corporate "persons" to sue governments in our courts occurs in public view under laws passed by the legislature, while Parliament remains supreme.

In the MAI panel process, corporations have rights equal to that of governments (or arguably, greater than governments); while citizens are entirely excluded from participation and information about the proceedings. The expropriation panels create the burden that governments must pay huge amounts to act in accordance with domestic public interest policies, or even constitutional law (e.g., constitutional Aboriginal rights). The "chilling effect" of adding investor compensation payments to every sector of public interest legislation is obviously considerable.

PURPORTED ENVIRONMENTAL PROTECTIONS

The October draft of the MAI reveals continuing discussions and controversies regarding three approaches to environmental issues.

First, some delegations proposed that the Preamble to the agreement contain wording indicating a commitment to environmental protection and conservation, or, alternatively, to the Rio Declaration on Environment and Development and Agenda 21. Since the Preamble does not include enforceable obligations, this wording does not provide actual protection for environmental measures.

Second, the drafters discussed a limit on the prohibition on performance requirements with regard to subsidies.[11] Depending on the final wording, this limit could reserve the possibilities of subsidies to promote local interests or green technologies. However, this self-serving corporate "advantage" is a small concession compared to the loss of regulatory possibilities the "Performance Requirements" article provides.

Third, the drafters debated whether to include wording on "not lowering standards"[12] in order to attract investment. They considered whether to use the non-binding NAFTA wording, or an actual prohibition on the practice.[13] The pattern of lowering and eliminating standards in Canada since NAFTA was signed demonstrates the futility of the inclusion of non-binding language, and support for more binding language does not appear to be strong.

The Canadian government has proposed "reservations" from the MAI which touch on a number of subjects with significant environmental impacts: energy, fisheries, Aboriginal affairs, and transportation, including water transportation. However, environmental protection and resource conservation measures are not removed from the ambit of the agreement, nor are reservations for provincial measures proposed.[14]

Negotiators clearly contemplate some degree of "standstill" (no future implementation of measures which don't accord with MAI protections) or "rollback" (eventual elimination of current non-conforming measures). OECD commentators specifically wish to prevent reservations that are of a "precautionary" nature.[15] These elements are antithetical to the need for further development of environmental protection laws and policies in Canada and other countries.

TRADE LAW IMPACTS ON THE CURRENT CANADIAN REGULATORY CONTEXT

For Canada, the MAI represents the fourth major international deregulation initiative, following the Canada-U.S. Free Trade Agreement, NAFTA, and the 1994 GATT/WTO agreements. They have established a web of international trade law and jurisprudence which provides the context in which the MAI will be implemented. The treatment of environmental and health protections under those agreements is instructive regarding their likely treatment in MAI-related disputes.

GATT ARTICLE XX: GENERAL EXCEPTION

Since 1947, the GATT regime has included a general exemption from the other disciplines of the agreement, including national treatment and most favoured nation principles. Article XX "permits" countries to maintain standards deemed necessary for protection of "human, animal or plant life or health" and for "conservation of exhaustible resources..."[16] This article was included in the Canada-U.S. FTA and NAFTA.[17]

With the conclusion of the Uruguay Round of GATT negotiations in 1994, and the implementation of the new World Trade Organization/GATT agreements, an increased number of trade disputes have arisen in which environmental or health standards have been in issue.[18] *In every case, the domestic standard that was at issue has been found incompatible with GATT (or the FTA), leading to a requirement that it be rescinded.*

It must be understood that trade law could have accommodated environmental and health concerns from the beginning, given the wording of Article XX. However, every case has gone against national standards, leading to the systematic elimination of governmental options previously thought available under the article. The interpretation of the MAI, whatever its final wording, will be carried out in GATT-style "confidential" dispute processes using these precedents.

In fact, the MAI doesn't even provide for such a general exemption. The only general exceptions proposed for the MAI are for "essential security interests," actions taken in time of war, actions regarding non-proliferation of nuclear weapons, "production of arms and ammunition," actions related to UN international peace obligations, and "prudential measures" relating to financial services.[19]

When environmental or health laws are contested by business using the MAI, there is very little chance that they will be held justifiable in themselves, without a need for the legislator to pay "compensation" pursuant to the expropriation article.

INTERNATIONALIZATION AND HARMONIZATION OF STANDARD SETTING

NAFTA was the first agreement which provided detailed wording on development of environmental (and other) standards through its chapters on Technical Barriers to Trade and Sanitary and Phytosanitary Standards. The 1994 GATT included similar chapters.[20] They include very specific wording regarding how domestic standards must be written to ensure compatibility with the trade regimes. They also specify a number of international bodies as standard-setters: the Codex-Alimentarius Commission; the North American Plant Protection Organization; the International Office of Epizootics; the Food and Agriculture Organization (regarding the International Plant Protection Convention); and the International Standardization Organization.

Environmentalists have seen that, as we predicted, the increased emphasis on internationalization and harmonization of environmental standard-setting has made it more difficult to achieve improved standards at home. These international bodies are largely inaccessible to citizens and environmental groups; some have considerable corporate participation; and they seek to set standards that can be achieved internationally, rather than standards that would be best for a particular country's environment or health requirements.

Further, the *Beef Hormone*[21] decision of a WTO/GATT panel, released in August 1997 in response to a Canadian complaint, makes explicit that international standards take precedence over domestic ones, even retroactively. The Canadian government complained to the WTO that the European Community's ban on hormone residues in beef contravened the Sanitary and Phytosanitary Chapter of the GATT, and won. The dispute panel found that, since the EC standards were more stringent than those of the Codex Alimentarius, they could not be maintained, thus confirming the primacy of international standards over domestic ones.[22]

Should investor-state claims arise under the MAI, based on local or national environmental standards, they will be judged against this jurisprudence and are unlikely to be held justifiable. It is likely that corporations will be contesting them using the "expropriation" articles of the MAI, a prospect that will make it even harder to achieve enhanced domestic protections in Canada and elsewhere.

Voluntarism to replace law

At both levels of government in Canada, environmental laws are being replaced or undermined by an increased willingness to rely on corporate "voluntary" initiatives for environmental protection. Globally, this is promoted by the enhanced role of the International Standardization Organization in the GATT, and its movement into policy areas where it has not previously worked, including environmental management regimes. (ISO 14000 series.) In Canada, we have seen the governmental and corporate collaboration in a sustainable forest certification scheme that has little environmental credibility.[23] Also, the 1996 proposed reform of the *Statutory Instruments Act*, the *Regulations Act* would have incorporated the wording of ISO standardization documents into Canadian law[24] in place of enforceable regulations.

The incorporation of the *OECD Guidelines for Multinational Enterprises*[25] in the MAI reflects this non-binding, voluntary approach to corporate responsibility. The MAI does not require mandatory corporate compliance with domestic public interest laws in the countries in which companies operate as investors.

Bilateral Investment Agreements (BITS)

Regardless of whether or not the MAI is eventually signed under the aegis of the OECD, Canada is already far down the road of deregulated international investment policy. Given that two-thirds of the foreign direct investment in Canada comes from the U.S., the NAFTA Investment chapter is arguably the most significant investment "treaty" Canada has signed. The NAFTA provisions are similar but somewhat less stringent than those of the MAI.

In addition, Canada has signed or is currently negotiating investment treaties with 59 countries in Eastern Europe, Asia, Africa, and the Middle East.[26] Those negotiated before 1994 were negotiated on the basis of a model agreement drawn from the OECD; since 1994, they are based on the level of investor protection found in NAFTA.

Relative to other OECD countries, Canada is a newcomer to these agreements. Germany and France have been concluding bilateral investment agreements since the early 1960s.[27] UNCTAD reports that by January 1997, there were 1,310 BITS world-wide, of which the largest number had been concluded by Western European countries. These include: Germany 109, United Kingdom 87, Switzerland 81, France 74, and Italy 53. At that time, the U.S. had concluded 38.[28]

U.S. business interests are currently proposing that negotiations for a Free Trade Area of the Americas (FTAA), to begin in April 1998, should include attempts to reach interim agreements by 2000 on investment, services, and market access. They propose a hemispheric Convention on Investment, to provide national treatment; right of establishment in already open sectors; "full and free" repatriation of capital, profits, and dividends; expropriation protections; and a prohibition against performance requirements.[29]

Despite this proliferation of agreements, it is fair to ask whether they actually provide benefits to Canada. As the government of British Columbia has noted, Canada does not appear to have benefited from the NAFTA investment chapter. Rather, Canada's share of foreign direct investment in North America has declined from 25.9% in 1985 to 16.7% in 1996.[30] Given this NAFTA experience, it is reasonable to question whether further deregulation of investment through the MAI will provide economic benefits to Canada.

The bilateral agreements, NAFTA, and the American proposals require that opponents of deregulated investment focus on a broader landscape than just the MAI. Given this NAFTA experience, it is questionable whether further deregulation of investment through the MAI will provide economic benefits to Canada.

Conclusion

Even more than previous international trade agreements, the MAI suffers from a lack of balance between commercial interests and the interests of citizens and the environment.

It protects countries' actions of war, arms, and arms production, but does not recognize the legitimate objectives of domestic protections of health, labour standards, social policy, culture, or local job creation.

It includes an extremely broad definition of investment and investors rights, with extraordinary "expropriation" claims, but no rights for citizens and governments to compensation for corporate pollution and negative community impacts.

It includes standstill and rollback provisions, but no protection for future necessary innovative policies for public interest goals. It provides investor-state legal claims, but no citizen-state or citizen-investor claims; and secret legal processes.

It provides no balancing of Northern industrial interests and Southern needs for poverty alleviation through development of protected local industries and resource allocation.

It requires mandatory compliance by national governments, but no requirements that corporations comply with public interest laws in the countries in which they operate.

If signed, it will provide corporations with powerful new tools to prevent regulation of their activities for social and environmental purposes.

Endnotes

1 For a review of the staggering pace of removal of environmental regulation in Ontario, see Environmental Commissioner of Ontario, *Annual Report 1996: Keep the Doors Open to Better Environmental Decision Making*, Toronto, April, 1997; and *Intervenor*, Canadian Environmental Law Association, Vol. 22, No. 5 & 6. At the federal level, despite 1993 Liberal Party Red Book commitments to improve the *Canadian Environmental Protection Act* and to adopt an *Endangered Species Act*, neither commitment has been kept.

At both levels of government, environmental ministries have experienced drastic cuts in budgets and staff levels.

2 References are to the draft MAI wording of October 6, 1997, DAFFE/MAI/NM(97)2. Investors include human and corporate persons, non-profit and for-profit private and public organizations. Investment covers "every" kind of property, claims to money or performance, contracts, concessions, licenses, permits, etc. (MAI Article II) The principle of national treatment provides that countries must provide to foreign investors and their investments "treatment it accords ...to its own investors and their investments with respect to the establishment, acquisition, expansion, operation, management, maintenance, use, enjoyment and sale or other disposition of investments." The most favoured nation principle requires that countries provide the same treatment to all investors and investments ("treatment no less favourable") that they provide to any one country's investors and investments. (MAI Article III).

3 Submission to the Sub-Committee on International Trade, Trade Disputes and Investment of the House of Commons Standing Committee on Foreign Affairs and International Trade regarding the Proposed Multilateral Agreement on Investment, by the Government of British Columbia, November 26, 1997.

4 MAI Article III.

5 Article IV, Investment Protection.

6 Lindgren, Richard and Clark, Karen, "Property Rights vs. Land Use Regulation: Debunking the Myth of "Expropriation Without Compensation", Canadian Environmental Law Association, February 3, 1994, pp. 5-8. Cases cited in this discussion include: *Manitoba Fisheries Limited v. R,* (1978) 6. WWR 496 (SCC); *The Queen in Right of British Columbia v. Tener et al* (1985) 17 DLR (4th) 1 (SCC); *Soo Mill & Lumber Co. Ltd. v. City of Sault Ste. Marie*, (1975) 47 DLR (3rd)1; *Sanbay Developments Ltd. v. City of London*, (1975) 45 DLR (3rd) 403; *Hartel Hldings Co. Ltd v. Council of the City of Calgary*, (1984) 8 DLR (4th) 321.

7 NAFTA Chapter 11, especially Article 1110.

8 Sforza, Michelle, and Nova, Scott, "The Multilateral Agreement on Investment and the Environment," The Preamble Collective/The Preamble Center for Public Policy, Washington D.C., 1997, p.12.

9 Personal Communication from Michelle Sforza, Preamble Collective, November 19, 1997.

10 *Hydro Quebec v. Attorney General of Canada*, [1997] 151 DLR [4th] 32, Supreme Court of Canada.

11 Article III, Performance Requirements, subsection 2.

12 Non-numbered article, pp. 49 and 50 of the October draft.

13 NAFTA Article 1114 states that "it is inappropriate to encourage investment by relaxing domestic health, safety or environmental measures. Accordingly, a party should not waive or otherwise derogate from, or offer to waive or otherwise derogate from, such measures as an encouragement" for investment. If a Party does so, another Party's only remedy is to request consultation; no dispute settlement process is available.

14 OECD: Canada: Draft Reservations, DAFFE/MAI/RES(97)15, February 25,

1997 and MAI Article IX Reservations. The question of whether the MAI will apply to provincial governments remains controversial. The federal government currently takes the position that it will not, while other governments including the US claim that it will apply to subnational governments. Whether the Canadian federal government has the constitutional jurisdiction to commit provinces to international trade and investment agreements which affect their jurisdictional powers also remains an unresolved and controversial legal issue in Canada. Cf. Hogg, Peter, *Constitutional Law of Canada*, Third Edition, Carswell, 1992 Chapter 11, "Treaties".

15 MAI COMMENTARY, Article IX, Reservations.

16 GATT Article XX: Measures which are applied in a non- discriminatory manner and are not "a disguised restriction on international trade" are permitted if: (b) necessary to protect human, animal or plant life or health; (g) relating to the conservation of exhaustible natural resources if such measures are made effective in conjunction with restrictions on domestic production and consumption.

17 *Canada-US Free Trade Agreement* Article 1201; *NAFTA* Article 2101.

18 *In the Matter of Canada's Landing Requirement for Pacific Coast Salmon and Herring*, 1989; *US Restrictions on Imports of Tuna,* GATT doc. DS21/R Sept. 3, 1991; *Thailand - Restrictions on Importation of and Internal Taxes on Cigarettes*, GATT Doc. 375/200; *US - Standards for Reformulated and Conventional Gasoline* WT/DS2/AB/R 1996 and WT/DS2/R 1996; *EC Measures Concerning Meat and Meat Products (Hormones), Complaint by Canada*, WTO WT/DS48/R/Can, August 18, 1997.

19 MAI proposed Article VI Exceptions and Safeguards; and Article VII Financial Services.

20 NAFTA Chapter 7, Section B; and Chapter 9; GATT Agreement on Sanitary and Phytosanitary Standards, and Agreement on Technical Barriers to Trade.

21 World Trade Organization, *EC Measures Concerning Meat and Meat Products (Hormones): Complaint by Canada*; WT/DS48/R/CAN; 18 August 1997.

22 See "Intervenor", Canadian Environmental Law Association, Vol.22 No. 4 August-September, 1997, for an analysis of the decision. The EC appealed the case to the WTO Appellate Body, which modified the panel's legal findings but upheld its decision. (EC Measures Concerning Meat and Meat Products [Hormones]: AB-1997-4; WT/DS26/AB/R and WT/DS48/AB/R; January 16, 1998.)

23 "An Environmentalist and First Nations Response the Canadian Standards Association Proposed Certifcation System for Sustainable Forest Management6," October 1995, CELA.

24 The *Regulations Act* was passed by the House of Commons in early 1997, but as the Senate had not adopted it prior to the June 1997 election, it did not become law.

25 MAI Article X, Relationship to Other International Agreements.

26 Personal communication from N. Lynn McDonald, Investment Trade Policy Division, Department of Foreign Affairs, December 16, 1997.

27 United Nations Centre on Transnational Corporations and International Chamber of Commerce, *Bilateral Investment Treaties, 1959-1991*, United Nations, New York, 1992.

28 UNCTAD Note to correspondents No. 22: BIT by BIT: Understanding the Development Implications of Bilateral Investment Treaties, 28 May 1997, http://www.unicc.org/unctad/en/ pressref/nc9722.htm.

29 "Americas Trade", Vol.5, No. 2, January 22, 1998.

30 Government of British Columbia Submission to the Sub- committee on International Trade, Trade Disputes and Investment, November 26, 1997, quoting *World Investment Report: Transnational Corporations, Market Structure and Competition Policy*, United Nations, 1997, p.313.

THE MAI AND CULTURE

by Gary T. Neil

Introduction

In 1997, two press reports of interest to Canada's cultural community appeared.

The first was a series of articles reporting on the merger between Cineplex Odeon, owned by Seagram Co. Ltd of Montreal, and U.S.-based Loews Theatres, which would transfer effective ownership of the Canadian cinema chain to the Sony Corporation.

Canada's Minister of Canadian Heritage, Sheila Copps, said she "has discussed the merger with Industry Minister John Manley, who has jurisdiction over Investment Canada, and the two Ministers agree the deal must be of net benefit to the Canadian cultural industry."

The reports proceed to discuss how the government will negotiate an appropriate package of commitments from Sony, including screen time for Canadian films, in return for approving the merger.[1] Early in 1998, the merger was approved, in part based on a commitment that "control of Canadian film distributor Cineplex Odeon Films will be sold to eligible Canadian investors in a reasonable amount of time."[2]

The second press item was a short article reporting that Viacom Inc., one of the world's largest U.S.-based entertainment conglomerates, was about to sell parts of its giant publishing arm, Simon and Schuster. The sale would include Ginn Publishing Canada, a major player in the Canadian educational publishing market and the subject of much public debate over the years.

In 1989, when Ginn's foreign parent company was acquired by another company, the Canadian government forced the sale of the Canadian educational publishing arm under the terms of the Baie Comeau policy restricting foreign ownership in the book trade. When no private Canadian firm could make a deal to acquire Ginn, it was bought by an agency of government, the Canada Development Investment Corporation. Five years later, amidst howls of protests from the Canadian cultural community, the new Liberal government sold its interest in Ginn back to Paramount (which in turn was purchased by Viacom)[3].

Under the terms of the Multilateral Agreement on Investment (MAI) being negotiated through the Paris-based Organization for Economic Cooperation and Development (OECD), the policies which underpin these attempts to promote the interests of Canadian cultural industries could not be maintained. These policies would violate a number of key elements of the MAI. Canada would be left powerless to intervene in transactions which could have enormous influence on Canadian culture.

These are but a few contemporary examples of the potentially serious consequences of the MAI on Canadian cultural measures. The MAI in turn is merely the latest, and by no means the last, in a series of international trade agreements which limit policy options as governments confront the serious challenges facing Canada's cultural sector.

While the MAI is still uncompleted, an understanding of its potentially negative consequences will permit informed input to the final negotiations, prepare for its possible implementation, and ensure that Canada is ready if the focus of investment talks shifts from the MAI to another forum, such as the World Trade Organization (WTO).

BACKGROUND

Canadian literary scholar Northrop Frye has said there are three aspects to a nation's *culture*. First, there is *culture* as lifestyle, shown by the way a society eats, drinks, clothes itself and carries on its normal societal rituals. Second, there is *culture* as a shared heritage of historical memories, mores, and values, usually transmitted through a common language. Third, there is *culture* as the creative output of society. The creative output includes literature, music, movies, architecture, scholarship, applied arts, television shows, theatre, painting, sculpture and all other dimensions of the "arts."

As a northern people with roots in every part of the world, Canadians enjoy a distinctive lifestyle and our shared heritage as Canadians stretches back hundreds of years. But what has and continues to be vulnerable in Canada is the third aspect of culture: the creative output of our society.

In the past, some argued that Canadian content productions were creatively inferior to the works of others. But the recent international artistic successes enjoyed in a variety of fields is evidence of the fallacy of the argument. Bryan Adams, Bill Reid, k.d. Lang, Shania Twain, Norman Jewison, Celine Dion, Margaret Atwood, Karen Kain, Michael Ondaajte, Alanis Morissette, Carol Shields, Robertson Davies, Roch Voisine, "Kiss of the Spiderwoman," Antonine Maillet, Michael Snow, Garth Drabinsky, Leonard Cohen, Jeff Wall, the National Ballet of Canada, le Cirque du Soleil, Robert Lepage, Jim Carrey, and hundreds of other individual Canadian artists and producers have put Canada on the world stage and brought increased financial success to Canada's cultural industries.

There is a growing recognition that our cultural development is fundamental to the nation. Artists are both a mirror of our society and our conscience. They show us who we are and challenge us to think about what we can become. The cultural industries are critical to our economic development and our entry to the knowledge-based economy of the next century. They comprise one of the few sectors of the economy which continued to grow throughout the past 20 years, providing hundreds of thousands of jobs to Canadians in every region of the country.

The direct economic impact of the arts and culture sector is estimated at $16 billion annually, or 2.7% of the total economy, and the work-force is more than 670,000 Canadians[4]. Human Resources Development Canada projects that employment in the arts, culture, sports and recreation sector will grow by 45% before 2005, the second fastest growing sector in Canada.

But, despite the artistic success and the growing financial strength, Canada's cultural output is not sufficient to provide a choice to Canadians whenever they want it. Canada is the most open market in the world for cultural products because Canadians believe passionately in the free movement of ideas, information and entertainment. But sobering figures exist in each sector of Canadian culture.

In television, despite the proliferation of new Canadian services, roughly 60% of what English Canada watches is U.S. programming, almost 95% of the time on Canadian movie screens is devoted to the films of others, over 84% of retail sales of sound recordings feature foreign content, 70% of the Canadian book market consists of foreign works, and 83% of the newsstand market is foreign magazines.

But Canadians also want to be able to see ourselves reflected in what we watch, hear and read, and to be able to choose to view the world from our own perspective, as well as that of others. It is difficult to provide the necessary range of quality Canadian choices on a purely commercial basis. Canada is a nation of only 30 million people, spread out over 6.5 million square kilometres, of whom 22 million share a language and idiom with the world's largest producer of cultural material.

Canadians expect and deserve to receive Canadian material that is equivalent in quality and price to the U.S. product, but our cultural producers do not have the economies of scale enjoyed by their U.S. counterparts, who produce for a primary market many times the size of our own.

- In the television industry, Canadian broadcasters typically contribute 25-30% of the production budget as a licence fee. In the U.S., broadcasters contribute 75-80% of the budget, a result of having substantially larger audiences to sell to advertisers.

- In book publishing, the average print run for a work of fiction in Canada is 1,500 copies, compared to 10,000 in the United States, which means the unit cost per Canadian book is much higher, yet the selling price must remain comparable to satisfy the Canadian consumer.

Faced with these competitive advantages enjoyed by our neighbour, Canada has developed a series of measures to level the playing field and permit our artists and cultural industries to emerge and succeed. The basic objective of these policies is to ensure that Canadians have choice in our own country.

Many of the policies so vital to our creative output are under increasing attack from the U.S. entertainment industry, which views any policy designed to encourage indigenous production activity as an impediment to its conquest of world markets and a threat to its hegemony.

- A WTO challenge to our magazine industry support measures launched by the U.S. was successful in 1997. The U.S. was close to commencing retaliatory measures in response to the CRTC decision to remove Country Music Television from the list of authorized services, and it may yet challenge the provisions of Canada's new *Copyright Act* under NAFTA. What we view as culture, the U.S. views as business. What we view as encouraging choice, the U.S. views as erecting barriers.

In this environment, the trade agreements entered into by Canada have served to limit policy options. In addition to the U.S. challenges, the European Union has commenced an appeal to the WTO of a Canadian government decision to restrict the proposed expansion of the distribution arm of PolyGram Filmed Entertainment. Perhaps even more insidious is the new mindset of government policy-makers, a kind of self-censorship, which sees bureaucrats who are confronting policy challenges straining to find solutions which conform to the new trade agreements and do not require Canada to claim the "cultural exemption" of the Free Trade Agreement and NAFTA.

Before the Canada/U.S. FTA, the policy options available to decision-makers were limited only by their imagination and domestic political concerns. With the FTA, Canada put a box around its cultural sector and declared that certain potential support measures fall outside that box and would not be implemented. With NAFTA and the WTO, we reduced the size of the box. The MAI represents the greatest threat to Canada's cultural policies and threatens to eliminate the box entirely.

KEY MAI PROVISIONS

The important elements of the MAI for Canada's cultural community include a range of provisions contained in the draft text. This analysis is based on the October 1997 version.

The MAI is designed to make it easier for individual and corporate investors to move assets—whether money, production facilities or intellectual property rights—across international borders. The proposed definition of investor includes both individuals and businesses, whether or not incorporated and whether or not they are operated for profit. The definition of investment is equally broad and covers "every kind of asset owned or controlled, directly or indirectly, by an investor..." Intellectual property rights, an underpinning of the cultural industries, are included as one of the assets listed.

National Treatment (NT) provides that each country which is signatory to the agreement must treat nationals of other signatory countries no less favourably than they treat nationals of their own country. This applies to laws, rules, regulations and practices, and prohibits the adoption of discriminatory policies, whether or not such discrimination is intentional.

Most Favoured Nation (MFN) provisions state that all foreign countries must be treated the same. This prevents the imposition of laws which require companies to cease conducting business in countries which have a poor human rights record, for example, and prohibits a country from providing treatment to a non-signatory nation which is more favourable than it provides to MAI signatories.

The MAI provides that approval for temporary entry to work will be granted by member nations to the investor and key personnel, including executives, managers and specialists who are "essential to the enterprise."

Significant sections of the MAI seek to prevent a country from imposing, in relation to an investment, any measure that requires the foreign investor to achieve certain standards of performance, including levels of export, percentage of domestic content, or purchasing of domestic supplies. This provision is drafted to require member nations to treat investors from non-signatory nations in an equivalent manner.

The MAI provides that nations cannot nationalize or otherwise expropriate an investment, either directly or indirectly, except where it is in the public interest, conforms with the due process of law, is undertaken on a non-discriminatory basis, and is accompanied by "payment of prompt, adequate and effective compensation."

Another section is designed to ensure that investors can move their capital and profits to and from nations without hindrance and in a currency which is freely convertible at exchange rates established by the marketplace. The draft text provides explicitly that NT and MFN treatment will prevail in any case where government decides to privatize a public resource or asset.

Final agreement has not been reached respecting the inclusion of tax measures and policy, except as they may be used as a means to disguise an expropriation.

Key provisions of the MAI establish how disputes under its terms will be resolved. Over the past eight years, Canada has become well-acquainted with the dispute settlement regimes of the FTA and the WTO, sometimes to our detriment, as was the case in the WTO decision striking down all three components of the Canadian government's magazine support measures.

The MAI provisions allow both individual investors and states to trigger the process. These provisions permit an individual investor from an MAI signatory nation who has sustained a "loss or damage" as a result of an action of another signatory nation to launch a formal complaint under the MAI. The dispute is submitted to an arbitration panel with one member selected by each of the disputing parties and a chair mutually agreed. In some cases, this creates enhanced rights for a foreign company, since a domestic one would have no access to international arbitration and would be limited to seeking redress through a domestic process.

Also, it is important to note that some of largest and most powerful firms in the world are key players in the entertainment industry. The agreement also establishes a comparable system for the resolution of disputes between nations. Each party nominates one person to be on a panel and mutually agrees on the chair.

As drafted, the MAI will apply not only to a national government which ratifies and signs the Agreement, but to all levels of government in that nation, whether state, provincial, municipal, local or otherwise. If these "sub-national" levels of government are included in the MAI, it creates the potential in Canada for foreign nationals to receive *more* favourable treatment than residents of other provinces—for example, from one of the film development agencies. Discrimination against foreign investors would be prohibited, but investors from other provinces would not enjoy the protection of the MAI.

As well, the draft text includes two possible approaches to ensuring that any entity created or delegated by the government to exercise authority is covered by the obligations of the Agreement. In the view of the MAI's proponents, these provisions are critical to ensure there is no circumvention of the basic rules.

There are limited exceptions found in the draft text, including actions necessary for the protection of "essential security interests" of a nation, temporary measures during balance of payments crises, and "prudential measures" with respect to financial services.

"Essential security interests" is limited to a physical threat to a nation, including measures taken during a time of war or armed conflict.

The agreement has bracketed text (indicating final agreement has not yet been reached) in several places concerning measures related to protection of the environment and "maintenance of public order."

Many international trade agreements permit individual nations to maintain specific measures that would otherwise violate the agreement by listing these "reservations" upon signing. While the scope and nature of country-specific reservations to be permitted under the MAI is still being discussed, several matters are firm.

Agreement has been reached that non-conforming measures can be listed, continued if they are renewed promptly, and changed if the amendment increases the degree of conformity of the measure. However, agreement has not been reached on a Part B which would permit the lodging of reservations for new measures taken in sectors of economic activity that countries would specify on signing the agreement. This is sometimes referred to as an "unbound" reservation, to distinguish it from the "bound" reservation that would exist in the absence of Part B.

The MAI's commentary section reviews two fundamental principles related to the country-specific reservations. The manner in which these principles would apply to the proposed Part B is not agreed. Where a nation lists a non-conforming measure, such measure would be subject to the principle of "standstill." The text provides:

> *"Standstill would result from the prohibition of new or more restrictive exceptions to this minimum standard of treatment. From this perspective, a violation of standstill would be a violation of the underlying MAI obligations (e.g., of National Treatment and MFN), and the dispute settlement provisions would apply to such breaches of the MAI obligations."*

There is a lengthy discussion of how these non-conforming measures can be eliminated over time. Several methods, including peer pressure, periodic review by the governing body, and directing future negotiations to remove non-conforming measures are reviewed. The intention is explicit:

> *"Rollback is the liberalization process by which the reduction and eventual elimination of non-conforming measures to the MAI would take place."*

THE CULTURAL SECTOR IN THE MAI TEXT

In the January 1997 draft text of the MAI, there was no mention of the cultural sector, either directly as a possible exception or inclusion, or indirectly. A review of that text results in the inevitable conclusion that the cultural sector would be covered fully by the MAI as drafted in January 1997, except as individual nations may list country-specific reservations.

In the commentary attached to the May 1997 draft text (but not in the Agreement's body), France tabled for discussion a proposed exception clause for culture, to read as follows:

> *"Nothing in this agreement shall be construed to prevent any Contracting Party to take any measure to regulate investment of foreign companies and the conditions of activity of these companies, in the framework of policies designed to preserve and promote cultural and linguistic diversity."*

This annex states that France has concluded that "the basic principles of this agreement raise application problems for cultural industries (notably the printing, press and audio-visual sectors)." It discusses restrictions on investment in the audio-visual sector and the difficulty of applying them to new technologies under the standstill provisions; linguistic and other requirements in the sector which violate National Treatment obligations; and the co-production treaties in film and television.

Notwithstanding this submission by France, there was no change in either the May or October of 1997 or the February of 1998 draft texts. No other country has been listed as supporting the French text, and no alternative proposal has been tabled. In addition, it should be noted that this proposal is contained in the commentary to the Agreement rather than in the main text. Ordinarily, when agreement language is proposed by a participating country, it is placed in brackets as appropriate in the main text, indicating the proposal has not been agreed to by all parties.

Canada's Role in Negotiations

Analysis of the text suggests that Canada is a major proponent of the MAI and plays a prominent role in the negotiations. In the text, there are more than 20 references to Canadian proposals. This is not hard to understand when you consider that Canada has a significant stake in the outcome, both as a nation which invests heavily in other countries and as a recipient of foreign investment.

Firms in certain sectors of Canada's economy have major foreign holdings: total Canadian investment abroad was estimated to be $171 billion in 1996. In that same year, it was estimated that foreign investment in Canada reached $180 billion[5].

The United Nations Conference on Trade and Economic Development has developed an index of transnationality of individual companies which analyzes the degree to which a company's foreign assets, sales and employment exceed its home country figures. In this index, Canada has three companies in the top 15: Thomson (2), Seagram (4) and Northern Telecom. Only Switzerland has more.[6]

Canada has advanced proposals in a number of key areas, including a draft article on "conflicting requirements" which seeks to limit the ability of one nation to impose measures that require an investor to act in conflict with the laws of another nation. While this article addresses Canadian interests in Cuba, it raises the intriguing possibility that, even when National Treatment is applied to a foreign investor, such investor may still have access to the dispute settlement mechanism of the Agreement. Canada has also noted its reservations concerning a number of articles in the draft text.

However, in the text and other documentation available publicly, the Canadian delegation has been silent on the question of the cultural sector. There is no indication in any section of the draft text that Canada has any reservations about the implications of the MAI for the cultural sector. Canada does not even record its support for the proposal from France for a cultural exception.

Furthermore, the draft list of country-specific reservations tabled by Canada during the process does not include any cultural measure. In fact, by listing certain telecommunications measures and noting that the reservation does not apply "to providers of enhanced or value added services," the provision may be worse than the status quo.

With convergence, programming services will soon be provided by means of telecommunications transport networks. Agreeing that such services are outside the reservation may render CRTC regulation of programming services delivered in this manner unsustainable. It should be noted that an equivalent provision respecting "value-added services" is contained in NAFTA.

CANADIAN CULTURAL MEASURES AT RISK

The provisions of the MAI as drafted would affect virtually every cultural support program and measure which Canada has implemented. Some of the more obvious and sensitive areas which are contrary to the commitments in the MAI are analyzed below.

A) Restrictions on Foreign Ownership

Canada prohibits, limits or restricts foreign ownership in most of the cultural industries.

Such provisions would violate the National Treatment obligation, as well as the prohibitions against performance requirements, uncompensated expropriation, and restrictions on movement of capital. Individual foreign firms, some of which have considerable financial resources, and foreign nations could take action against Canada under the dispute settlement provisions. The current policies which are vulnerable to a challenge include:

- No foreign company can own more than 33 1/3% of a Canadian broadcaster or distribution undertaking (cable company, satellite broadcaster or other). Similar limitations are found in the telecommunications field.
- The policy in the book trade generally prohibits a Canadian company from being sold to non-Canadian interests and provides that a foreign company is not permitted to establish a new business in Canada. This policy in the past has resulted in the forced sale of assets to Canadians in the Ginn Publishing case, with the government acting as the buyer of last resort (potentially, an "expropriation" under the MAI).
- Indirect acquisitions in the book trade are reviewed by Investment Canada and are approved only if they are of "net benefit" to Canada and the Canadian-controlled sector. The "net benefit" test typically involves the negotiation of undertakings by the foreign investor to support Canadian authors, acquire Canadian products for distribution, and provide jobs to Canadians.
- The policy in film distribution prohibits a foreign company from establishing a new business in Canada, except to distribute its own productions. Any increased foreign ownership in film distribution is reviewed by Investment Canada under the "net benefit" test. It is under the terms of this policy that PolyGram has

been prevented from expanding its film distribution business in Canada beyond "proprietary" productions and Loews Theatres/Cineplex Odeon has been required to make certain commitments to government.

- Increased foreign ownership in the sound recording business is reviewed by Investment Canada under a similar "net benefit" test to that used in the book trade.
- Ontario's *Periodical and Publications Distribution Act* and several Quebec statutes require Canadian ownership (or provincial ownership) as a condition for establishing a business in certain cultural fields.

B) Funding Programs Limited to Canadian Individuals and Firms

Access to most funding programs is denied to non-Canadian companies and individuals.

Even if a foreign company is producing Canadian content material, publishing Canadian writers or recording Canadian artists, it is not entitled to apply for funding support. Such restrictions may well be contrary to the MAI's NT provisions.

- Funding support for film and television production activity through the $200 million Canadian Television and Cable Production Fund (CTCPF), which is a cornerstone of the current production boom, as well as Telefilm, the provincial agencies and Canada Council, is limited to Canadian firms. If taxation is "carved-in" to the MAI, the support through the Refundable Investment Tax Credit and the companion provincial schemes is put at risk.
- The CRTC has mandated the creation of private sector production and talent support programs in both the television and sound recording industries by directing licensees to provide certain percentages of revenues for these purposes. The total value of these funds is close to $100 million annually. The programs are

generally not available to foreign firms, even if they have a Canadian subsidiary and are producing Canadian content records, television programs and movies. The funds have become a critical component of the industries and promote individual artists, actors, technicians, designers, directors, musicians and others, by making possible a wide range of production. Because the CRTC would be included as a government regulatory agency under the MAI disciplines, access to these funding programs could not be limited to Canadians. The obligatory nature of the funding requirement may be at risk if the ownership restrictions on Canadian broadcasters are removed.

- Access to the Book Publishing Industry Development Program, the Block Grant Program of the Canada Council, and the Publications Assistance Program, which together provide more than $100 million support, is limited to Canadian book and magazine publishers. These programs ultimately support individual writers, editors, artists, and others involved in the book and magazine industries, particularly emerging authors. Again, under the MAI, while it is likely the programs could continue to support certain genres of activity, access could not be limited to Canadian firms.
- Access to the limited number of funds which support new media productions has been generally limited to Canadian firms.
- The Cultural Industries Development Fund administered by the Federal Business Development Bank provides assistance only to Canadian firms.
- Since the definition of investor in the MAI includes organizations and associations operated on a not-for-profit basis, direct and indirect funding of their activities may be subject to challenge if access is denied to a foreign association or organization having a Canadian presence or asset.
- To qualify for funding from the various arts, heritage and museums programs, the institution or individual must be Canadian. Where a foreign national owns a Canadian asset in this field (and remember, this may include an intellectual property

right), the MAI would require National Treatment for such a foreign "investor" to the extent they might otherwise be eligible to apply for funding support. This has the potential to affect all of the programs of the Canada Council, provincial and local arts councils, the Museums Assistance Program, Cultural Initiatives Program, and the Arts Stabilization Projects, although the final language both of the intellectual property rights provision and the exceptions clause will be determinative.

C) Canadian Content Requirements

For a television program to qualify as Canadian Content (Cancon), the producer of the material must be Canadian.

This requirement would be considered a violation of the National Treatment obligation of the MAI.

- Cancon rules, such as those in television and radio, are an underpinning of the music and audio-visual production industries. In most cases, even if foreign film and television producers create programs which satisfy the Cancon definition (6 or 8 out of 10 points), they would not be entitled to the CRTC Cancon number, nor be eligible for the various funding programs. While a foreign record company's Canadian subsidiary which creates a Cancon sound recording (two out of four elements) can obtain a CRTC number, it is not entitled to other benefits of such designation.
- More fundamentally, there is a relationship between Canadian content rules and the ownership of broadcast undertakings. Should the limitations on non-Canadian ownership in the sector be removed as a consequence of the MAI, it would be difficult to maintain obligatory Cancon requirements on the new foreign owners of Canadian broadcasters, as these would be in the nature of prohibited performance requirements.

- In an MAI world, the CRTC may be limited to voluntary commitments, extracted during the licensing process. This would apply both to requirements to fund independent production activity and the Foundation to Assist Canadian Talent On Records (FACTOR) and to maintain Cancon levels.

D) Other

- The *Cultural Property Export and Import Act* in some cases limits the ability of foreign investors to move their assets from Canada.
- New measures to encourage production and distribution of new media materials, including incentives and such things as the sale of digital rights by museums and galleries, could not be limited in application to Canadians.
- As France noted in its intervention to the MAI text, Canada's 36 co-production treaties which encourage partnerships in film and television with producers in countries other than the U.S. would violate NT and MFN obligations.
- If public cultural agencies or assets are privatized, foreign interests could be allowed to acquire them. Potentially, this could affect decisions to privatize TVOntario, the CBC, museums, the National Film Board, the National Arts Centre, etc.
- The CRTC maintains a range of regulations which discriminate against foreign services. These include the cable substitution rules, the list of eligible foreign programming services which can be distributed in Canada, and other policies which provide preferential access for Canadian services to the distribution undertakings. All would be at risk under the MAI as violations of NT obligations.
- If taxation is "carved-in" to the MAI, foreign interests may be able to claim that restrictions on Canadian firms advertising in U.S. magazines and on U.S. border stations (which are provided in the *Income Tax Act*) are a violation of their right to be treated equally to Canadians (National Treatment).

- Canada's immigration regulations could not sustain policies which restrict the flow of foreign performers and other cultural workers into Canada to work on foreign-financed film, television and performing arts productions.
- Measures encouraging exports in the cultural industries would be in violation of the NT obligation if they are not available to foreign companies which create Canadian material.
- The section of the MAI which provides that government commissions, enterprises and agencies must act in a manner which is consistent with the obligations of the Agreement would have far-reaching consequences for Canadian institutions and agencies with cultural implications. This includes not only the Canada Council, Telefilm, CBC, CRTC, National Arts Centre and museums, but also schools and libraries. This is particularly the case in areas such as acquisition of Canadian-produced materials.

EXCEPTIONS AND RESERVATIONS

As debate on the MAI has been engaged in Canada, there is a widely held consensus that Canada cannot enter the Agreement unless there is a comprehensive exception for Canadian cultural measures. Even the newspapers and magazines which support the MAI call editorially for such an exception and politicians otherwise kindly disposed to the Agreement argue this is a "deal-breaker" for Canada. Bill Dymond, Canada's chief MAI negotiator, told a meeting of the Canadian Conference of the Arts (CCA), a national umbrella organization of artists, producers and associations, that he has conveyed the message to Canada's partners that a complete exception is required in this field. But what does this really mean?

Three different approaches to this question are being discussed publicly:

- The proposal by France for a cultural exception, contained in the commentary section of the Agreement is the approach favoured by most.
- At his November 4, 1997 appearance before a House Committee examining the MAI, Canada's Minister for International Trade, Sergio Marchi, stated that Canada would achieve an exception no less favourable than that found in the North American Free Trade Agreement.
- Use of a Country-Specific Reservation approach.

In dealing with exceptions to trade rules, experience suggests that international panels interpret language narrowly, since they are comprised of individuals who generally support attempts to liberalize trade. The recent WTO panel decision which struck down Canada's magazine support measures is instructive in this regard. The panel determined that Canadian and U.S. magazines are "like" products, or basically interchangeable. They did not view the substantially distinct editorial content of Canadian publications as having any relevance in their determination. They cited as the leading legal precedent a case which involved Japanese beer and liquor.

The language proposed by France is narrow and would not cover adequately all current forms of artistic expression, let alone those that could emerge in the next century. It could well be limited in application to measures supporting culturally-significant work or works in minority languages. An international panel of trade experts, with no understanding of cultural imperatives or sympathy for the Canadian reality, could find that, since Canada has already achieved "cultural and linguistic diversity," a particular measure is attempting to hide behind the cultural exception and is really an economic measure in a cultural disguise.

The French proposal would certainly not exempt policies which are designed to build and maintain a strong cultural infrastructure, such as the recently announced foreign production services tax credit or measures which promote advertising on Canadian broadcasting services.

The principal concern of the French, as it was during the GATT talks, is maintaining the European content quotas in television. Their publishing and other cultural industries have grown and matured with the protection of language and a thousand years of common history. In the endgame of MAI negotiations, the French may well be prepared to settle for a narrow exception clause that preserves these quotas.

The NAFTA exception clause is a verbatim repeat of the FTA's language. It has an industrial focus and defines only the forms of expression currently used by artists, including film, television, publishing and sound recording—the cultural industries. While it is a thorough list of existing cultural industries, it does not include the heritage sector, nor performing arts, visual arts and crafts. Because it was drafted in the late 1980s, it cannot possibly include the forms of cultural expression that will emerge in the next century.

The NAFTA provision also repeats the FTA's infamous "notwithstanding" clause, thereby authorizing retaliation against Canadian cultural measures and not limiting retaliatory measures to the cultural realm.

The dangers in a Country-Specific Reservation approach are enormous. While final language has not been agreed upon, it is impossible to list measures that have not yet been implemented. Furthermore, it would be impossible to list future culturally-significant sectors since artists have not yet begun to create in these media. It would be difficult, therefore, even with an unbound reservation, to safeguard all prospective cultural policy mechanisms.

According to the October draft MAI text, existing measures can be maintained but they cannot be strengthened, nor can new ones be implemented. To the extent that the principle of "rollback" applies to these listed measures, they may disappear completely over time.

Most particularly at risk in each of the proposed approaches are the new forms of cultural expression which will emerge in the decades ahead and which, by their very definition, cannot possibly be contemplated today.

For this reason, if the MAI proceeds, it is vital that the Canadian government work actively with France and other nations in the OECD to seek a broad general exception for the cultural industries, arts and heritage, using the French proposal only as a starting point.

CONCLUSION

Potentially, the MAI could have a profound negative effect on a range of Canada's cultural support measures and touch all sectors of the arts, culture and heritage communities in Canada. It is a more serious threat than any of the other trade agreements to which Canada has acceded in the past decade.

If Canada's sovereignty on cultural matters is to be protected, a comprehensive cultural exception is an absolute prerequisite. The elements of such a complete exception are:

- A comprehensive definition of culture, which includes not only the cultural industries of radio, film, television, book and magazine publishing and the music industry, but also new media and key elements of the telecommunications sector. It should explicitly include the performing arts, visual arts, crafts and heritage sectors, as well as individual artists and other creators.
- Agreement that the exception is self-defining for each nation, to permit it alone to determine what is a "cultural" measure, and to change this determination over time.
- Provision that adjudication of any dispute arising from the interpretation of the cultural exception is referred to a panel of cultural experts empowered to determine if a given measure is "cultural."
- Adequate language to ensure that the exception is not confined to certain parts of the agreement, but rather overrides all of the obligations and is not subject to the principles of "standstill" and "rollback."

These principles should apply to all negotiations which Canada enters into with its global trading partners. Furthermore, obtaining an adequate cultural exception should be an absolute pre-requisite to Canada agreeing to any new trade agreements or to renew existing ones.

ENDNOTES

1 The Globe and Mail, Thursday Oct. 2 1997, pg. C-1
2 Playback, January 12, 1998, pg. 1
3 The Globe and Mail, Friday Jan. 16 1997, pg. C-10
4 All figures in this article are from various publications of Statistics Canada, unless stated otherwise. These figures are for 1996.
5 Notes for an Address by Hon. Sergio Marchi, Minister for International Trade to the Standing Committee on Foreign Affairs and International Trade, Ottawa, Nov. 4 1997
6 The Economist, September 27-October 3 Edition, pg. 115

THE MAI AND PUBLIC AND SOCIAL SERVICES

by Matthew Sanger

INTRODUCTION

The logic of the MAI is directly opposed to the principles on which Canada's health care and social services systems are founded. The MAI would establish a "level playing field" for international investment by providing investors in all participating countries with a common set of rights. These rights constrain government action, including the ability to administer and direct the evolution of our health and social services programs.

While few would argue against the desireability of ground rules for the treatment of international investment, the MAI goes far beyond what most people would consider appropriate. The extremely broad definition of what constitutes an investment means that the range of government measures affected by MAI rules extends far beyond the regulation of commercial activity. Legislation and regulations in social policy, which may affect commercial investors only incidentally, will nevertheless be constrained by the far-reaching rights accorded to investors.

It is important to note that Canada's health care and social services are provided through a complex mix of public and private institutions. Self-employed physicians provide much of our health care services, which are paid by a publicly funded and administered system of Medicare. Most regulated child care is provided by non-profit community-based organizations, funded both by government subsidies and fees from parents. Home-care services in most parts of the country are provided by different—and shifting—mixes of public and private organizations.

Government legislation and regulation in these areas inevitably have implications for the private individuals and organizations involved, directly and indirectly, in the provision of health and social services. It is vital that governments have the ability to administer and direct these programs to meet the changing needs of their citizens. This includes the ability to adjust and experiment with the mix of public, private and non-profit funding and delivery of health and social services.

The MAI would restrict this ability. By giving private individuals and commercial enterprises very strong rights to compensation, the MAI would effectively prevent legislation and regulations which have the effect of limiting returns on an investment. By preventing governments from targeting subsidies, it would remove an important tool for governments to direct how social services are provided. The only direction of change permitted by the MAI would be to increase opportunities for private individuals and commercial enterprises.

The first section of this essay begins with a discussion of the federal government's claim that health and social services will be protected in the MAI, then proceeds to review the specific elements of the MAI which pose a threat to health and social services.[1] The second section illustrates these dangers using the example of Québec's new family policy.

"A HIGH STANDARD OF INVESTMENT PROTECTION"

Proponents of the MAI maintain that the aim of the current negotiations is to reach agreement on a set of ground rules which "set a high standard of investment protection".[2] Their acknowledged aim is the make a strong agreement, negotiated by the world's wealthy industrialized countries, the standard for a wider agreement to include developing countries which are more vulnerable to sudden shifts in international investment flows.

Negotiators have tried to achieve this aim by proposing a text that is virtually all-encompassing. This point is affirmed by the negotiations chairman in the official communiqué issued following the February 1998 meeting of negotiators:

Delegations confirmed that the MAI is to be an ambitious, comprehensive agreement covering, in principle, all sectors and economic activities. Exceptions will nevertheless be needed for overriding and widely-shared policy reasons, such as national security, and to respect political sensitivities and priorities, taking into account other international agreements [3]

Before reviewing the specific articles of the MAI which threaten health and social services, it is necessary to consider the scope of the agreement in more general terms.

Reservations

There is no general provision that would exclude health and social services from the MAI rules. The only general exclusions in the proposed text are for government measures relating to national security (including arms production), the maintenance of public order, monetary and exchange rate policies.[4]

The MAI would also allow a government to take special measures inconsistent with its rules in two very specific circumstances: to regulate transfers of capital in order to stabilize a serious balance-of-payments or exchange rate problem, and to regulate financial services to protect investors. [5]

It is conceivable that other government measures will be excluded in the final text, as suggested by the communiqué quoted above. The French government, for example, is demanding a "general exception" for culture. However, there is no discussion of a general exception for health and social services. Given the strength of the commercial interests involved, particularly in the United States, it is highly unlikely there would be agreement to completely carve out health and social services from the agreement.

Country-specific reservations would provide a weaker form of protection for health and social services than would a general exception. Canada and other countries can propose reservations which exempt specific government measures from certain MAI rules. These reservations apply only to the countries which propose them and must be agreed to by other countries. They are also narrower than a general exception in that they provide protection only from the MAI articles specified in the reservation; the measure in question remains subject to all other parts of the agreement. Furthermore, international treaty law requires that country-specific reservations be interpreted narrowly when there is a dispute over the level of protection provided.[6]

It is through these country-specific reservations that the Canadian government proposes to protect health care and social services. Public information produced by the Ministry of Foreign Affairs and International Trade makes the following commitment:

As in NAFTA, Canada will retain, through exceptions, the ability to preserve the integrity of Canada's health care system.[7]

Canadian negotiators have filed a long list of Canadian government measures which they want reserved from certain parts of the MAI. The proposed reservation for health and social services reads as follows:

> *Canada reserves the right to adopt or maintain any measure with respect to the provision of public law enforcement and correctional services, and the following services to the extent that they are social services established or maintained for a public purpose: income security or insurance, social security or insurance, social welfare, public education, public training, health and child care.*

Unlike NAFTA, the MAI includes no agreed list of the kinds of measures for which countries may take reservations. This adds to the uncertainty that Canada's proposed reservation for social services, or any other proposed reservation, will be accepted by other countries with very different health and social services regimes.

Canada's proposed reservation for social services would apply to any existing or future measures taken by the federal government. Several delegations are opposed to any such "unbounded" reservations. They insist that any reservation must be limited to existing measures ("standstill") and that there be a commitment to progressively reduce the scope of any such reservation ("rollback"). These objections cast further doubt on the Canadian government's ability to secure acceptance of its proposed social services reservation.

If it is accepted, the proposed Canadian reservation would reproduce the weaknesses contained in the NAFTA reservation on which it is modelled (Annex II-C-9). Because of the qualification that health and social services are protected only "to the extent that they are social services established or maintained for a public purpose," there is enormous uncertainty over the level of protection provided by this NAFTA reservation. This uncertainty would apply equally to Canada's proposed MAI reservation.

No dispute panel has provided an interpretation of Canada's health and social services reservation in NAFTA Annex II-C-9. While the Canadian government claims that the great majority of our social services including health services, have a public purpose, the U.S. government asserts a much more narrow interpretation.

Guidelines issued by the United States Trade Representative state that:

> *If private investors/service providers are permitted to supply services similar to those provided by a government (i.e., day care, drug treatment, law enforcement, social welfare, education, etc), Chapter 11 [Investment] and Chapter 12 [Cross-border trade in Services] apply to the provision of those activities by NAFTA investors/service providers.*[8]

In other words, the view of the USTR is that the NAFTA rules apply to health and social services in all cases where there is a mix of public and private funding or service delivery. If this interpretation prevailed in a dispute, it would expose our health care system, and many other social services, to challenge by foreign commercial interests.

It is reasonable to assume that the United States would assert the same narrow interpretation of the social services reservation Canada has proposed for the MAI.

Leaving aside strong doubts that other MAI countries will accept Canada's proposed reservation, it seems an enormous gamble to entrust the protection of our health and social services to such an ambiguous and untested reservation.

A further weakness of Canada's proposed reservation is the fact that it applies only to areas of federal jurisdiction, providing no protection for provincial measures.[9] Health care and social services are areas of provincial jurisdiction in Canada. Notwithstanding the importance of the Canada Health Act and the significance of federal-provincial transfers, most social policy is determined by provincial legislation and regulations.

By contrast, Canada's social services reservation in NAFTA applied to both federal and provincial measures. Even then, provincial governments were concerned that NAFTA Annex II-C-9 did not provide sufficient protection for health and social services. In response to provincial concerns, and to the publicity generated by critics of NAFTA, the Canadian government signed a formal letter of agreement with the United States and Mexico to confirm that all provincial and state legislation and regulations in existence when NAFTA took effect are fully protected. This resolution provides stronger protection for health and social services because it does not rest on an interpretation of the meaning of Annex II-C-9.

Given that many MAI countries are unitary states, it is unlikely that Canada could secure agreement for a similar general reservation for existing measures of sub-national levels of government. Countries with unitary states would consider this inequitable because it would reduce the scope of the MAI in federal states only.

The Canadian government has promised to add provincial measures to its proposed social services reservation. It is unclear why it is leaving this to a later stage in the negotiations. Again leaving aside doubts about Canada's ability to get agreement on such a proposal, the inadequacies of this reservation for federal measures apply equally to provincial measures affecting health and social services.

Canada's proposed reservation is wholly inadequate to ensure the level of protection which the federal government has promised Canadians it will secure for health and social services. Even the Liberal-dominated House of Commons committee which examined the MAI recognized the inadequacies of the federal government proposals. In its majority report[10], the Committee recommended that a list of provincial-level reservations be finalized as soon as possible in consultation with provincial governments, and that this list be made publicly available.

It also stated that "Canada must achieve an unbound reservation for health, education and social services" in consultation with sub-national levels of government. While these recommendations would enhance the level of protection currently proposed, they would be weaker than a general exception which would completely carve out health and social services from the MAI.

Specific threats to health and social services

What are the dangers to health and social services, given the strong probability that these sectors will not be adequately shielded from the MAI? How will specific elements of the agreement undermine our social programs?

The following is short review of the most significant elements of the MAI, which are discussed in greater detail in other sections of this volume.

Investment incentives

Among the most significant elements of the MAI affecting health and social services is the chapter on investment incentives.[11] The primary purpose of the proposed article is to prohibit governments from targeting subsidies to attract or maintain foreign investment in the form of industry and other enterprises. However, the MAI rules are cast so broadly that this chapter could enable commercial providers to claim equal access to public subsidies for health and social services. This power could effectively prevent any new initiatives, such as Quebec's new Family Policy, which target subsidies to specific organizations such as community-based non-profit agencies.

Under the proposed article, investment incentives would be subject to the central principles of National Treatment and Most Favoured Nation. In contrast to NAFTA, which explicitly excludes government subsidies and grants, the MAI defines investment incentives extremely broadly as a "grant of a specific advantage arising from public expenditure".[12] In the absence of a strong protection for health and social services, this broad definition would capture government subsidies in areas where there is a mix of public and private provision.

The impact of this article would be amplified by a proposed paragraph which remains bracketed, indicating that there is not full agreement to include it in the text. This paragraph would allow a government to challenge incentives provided by another government if it considers that the incentives have a discriminatory effect, even if they are not targeted in a discriminatory manner. This would further restrict government powers because the effect of a government measure is conditioned by circumstances beyond its control, including the prevalence of commercial social service providers in other countries.

INVESTMENT PROTECTION

Government initiatives in health and social services could also be affected by the MAI rules drafted to protect investments.[13] Commercial providers could use these rules to seek compensation for any legislation or regulations which reduce their expected profits or other gains from investment.

As noted in other contributions to this volume, the MAI would require governments to compensate private investors for measures which fall far short of the physical expropriation of an investment. This is because the MAI uses an extremely broad definition of what constitutes an investment, and because it gives very strong rights to compensation for any measures which affect an investment.

The MAI defines an investment as "every kind of asset owned or controlled, directly or indirectly, by an investor." The definition makes clear that this includes a very broad range of assets, including intangible property such as rights conferred by concessions, licenses and permits.[14]

The MAI requires governments to give investors from another MAI country "full and constant protection and security."[15] Governments are prohibited from expropriating an investment and from taking "any measure or measures having equivalent effect." Given the broad definition of investment in the MAI, this protection would apply to any measures that reduce the market for an investor, or otherwise reduce anticipated profits.

Expropriation is permitted "for a purpose which is in the public interest," provided that foreign investments are not targeted. However, even in these cases, a government is required to provide prompt compensation. Because the definition of investment encompasses a very broad range of assets, investors could claim very high levels of compensation for any health or social policy measure which significantly reduces commercial markets. This liability would effectively prevent governments from taking such initiatives.

Quebec Family Policy

This section uses a specific example—Quebec's new Family Policy—to illustrate how the rules discussed above would constrain governments from achieving legitimate policy objectives in the area of health and social policy.

Although the following example is specific to child care programs in the province of Quebec, the dangers are similar for all health and social services which are funded and delivered by a combination of private and public institutions and individuals.

A new Family Policy was announced by the Quebec government at its Summit on the Economy and Employment in October 1996. This announcement was central to the provincial government's efforts to gain support from business, labour, and other sectors of Quebec society for tough economic and fiscal measures to address a large deficit and continued high levels of unemployment.

The Family Policy announced at the Summit encompassed initiatives in three areas: 1) early childhood services, 2) financial support for families, and 3) paid leave for parents.[16]

The last initiative would have used unemployment insurance premiums to greatly expand the parental leave benefits available to new parents resident in Quebec. Nothing has come of this proposal, as it required the agreement of the federal government. It was likely less a serious proposal than a gesture to shore up public support for separation by fuelling Quebec's ongoing dispute with the federal government over jurisdiction for social policy.

The second initiative integrates various child allowances and targets them to low-income families, including both working families and those on social assistance. This initiative was coordinated with other provinces and the federal government. As in other provinces, the support is provided through an enhanced federal tax benefit.

The first initiative of the Family Policy has been the most significant. It includes the creation of full-time kindergarten for five year-olds, free child care and educational services for underprivileged four year-olds, and an enormous expansion of low-cost child care available to all children between one and four years old.

The promise of quality child care for all children for $5 a day became the *leitmotif* for the entire Family Policy. It is being introduced in phases, beginning in September 1997 with the provision of $5 a day child care for all four- year-olds. By 2001 all children between the ages of one and four will have access to low-cost child care.

The following are the main features of the Quebec government's initiative to expand early childhood services:

- Existing regulated not-for-profit child care providers are directly subsidized by the provincial Ministry of Family and Children's Services. The subsidy covers the difference between the $5 fee paid by parents and the actual cost of providing a child care space. To be eligible for subsidies, these centres must meet provincial requirements regarding non-profit status, area serviced, and parent representation on the Board of Directors.
- 73,000 new child care spaces will be created between 1997 and 2001. Many of these will be in centres established to service specific geographic areas. These Early Childhood Centres (Centres de la petite enfance) will be community-based, not-for-profit centres controlled by a local Board of Directors on which two-thirds of the seats are reserved for parents. These centres will receive provincial subsidies on the same basis as existing providers.
- Both existing providers and the new Early Childhood Centres will be required to provide family-based care as well as centre-based care.
- Subsidies will be allocated with the aim of coordinating services so that in every community a single agency provides the full range of child care and family support services required. This includes evening and weekend care, part-time and respite care.

Providing universal access to low-cost early childhood services is arguably as significant in our day as the creation of Medicare was in the 1960s. It addresses social needs created by the increased participation of women in paid work and changes in family composition. The Quebec initiative is all the more significant given the withdrawal of support for child care by other provincial governments and the federal government's failure to support an expanded system of child care, as promised in the 1993 federal election.

Commercial child care providers initially resisted the new Quebec Family Policy, just as doctors resisted public health insurance when it was initiated in Saskatchewan. Fortunately, commercial child care providers have less political power than doctors wielded in the 1960s (and continue to exercise).

How could the MAI impede the Quebec government if it were in effect when the Family Policy was introduced?

Firstly, commercial child care providers could greatly increase the cost of the initiative by claiming rights to compensation for loss of their investments.

Commercial child care providers in Canada, including Quebec, are predominantly small "Mom and Pop" enterprises wholly owned by Canadian residents. These domestic investors could not directly exercise rights which the MAI confers on international investors. However, the MAI would set a standard for compensation which is far more stringent than the current practice. If domestic investors were not treated as favourably as international investors, they would have grounds to claim a form of reverse discrimination.

The large chains that predominate in the United States have sought to gain a foothold in the Canadian market. The Canadian market is becoming more attractive to large commercial providers as other provinces withdraw public support, relax regulations, and contemplate replacing institutional subsidies with individual vouchers. A foreign commercial chain with any investment in Quebec, even a minority interest in a single centre, would have rights under the MAI to claim compensation.[17]

While domestic investors would not have the same legal right to compensation, their bargaining leverage in negotiations with the provincial government would be greatly enhanced by the MAI. As Ian Robinson argues elsewhere in this volume, the MAI will restrict the scope of government policy as much by strengthening the hand of private enterprise in negotiations with government as by directly prohibiting certain measures.

Even without the MAI in effect, commercial providers had enough clout to force extended negotiations with the Quebec government. These negotiations resulted in significant changes to the implementation of the Family Policy. Even these concessions to commercial operators could have been challenged, had the MAI been in effect.

As a result of these negotiations, commercial providers have three options: 1) convert to non-profit status to qualify for the provincial subsidy; 2) remain private commercial providers without access to the subsidy; or 3) enter a partnership arrangement with a local Early Childhood Centre.

The partnership option is available where an Early Childhood Centre needs additional capacity to meet the demand for child care in the community it serves. The Centre agrees to "rent" spaces which the commercial provider can offer at the $5 fee. The Ministry subsidizes the cost of these spaces at a lower level than the subsidy provided to not-for-profit centres. These rental agreements must be renegotiated each year and are subject to the commercial provider meeting stringent quality standards.

The MAI would enable commercial providers to claim greater access to provincial subsidies. They could base this claim on at least three different grounds:

1. A commercial chain based in the United States, or in any other signatory to the MAI, would be able to challenge the Quebec government's requirement that child care providers be locally controlled as a condition for receiving subsidy. Targeting subsidies to domestic providers would likely be seen as discriminatory treatment in violation of the National Treatment requirement for investment incentives.
2. Commercial providers could claim a right to the same level of subsidy as not-for-profit providers. This would also constitute discriminatory treatment under the MAI. Canadian-based providers could not directly exercise MAI rights, but their bargaining power would be enhanced by the ability of foreign providers to do so.
3. Commercial providers based in the United States could claim that the preference given to not-for-profit providers has the effect of excluding American child care providers from the Ca-

nadian market. Taken on its own, the requirement of not-for-profit status as a condition for receiving subsidies is non-discriminatory because it applies to all providers regardless of where they are based. However, American investors could argue that this policy has a discriminatory effect because it excludes commercial chains, which are the predominant form of child care provider in the United States.

A successful challenge on any of these grounds would undermine a central feature of the Quebec family policy. The government would be prevented from allocating subsidies to develop an integrated "hub" model of early childhood services in which a single agency provides the full range of child care and family support services required in a community.

In summary, the MAI would not directly prohibit the implementation of the Quebec Family Policy. However, it would greatly impede this important social policy initiative by increasing the ability of commercial providers to exact concessions, including compensation payments, and by preventing subsidies from being targeted to ensure a coherent provision of services. These obstacles would effectively prevent a new public initiative as ambitious as the family policy.

CONCLUSION

This essay has used the example of Quebec's Family Policy to illustrate the dangers which the MAI poses for our health and social services. Similar dangers apply to other areas of social policy in which there is a mix of public and private funding and delivery. Home-care is an example of such a service for which there is a growing recognition of the need to expand public support.

Public attention to child care and home-care is a reflection of the changing needs of Canadian citizens. Government initiatives in these areas could be as significant for our generation as the creation of Medicare was for a previous generation. Private companies and individuals could resist any infringement of their commercial gainsas hotly as doctors initially resisted Medicare. By restricting the targeting of government subsidies and by strengthening the hand of commercial investors, the MAI would greatly reduce the ability of governments to respond to the changing social needs of Canadians.

ENDNOTES

1 All references in this chapter to the MAI are to the February 18 1998 version of the MAI negotiating text, unless otherwise noted.

2 Foreign Affairs and International Trade web site: "Multilateral Agreement on Investment, MAI: An Introduction" January 14 1998.

3 OECD News Release, High Level Meeting on the Multilateral Agreement on Investment, February 18 1998 (posted on OECD web site).

4 MAI text, part VI.

5 MAI text, pages 74-76.

6 Legal opinion dated November 14 1997 by Appleton and Associates (prepared for the Council of Canadians).

7 Foreign Affairs and International Trade web site: "Multilateral Agreement on Investment, MAI: An Introduction" January 14 1998.

8 Reprinted in Inside Nafta, April 17 1996, p.13

9 For a more detailed discussion of the implications of the MAI for provincial government powers, see Ian Robinson's chapter in this volume.

10 First Report of the Sub-Committee on International Trade, Trade Disputes and Investment, Canada and the Multilateral Agreement on Investment, December 1997. (Available on the Parliamentary Internet site: http://www.parl.gc.ca).

11 MAI text, pages 42-44.

12 MAI text, page 44.

13 MAI text, pages 52-57.

14 MAI text, page 11.

15 MAI text, page 52.

16 The Quebec Family Policy is described in detail in the White Paper issued by the Quebec Secrétariat de la famille, "Nouvelles dispositions de la Politique familiale," 1997. A good English language summary is Quebecs New Family Policy, a fact sheet prepared for the Childcare Resource and Reserch Unit, University of Toronto, September 1997.

17 This right could extend to foreign based commercial providers with investments in any other Canadian province, if the exclusions for health and social services were removed from the Agreement on Internal Trade, as has been threatened. See Bryan Schwartz, Implications of Expanding the Scope of the Agreement on Internal Trade to Include Health and Social Services, a legal opinion prepared for the Canadian Union of Public Employees, February 1998.

THE MAI AND THE MUNICIPALITIES

by Barry Appleton[1]

Over 30 years ago, Marshall McLuhan used the term "global village" to describe a new trend. McLuhan's global village referred to how modern technology, like jet air travel, television and satellite-based long distance telephones, linked remote areas of the world together in new ways.[2] Decisions made thousands of miles away could have an impact at home, and local actions could have immediate impact abroad.

As we enter a new millennium, few knew then how correct Prof. McLuhan would be. We find ourselves constantly coping with the impact of change. New technology has resulted in shorter time frames and has extended a global reach for business. We need no better proof of this development than to see how financial issues half a world away in Asia have had a direct effect on our domestic stock markets and interest rates. Our new reality is defined by CNN, the internet and corporations which operate on a global basis. As a result, today local issues can immediately have international effect and many types of local issues are now the stuff of global agreements.

Thus, it should not be surprising to find that today the most local of our institutions, civic government, is now the subject of international agreements. This paper will look at how global investment treaties can have an impact on the municipal government. Part I looks at how this change has occurred, Part II examines the key instrument of this change, Part III gives examples of this change; and Part IV deals with general conclusions.

HOW THIS CHANGE OCCURRED

The impact of international law on local government has not occurred overnight, but has been influenced by a number of factors over the last 50 years.

The shift away from tariffs

From the late 1940s and onwards, international agreements were preoccupied with the issue of reducing tariffs. Since the reduction of tariffs resulted in lower protection for domestic industries, it took a considerable effort to achieve meaningful agreements. At first, the focus of international agreements was to local customs duties. By the late 1970s, most duties had been reduced or removed and the focus of attention shifted to new areas: non-tariff barriers.[3] The first international agreements were concerned with issues such as product standards or government procurement. However, developed states, like Canada and the United States, continued to push for controls on a new area: foreign investment.

The creation of investment treaties

After the Second World War, American negotiators began to include clauses in American treaties that gave protection to the investments owned by American's abroad. These clauses usually permitted the U.S. government to bring a claim before an international tribunal in order to seek restitution for lost property. Eventually, these investment protection clauses became codified into a form of treaty known as a Bilateral Investment Treaty (BIT). The BITs were generally negotiated with developing states and they guaranteed compensation to American investors in the case of expropriation or a failure to provide fair and equitable treatment.[4] The World Bank's International Centre for the Settlement of Investment Disputes (ICSID) reports that since 1987 more than 800 BITs have been concluded.[5]

The successful negotiation of the North American Free Trade Agreement (NAFTA) in 1994 created the first broad investment agreement between developed and developing states. While this agreement also looked at trade issues, it marked the first time that two developed states ever agreed between themselves to accept the onerous provisions of a bilateral investment agreement. The NAFTA contains a broad set of investment obligations. While these obligations applied to all levels of government in Canada, most of the obligations did not apply to municipalities because of technical exceptions and reservations. However, some NAFTA obligations still applied to the actions of municipalities—a fact that the federal government failed to clearly convey to municipalities across Canada.

The NAFTA was the first multilateral agreement to contain a controversial process that permitted individuals themselves, rather than governments, to police these agreements. If a government action violated an obligation in the NAFTA's Investment Chapter, an individual from another NAFTA Party or its investment could directly challenge that measure before a fast-track international tribunal without the agreement of its home government.[6] The "investor-state" dispute settlement process provides for a fast and effective means of settling disputes between investors and governments by bypassing domestic courts completely.

The Investor-State dispute settlement process established in the NAFTA has been described as "an untapped source of extensive private investor rights, including guaranteed access to a NAFTA panel for a private party."[7] Designed to provide protection for foreign investors in developing countries, the investor-state dispute settlement process focuses strictly on settling investment disputes between individuals and governments.

While the NAFTA was the first step in this process of creating international responsibility for municipal governments, the most significant development in this process is currently at hand—the Multilateral Agreement on Investment.

THE INSTRUMENTS OF CHANGE

The Multilateral Agreement on Investment[8] (the MAI) is an international investment agreement currently under negotiation by the 29 member countries of the Organization for Economic Cooperation and Development in Paris. The goal of the MAI is to establish international standards on how governments treat foreign investors and their investments. The MAI is built upon the framework of the NAFTA's Investment Chapter. The MAI, in distinction to the NAFTA, is a much broader agreement in that its terms apply to all levels of government without exception[9]. As currently negotiated, the MAI's obligations will directly apply to the acts of all levels of government, including municipal governments.

Like the NAFTA, the MAI includes a special process to protect the "rights" of foreign investors by allowing them and their companies to challenge local measures that violate their international rights. The Investor-State dispute settlement process allows a foreign investor from an MAI country (both individuals and corporations) to directly bring a compensation claim against another MAI government. These claims are heard before a special international arbitration panel that can award financial compensation to investors that have been harmed by governmental action which violates the MAI's investment obligations. The panels cannot strike down MAI-infringing measures, but the threat of paying enforceable damage awards can be chastening to government policy initiatives.

MAI investors are entitled to dispute government measures. These measures are not limited to legislation but extend to all acts attributable to governments, including regulations, governmental policies and practices. Not only are national governments covered by this Agreement, but so are state, provincial, territorial and local governments. An example of the scope of application of the Investor-State process is described by American trade lawyers Gary Horlick and Alicia Marti, as follows:

If Arlington County, Virginia was to deny a zoning variation to Goldstar U.S., while granting a similar one to Micron (or Sony U.S.), could Goldstar Mexico bring the U.S. to an arbitration panel under Chapter 11B? An important issue would be whether Goldstar Mexico had incurred loss or damage by reason of the denial.[10]

The MAI requires that there be some international participant involved in an investment dispute. Any individual resident in an MAI country, or a business owned by that individual, can launch a claim against the government of another MAI country. For example, Canadian investors are not eligible to bring disputes against the Government of Canada; however, American or Japanese investors can. A major exception to this rule is that Canadian corporations "owned or controlled directly or indirectly" by a citizen of another MAI country can bring a claim against Canada.

This results in the situation that foreign investors and their investments in Canada have access to the investor-state dispute process, while other Canadians may not. In essence, foreign investors are provided with a better legal remedy than Canadians under these rules.

MAI "Rights"

The MAI deals with a number of important government obligations. Among these obligations are the following:

National Treatment

- The concept of national treatment is one of the cornerstones of the MAI. It requires governments to treat all investors the same, irrespective of their nationality. This obligation ends government policies that favour local business. For example, national treatment prohibits the imposition of differential fees based on the residency of an investor, such as out-of-district levies for services such as garbage pick-up or education.

Performance Requirements

- The MAI restricts the ability of governments to impose a wide variety of practices known as performance requirements. For example, governments cannot require a foreign investor to purchase local goods or services. Governments may also not require an investor to hire local residents as a condition for receiving any benefit, such as a tax concession. Thus, common investment incentives provided by municipalities on the condition that a foreign business locate in the area are effectively removed by the MAI.

Expropriation

- The expropriation provisions of the MAI are perhaps the agreement's most controversial element. The MAI forces governments to pay compensation whenever there is an expropriation or "a measure equivalent to an expropriation."[11] Under international law, the term "expropriation" is very broad. It applies to any act where a governmental authority denies a person or company some benefit of property.[12] The government does not need to take title to the property; all it has to do is deny the benefit of the investment to the investor.[13] This international definition of expropriation is not the same as the definition of expropriation under Canadian law—it is far wider.
- The MAI is a very generous treaty when dealing with quantifying investor compensation. An investor must receive fair market value for its expropriated property.[14] This valuation basis provides compensation at levels that could be higher than those established under Canadian domestic law. This generous compensation standard augments the broad definition of what constitutes an expropriation under the MAI.

Minimum Standards of Treatment

- This obligation requires governments to provide due process to foreign investors and their investments. Even if a country treats foreigners as well as locals, this obligation sets a minimum standard of conduct that no country can fall below.

The impact of these MAI obligations is made greater on account of the absence of key limitations in the MAI that are found in other international investment agreements, like the NAFTA. For example, the MAI applies to *all advantages* granted by governments. The term "advantage" is a broad term which may cover any government subsidy, concession or incentive. The NAFTA specifically exempted subsidies from the application of several parts of the Investment Chapter.[15] Provincial and municipal government subsidies that discriminate on the basis of residency, or that require local residency, could be maintained under the NAFTA, but may be prohibited by the MAI.

A similar expansion of the MAI occurs because of the broad definition of the term "investment." Under the MAI, the term "investment" encompasses every kind of asset owned or controlled, directly or indirectly, by an investor.[16] This term is more broadly defined in the MAI than in the NAFTA or the Canada-U.S. Free Trade Agreement.

EXAMPLES

While municipalities are not "parties" to the MAI, they are subject to the full extent of the obligations in the MAI, although they have absolutely no right to participate in any investor-state dispute hearings that would question their actions.

Public Health and Safety

- The MAI contains no public policy exception to the requirement to pay compensation in the event of an expropriation. Thus, if a civic government takes an action to shut down a local business for dumping harmful waste into the local water supply, this action would not relieve the civic government from liability for compensation. The federal government has not included any wording in the MAI that would permit actions to conserve and protect the Canadian environment, public health or safety. Except for a very specific exemption from the performance requirements obligations, the MAI does not have any environmental exceptions. This single limited environmental exemption in the MAI only permits governments to require domestic content or provide a preference to local goods or services only if:

- the measure is not arbitrary or unjustifiable;
- is not a disguised restriction on investment; and
- is necessary to protect human, animal or plant life or is necessary for the conservation of living or non-living exhaustible natural resources.

Without the inclusion of broad, easily accessed environmental or public health and safety exceptions or reservations, the MAI's broad investment rules may result in new limits on the ability of governments to freely meet environmental challenges.

Municipal Licenses

- The MAI's obligations extend to the governmental allocation of concessions and licenses. Thus, issues regarding the awarding of licenses can be the basis of an investor-state dispute. Indeed, the refusal of a municipal government in Mexico to issue a civic license for a waste facility is currently the basis of a $50 million NAFTA expropriation action.

Land Use Regulation

- Municipal policies respecting land use regulation regularly impose costs upon investors. Changes in zoning that could restrict the use of land, even including historic designation, could result in effective claims under international law definitions of expropriation. While under domestic law, there can be no compensation for losses caused by changes in land use regulation; this is not true under international agreements such as the NAFTA or the MAI.

Subsidies and Investment Incentives

- The MAI national treatment obligation applies to all government measures,[17] including subsidy programs and other "advantages" provided by the government. This is a significant expansion of the "national treatment" requirement in the NAFTA. Because of the national treatment requirement, any advantage provided by a civic government must be offered to any other foreign investor. The only discrimination that is permitted is against Canadian citizens.
- The MAI requires that any investment incentives offered to local persons must be made equally available to foreign persons.[18] These incentives cannot be based on performing specified requirements. Since small businesses are predominately local, programs that assist them must be equally available to foreign investments, even if they are larger.

Municipal Procurement

- The MAI, as currently drafted, contains no exemption for municipal government procurement policies. At a minimum, the MAI performance requirements' obligations would severely restrict procurement policies at all levels of government. This could harm the ability of governments to assist community-based suppliers. As currently drafted, the MAI could require municipal governments to provide "transparent" procurement procedures for procurement bids. These bids could be subjected to potential investor claims alleging a violation of national treatment or minimum standards of treatment. The coverage of municipal procurement into the obligations of the MAI would result in increased paperwork and cost for municipal procurement.

In summary, a broad range of municipal functions would be affected by the MAI. In addition, there are existing implications of the NAFTA for the municipal sector. While the NAFTA does not apply to subsidies or to municipal government procurement, it does apply to new expropriation, national treatment and performance requirement measures made after January 1, 1994.

RESERVATIONS

Reservations are special forms of exceptions to international agreements which permit a member to be excused from meeting a specific obligation in a specific way. Because a reservation is a deviation from the objectives of the international agreement, reservations are interpreted very narrowly by international tribunals.

In a document entitled "CANADA: DRAFT RESERVATIONS,"[19] the federal government proposed to make a number of reservations to the MAI. These reservations appear to be identical to reservations made by Canada under the NAFTA.[20] No reservations were taken to exempt municipal governments from the obligations of the MAI. In addition, no exceptions were included in the text of the MAI to otherwise exempt municipalities.

Even if reservations were to be made to the MAI for municipalities, it must be pointed out that, under the "rollback" provisions of the MAI, these reservations could become subject to eventual negotiation for elimination.

CONCLUSIONS

Canadian businesses claim that their investments abroad will be able to obtain advantages from the strong investment protections provided by the MAI.[21] Canadian governments, at all levels, will be forced to comply with these protections in Canada. Canada has shown itself to be an attractive place for foreign investors to do business. As a result, Canada has become the host state to a significant amount of foreign investment. With the country's existing base of foreign investors from the United States, Japan and Europe, the implications of the MAI will immediately have effect throughout the county.

The MAI creates an entirely new multilateral dispute process, vastly different from the GATT or WTO. The ability to allow individuals to directly bring cases against governments (even without the consent of their home government) will have unpredictable results. What is clear is that the MAI creates a speedy and enforceable process to settle disputes with governments. This is likely to result in investors carefully scrutinizing government practices to find an MAI provision on which they can base a claim. Thus, policing of the MAI will move from governmental channels over to businesses, with enforcement done through the use of international tribunals.

With the expansion of Investor-State dispute settlement throughout the world's most-developed nations, this trend will only continue to grow.

The MAI investment provisions have quietly created a looming economic constitution that protects the rights of foreign MAI investors investing in each MAI country. The need to take policies that are consistent with these rights will have a number of implications for civic governments:

1. *The rules of the game are changing.* Municipal governments will find that the rules that apply to them have changed. Appreciating these changes will be even more difficult for municipalities, as they traditionally do not have experience interpreting international investment agreements.
2. *"Governments would rather switch than pay."* Faced with budget restraints and lacking expertise in international investment law, civic governments will need to modify their policies to avoid the high damage awards that panels could assess. However, the simple fact that large damage awards can be assessed for internationally-inappropriate behaviour could leave municipalities unwilling to take actions that could leave them susceptible to later international tribunal review.
3. If a government persists in its goal of implementing MAI-inconsistent actions, *that government may be forced to rent back*

jurisdiction. Governments are able to function freely, but they may have to pay compensation to do what they were elected to do.

Clearly, municipal governmental concerns have not been an important factor in shaping the MAI. Instead, the desire of investors to obtain protection from municipal regulation has been reflected. While there is still time to change the MAI, the basic structure and content of this Agreement appears to be complete. There is little doubt that this MAI and its investor-state dispute system will play a major role in how business will be done in North America over the next decade.

Municipalities are directly affected by this proposed agreement and it appears that there has been little thought by national governments in finding ways to exempt them. Indeed, some participants in the MAI negotiations have made it clear that they are opposed to any blanket reservations or exceptions for "sub-national" governments, since they fear that they will be used as a loophole to provide local preferences for local business.

Agreements like the MAI can be helpful in assuring foreign investors that their investment is safe in Canada. At the same time, however, this Agreement will impose significant restraints on all levels of governments. These restraints include the costs of paying compensation awards of foreign investors and the imposition of new limits on how civic governments can operate with respect to foreign businesses.

Change is here, whether municipalities are ready or not. Prof. McLuhan's global village has come to your village, leaving municipalities with the burden of coping with the change that is before them.

ENDNOTES

1 Barry Appleton is the Managing Partner of Appleton & Associates in Toronto and New York City. He is the author of *Navigating NAFTA: A Concise User's Guide to the North American Free Trade Agreement*. This short paper is based on an address made to the Annual Civic Night Dinner for the Simcoe County Kiwanna's Club on January 19, 1998.

2 Marshall McLuhan, *Understanding Media: The Extensions of Man* (1964).

3 See John Jackson. *The World Trading System: Law and Policy of International Economic Relations* (Cambridge, MA., MIT Press; 1989) at 52-57 .

4 A full examination of BITs can be seen in Rudolf Dolzer & Margrete Stevens. *Bilateral Investment Treaties* (International Centre for the Settlement of Investment Disputes: Washington D.C., 1995).

5 *Bilateral Investment Treaties 1959 - 1996: Chronological and Country Data Bibliography* (International Centre for the Settlement of Investment Disputes, Washington D.C., 1997) Doc. ICSID/17 at p. v.

6 This process is contained in Section B of NAFTA Chapter 11.

7 Gary Horlick & Alicia Marti, "NAFTA Chapter 11B, A Private Right of Action to Enforce Market Access Through Investments," *Journal of International Arbitration*, Vol. 14 No.1, March 1997, at 54.

8 All references in this submission are to the May 14, 1997 text. DAFFE/MAI (97) 1/REV 2 unless otherwise noted.

9 Governments are currently negotiating country-specific reservations to the MAI but the scope and impact of these reservations is still under negotiation.

10 Gary Horlick & Alicia Marti, "NAFTA Chapter 11B" at 53.

11 Any direct or indirect expropriation of an investment must satisfy all of the following requirements. The MAI provision requires that it must be:
i. for a purpose which is in the public interest; ii.on a non-discriminatory basis; iii.in accordance with due process of law; *and* iv.accompanied by payment of prompt, adequate and effective compensation.

12 The expropriating government need not take formal title to the property in order for there to be an expropriation. The Iran-U.S. Claims Tribunal gave the following definition of expropriation: *It is well settled in the practice of the Tribunal, as elsewhere, that property may be taken under international law through interference by a State in the use of that property or the enjoyment of its benefits amounting to a deprivation of the fundamental rights of ownership.*
Sola Tiles Inc. v. *Iran (1987),* 14 Iran-U.S. C.T.R. 223 at 231-232, par. 29.

13 For example, see *Harza Engineering Co.* v. *Iran*, (1982) 1 Iran-U.S. C.T.R. 499 at 504.

14 MAI Part IV: Investment Protection: Expropriation Articles 2.2 - 2.5.

15 NAFTA art. 1108(7)(b).

16 This description includes, but is not limited to, enterprises, debt, equity, contract rights, claims to money, intellectual property, rights granted by laws, such as licenses, and any other tangible or intangible property, whether real or personal, and any related property rights.

17 The national treatment obligation does not apply to revenue taxes (such as

income taxes), but it does apply to other taxes such as capital taxes.

18 MAI: III: Treatment of Investors and Investments: Special Topics: *Investment Incentives*, page 44.

19 DAFE/MAI/RES(97)15 dated February 24, 1997.

20 It is important to note that there are significant differences in the effect of the MAI reservations because of the difference in wording between the obligations in the MAI and the NAFTA.

21 For example, see the Press Release of the Canadian Alliance of Manufacturers and Exporters of December 5, 1997 endorsing the MAI.

THE MAI AND TELECOMMUNICATIONS

by Andrew Reddick and Sid Shniad

> *"You might say that, as International Trade Minister, I am Canada's 'minister in charge of deals'....[M]y job really comes down to one thing: Helping Canadian businesses—and through them the Canadian public—get the best possible deals...*
>
> *"But I'm also aware that my job isn't just to go out and get a deal—any deal. Just as the first rule of medicine is 'Do no harm,' the first rule for a trade minister is: 'Accept only deals that are good for Canada.'...[A]t the end of the day, a deal is only worth accepting if it supports our Canadian values and advances Canadian interests."*
>
> —Notes for an address by the Honourable Sergio Marchi, Minister for International Trade, to the Centre for Trade Policy and Law, Ottawa, Ontario, February 13, 1998.

> *"It doesn't matter whether it comes in by cable, telephone lines, computer or satellite. Everyone's going to have to deal with Disney."*
>
> —Disney chair Michael Eisner, quoted in *The Media Monopoly*, 5th edition, Ben H. Bagdikian, Beacon Press, 1997.

Liberalization of Telecommunications: The Domestic Situation

In today's globalized world, corporations and governments are turning back the clock, dismantling programs, services and regulations that society has taken for granted for more than 50 years.

This destructive collusion has been very dramatic in the field of telecommunications. Now, after more than a decade of deregulating communications via changes to domestic laws and regulations, governments have upped the ante by attempting to enshrine the liberalization of telecommunications in international trade and investment agreements.

Policy changes related to competition and liberalization have primarily benefited large domestic and international companies such as banks, which rely heavily on telecommunication networks and services to conduct their business activities. These policy changes have resulted in a restructuring of the industry from a monopoly to an oligopoly market dominated by three or four large companies. For the public, these changes have resulted in an overall increase in costs, as well as the end of governments' pursuit of social objectives.

Under the rules that governed the telecommunications industry for the first eighty years of this century, long- distance voice service—the bulk of it used by big business —was priced significantly above cost. A major portion of the resulting revenues was used to defray the cost of providing local service, thereby benefiting the general public. This arrangement, known in the industry as cross-subsidization, was the basis for the spread of universally available, affordable telephone service throughout North America.

Phone companies were never thrilled with this arrangement, but they tolerated it because the deal gave them a legal monopoly over the lucrative portion of the business. Big business users, by contrast, detested the fact that socially-determined telephone rates raised their telecommunications costs, forcing them to foot the bill for this cross-subsidization.

Determined to reshape the industry, large business users mounted well-financed campaigns in the decades of the 1970s, 1980s and 1990s to convince government and regulators to deregulate the provision of telephone service. These corporate efforts were complemented by interventions from universities, experts in the field, economic think tanks, and a shift to the ideological embrace of a pro-market agenda by a number of government policy advisors.

In a forerunner of the process that has since come to be known as globalization, the corporate sectors of the United States, Britain and Japan pressured their respective governments to abandon social oversight of the telecommunications industry and to allow competition in the highly profitable long-distance part of the business with a view to reducing their communications costs and reshaping the industry so that it more closely met their organizational needs.

In the resulting deluge of policy and regulatory changes, the social regulation which prevailed in telecommunications for the first 80 years of the century has been dismantled. While liberalization and competition have generated lower communications costs for large corporate users and individuals at the high end of the income pyramid, the vast majority of phone customers have seen their overall bills increase significantly as the rates charged for plain old telephone service have skyrocketed.

Residential customers, as well as people living in rural areas and small towns, are facing significantly higher costs for their basic service. At a time when the Information Highway is being promoted as the cure for a range of social and economic ills, liberalization has placed access to basic telecommunications services subscribers at risk of being left without.

Although politicians insist that the communications sector will be the source of countless new jobs, deregulated phone companies have reduced their staffing costs and increased their profits by neglecting service quality. As a result, tens of thousands of telephone workers have lost their jobs.

On the eve of divestiture [in 1984], AT&T was the world's largest private employer with over one million employees...Since divestiture AT&T has eliminated some 140,000 bargaining unit jobs, while it has established and purchased major nonunion subsidiaries...Since October 1993, major corporate restructuring accelerated ...U.S. West announced the elimination of 9,400 jobs ...Bell South said it was eliminating 10,800 jobs...GTE announced the elimination of 17,000 jobs...Pacific Telesis said it would downsize by 10,000 jobs at Pacific Bell...AT&T declared it would eliminate another 15,000 jobs on top of already scheduled force reductions of 6,000 operator and call servicing positions, and 7,500 jobs at Global Information Solutions, formerly NCR...Ameritech said it would reduce its workforce by 6,000...NYNEX scaled back its plans to eliminate 22,500 jobs to 16,800 positions...

From the standpoint of labour-management relations, this massive industrial restructuring is in jeopardy of severing the traditional link between high productivity growth through rapid technological change and rising employee incomes with employment security.[1]

Similar disruptions and job losses have occurred in Canada as Canadian telecommunications companies have emulated their American counterparts. In the words of one observer,

The *Human Resources Study of the Canadian Telecommunications Industry* (1996) indicates that ...job losses occurred to clerical, communication equipment installation and repair, managers, telephone operators and fabricating and assembly workers, between 1991 and 1995, amounting to the elimination of 13,000 jobs. The report states that these losses have been offset by significant growth, in the same time period, in sales and marketing, electrical and electronic engineers, and computer hardware and software specialists (Department of Human Resources, 1996:11; *Interim Report*, 1995:51-52). This so-called job growth, however, only amounts to 2,800 jobs. The net loss amounts to approximately 10,000 workers. Recent figures compiled by the Department of Industry Canada paints a far bleaker picture. Over a six- year period, the traditional wired telecommunications carriers lost a total of 35,433 jobs...Jobs created as of 1995 by the alternative long-distance carriers (2,800) and the resellers (220) have only amounted to 3,020. The net loss in the Canadian telecommunication service sector has amounted to 32,000 (Industry Canada, 1997:8).[2]

Overlooking the adverse social effects brought on by the liberalization of telecommunications, the federal government's corporate-dominated Information Highway Advisory Council (IHAC) [3] embraced the deregulated market as the model for the development of this sector. Boosters of this vision are resolutely ignoring the fact that liberalization of Canadian telecommunications is stratifying the population, separating entire regions into information haves and have nots, and causing massive job loss.

DEREGULATION AND THE PURSUIT OF SOCIAL GOALS

Although there has been a tremendous push to deregulate Canadian communications, government continues to compel corporations to meet social and economic requirements as conditions for obtaining operating licences or providing service. The core of Canada's communications policies are laid out in the *Telecommunications*, *Radiocommunications* and *Broadcasting Acts*, which detail the objectives that Ottawa has established for Canadian communications as well as the economic and social obligations that companies are required to meet if they want permission to operate in this sector.

Despite corporations' best efforts, significant portions of these laws guided by values related to the public interest, continue to impede the push for liberalization. Wording contained in these three *Acts* stipulates that all Canadians have the right to access communications services to meet their social, cultural and economic needs. Section 3 of the *Broadcasting Act 4, for example, entitled Broadcasting Policy for Canada, sets out a broad framework of objectives and operating procedures for public and private broadcasters. The Act* defines the overall broadcasting system as including a mix of public, private and community elements. In addition, it defines public service goals relating to the promotion of national identity, cultural sovereignty, social participation, economic development, and diversity of opinion and information. According to the *Act*, these goals are to be promoted through performance conditions requiring would-be licensees to undertake initiatives related to programming and content provision, including the creation of production funds and requirements to provide physical access.

The Minister of Industry has responsibility for radio communications in Canada. The *Radiocommunications Act*[5] *gives the Minister broad power to apply conditions to licensees, requiring them to meet economic and social-cultural goals. For example, Section 5 of the Act* states that the Minister may "take into account all matters that the Minister considers relevant for ensuring the orderly establishment or modification of radio stations and the orderly development and efficient operation of radio communication in Canada."6 In pursuit of these goals, the *Act* allows the Minister to stipulate technical requirements and standards, to issue certificates and licenses, to require companies to engage in research and development activity, and to promote social objectives.

Similarly, Section 7 of the *Telecommunications Act*[7] *lays out the country's objectives in this key sector. These objectives are:*

- to facilitate the orderly development throughout Canada of a telecommunications system that serves to safeguard, enrich and strengthen the social and economic fabric of Canada and its regions;
- to render reliable and affordable telecommunications services of high quality accessible to Canadians in both urban and rural areas in all regions of Canada;
- to enhance the efficiency and competitiveness, at the national and international levels, of Canadian telecommunications;
- to promote ownership and control of Canadian carriers by Canadians;
- to promote the use of Canadian transmission facilities for telecommunications within Canada and between Canada and points outside Canada;
- to foster increased reliance on market forces for the provision of telecommunications services and to ensure that regulation, where required, is efficient and effective;
- to stimulate research and development in Canada in the field of telecommunications and to encourage innovation in the provision of telecommunications services;

- to respond to the economic and social requirements of users of telecommunications services; and
- to contribute to the protection of the privacy of persons.

Fully eight of the nine objectives listed address a range of economic and social goals, including the protection of Canadian ownership, the rendering of affordable access, the protection of privacy, stimulation of research and development, and the provision of access in rural areas. Under existing legislation, these objectives are to be met through the enforcement of various performance requirements, the levying of contributions and other requirements imposed upon service providers.

THE GROWING IMPORTANCE OF THE TELECOMMUNICATIONS SECTOR

The magnitude of the economic stakes in the telecommunications sector have generated tremendous pressure to deregulate it. In 1995, Canada's telecommunications providers generated more than $19.5 billion in revenues, accounting for more than 70% of the information technology market.[8] In the United States, the share of personal consumption expenditures on information products and services increased from 9.9% to 12.5 % between 1980 and 1992.

Between 1989 and 1992, worldwide demand for wireless services grew by an estimated 45% a year. In 1995, the global market for telecommunications services was estimated at more than US$500 billion. By the end of 1997, international telecommunications services revenues represented a market of $800 billion (U.S.) This figure is expected to reach $1 trillion by the year 2000.

Price Waterhouse's 1997 Technology Forecast[9] indicates that Internet commerce amounted to $183 million last year, while intranet commerce totalled $679 million. The same report predicted that electronic commerce over the Web will accelerate, reaching at least US$12 billion worldwide on the public Internet by 2000, with at least another $32 billion from corporate intranets.

In the words of the International Telecommunications Union (ITU), Technological and market forces are changing the telecommunications industry from a state industry with special status (and often under state ownership) to one in the mainstreams of trade. The globalization of national economies, the trend towards "information economies" and open access, the greater interest of the state in telecommunications as a key factor in national development, the significant decreases in costs in the sector which have facilitated entry, the fact that telecommunications is an essential infrastructure to facilitate trade in goods and services now being covered within the trade framework, such as financial services, and the creation of global telecommunications companies and consortia, all have contributed to bringing about this change. Telecommunications is now seen as the modern trade route.[10]

According to the ITU, "The convergence of the telecommunications sector with the computer and broadcasting worlds is creating new synergy, most evident in the growth of the Internet, which continues to double in size every year. At the start of 1997, there were more than 16 million host computers connected to the Internet and more than 50 million users."[11]

While domestic markets are significant, corporations' real preoccupation is the desire to capture a portion of the enormous world markets in telephone, radio, television, cable, telecommunications, computing and information services. At the same time, the creation of a powerful global information infrastructure has the potential to help realize the corporate goal of transforming national and regional economies into a single global economy, permitting transnational companies to coordinate far-flung production activities, as well as financial transactions, at the speed of light.

It should be noted, in this context, that transnational corporations generate 90% of international telecommunications traffic.[12] It makes sense, therefore, that having succeeded at the domestic level, the corporate champions of telecommunications liberalization have moved to promoting it internationally under the rubric of free trade and security for international investments.

There is an interesting political angle to these changes. To deflect attention from their own role in the promotion of anti-social, pro-corporate policies, our public officials have taken refuge in Margaret Thatcher's argument that There Is No Alternative because global economic forces— particularly terms and conditions included in international trade agreement—have compelled them to embrace liberalization. This is a convenient but erroneous explanation of the regressive changes which Canadian politicians have facilitated and embraced under their own steam. It is particularly inaccurate in the area of telecommunications, where the history of regulatory change shows clearly that our governments and politicians acted on their own initiative, following the advice of their corporate allies and that of right-wing policy analysts.

INTERNATIONAL TRADE AGREEMENTS AND TELECOMMUNICATIONS

As the corporate promotion of liberalization has moved to the international arena, the nature of international trade agreements has changed profoundly. When the international trade body known as the General Agreement on Tariffs and Trade (GATT) was established in 1948, its modest mandate was to reduce tariffs on a specific set of internationally traded goods.

Over the ensuing 30 years, GATT achieved this goal. By the start of the Tokyo round of international trade negotiations in the 1970s, tariffs on the goods specified in the original Agreement had been largely eliminated. But by the time GATT achieved its original purpose, several countries were promoting a different, more ambitious role for the international trade negotiation process.

In the Uruguay Round of negotiations that began in the mid-1980s, American, European and Japanese representatives tried to extend the GATT framework to create a series of trade-related investment measures whose purpose was to deregulate international investment by limiting governments' ability to impose performance requirements on foreign investment. In addition, they extended the reach of their discussions, establishing the General Agreement on

Trade in Services (GATS) to govern banking and telecommunications services.

The Uruguay Round was the largest set of trade negotiations ever held. The range and complexity of issues addressed there was enormous. Tensions between the First and Third Worlds were high. At times the talks verged on failure.

First World proponents of further liberalization— particularly those in the United States—worried that, once the Uruguay Round had ended, there might be no further opportunity to institutionalize liberalization at the international level. It was in this context that the U.S. government took to promoting the bilateral Canada-U.S. Free Trade Agreement (FTA) and the trilateral North American Free Trade Agreement (NAFTA).

These agreements gave the United States the ability to promote economic liberalization by applying pressure on Canada and Mexico, two of its most significant trading partners, in negotiations isolated from other countries. The American purpose was to create precedents in the FTA and NAFTA which could be included in multi-party trade agreements. At the same time, the U.S. continued its multi-country efforts to promote economic liberalization by promoting the altered role for international organizations like GATT.

Canadians are familiar with the Mulroney government's efforts to promote the Canada-U.S. Free Trade Agreement and NAFTA. What is not so widely known is that Canadian government and corporate representatives embraced the American campaign to deregulate international telecommunications, as well. In May 1994, Muriel Bradford, assistant vice-president of corporate affairs at Teleglobe Canada, delivered a speech to the Telecommunications Superconference in Toronto.[13] (Prior to being hired by Teleglobe, Ms. Bradford worked at Canada's Department of External Affairs and participated in the negotiations leading up to the Canada-U.S. Free Trade Agreement, NAFTA, and the Uruguay Round of GATT.)

In her speech, Ms. Bradford argued that Canadian telecommunications policy was being driven by an increasing preoccupation with trade liberalization. She declared that, as a consequence of this liberalization, government bodies like the Canadian CRTC and the U.S. Federal Communications Commission would have less and less control over telecommunications activities within their domestic jurisdictions.

Ms. Bradford insisted that "Domestic economic policy-makers and regulators will be left with fewer options than ever before, and domestic carriers will no longer be able to expand and upgrade their networks secure in the knowledge that their national markets will remain shielded from foreign competitors." She saw these developments as providing her new employer with an opportunity to gain market share in foreign markets, since at that time Teleglobe was anticipating that it would move from seventh to third place among intercontinental carriers by the end of the century.

The determination to alter the institutional nature of the GATT on the part of free traders like Ms. Bradford came to fruition when the World Trade Organization (WTO) was created in 1995. This marked the most significant institutional change in the area of international trade since the GATT organization was established in 1948. Where GATT had been restricted to trade in goods, the WTO's purview was designed to include services and intellectual property, as well—reinforcing the role that was already being played by GATS.

In addition to broadening the mandate of international trade organizations to deal with services, the new WTO sought to do away with what the corporate sector calls "technical barriers to trade"—national laws and regulations deemed to impede the pursuit of profit. By expanding the mandate of the trade negotiation process in this manner, governments sympathetic to corporate priorities have been able to use such forums to enhance corporate freedom by limiting government regulation and other social constraints.

The WTO has made ground-breaking moves in the liberalization of international telecommunications. In a recent pact negotiated at the WTO, countries agreed to liberalize their domestic markets in telecommunications services[14] *and to be bound to a dispute-settlement mechanism governed by WTO rules. Canada will maintain foreign ownership restrictions in telecommunications, which remain at 46.7% direct and indirect ownership and control, as defined in Section 16 (3) of the Telecommunications Act* of 1993.

Other items under the WTO pact included:

- the commitment to end Teleglobe Canada's monopoly on overseas telephone traffic, effective October 1, 1998;
- the commitment to end Telesat Canada's monopoly on fixed satellite services March 1, 2000;
- the commitment to alter Canadian legislative restrictions which prohibit investment in Teleglobe by foreign carriers;
- the decision to allow 100% foreign ownership and control of companies functioning in the resale sector (without imposing a licensing regime on these service providers);
- agreement to allow foreign ownership and control of overseas underwater cable landings as of October 1, 1998;
- commitment to allow mobile foreign satellites to provide services to Canadians as of March 1, 2000 except for direct-to-home (DTH) and direct- broadcast-satellite (DBS) services;
- agreement to remove traffic routing rules for all international telephone services and satellite services by March 1, 2000; and
- agreement to maintain an open, competitive market and the existing deregulatory regime.

With the implementation of the WTO agreement, the world clearly took a major step toward deregulating the telecommunications sector. As with the U.S.-Canada FTA and NAFTA, however, the substantive impact that this agreement had on telecommunications was less than the proponents of liberalization had wanted because signatory governments ended up protecting their national markets by applying reservations and exclusions which limited the deregulatory impact on this sector. Enter the Multilateral Agreement on Investment.

THE ORIGINS OF THE MULTILATERAL AGREEMENT ON INVESTMENT

Third World governments have never shared European and North American enthusiasm about the liberalization of corporate behaviour. In fact, they have seen this effort as a modern- day version of colonialism. For the time being, therefore, it proved impossible for corporate deregulators to use the WTO for their purposes. Frustrated in their efforts to promote international liberalization and to enhance corporate rights via the WTO, but unyielding in their dedication to this cause, corporate interests made the tactical decision to circumvent Third World opposition by shifting their efforts to the Organization for Economic Co-operation and Development (OECD).

The 29-member OECD is dominated by the richest and most powerful countries in the world. In May 1995, the organization's Paris-based Council initiated highly secret negotiations aimed at reaching a Multilateral Agreement on Investment (MAI). The goal was to create a framework which would definitively secure the liberalization of international investment, protect such investment from government actions, and create dispute settlement procedures conferring unprecedented powers on corporations in their relations with governments. The longer-term purpose was to compel non-OECD countries to acquiesce to a radically deregulated world economy by forcing them to sign on to a "high quality" deregulatory treaty.

International Trade Minister Sergio Marchi explains his reason for supporting the MAI:

The MAI is an attempt to negotiate an internationally accepted set of rules for the treatment of foreign investment...The current negotiations are limited to the 29 member countries of the OECD. But the game plan for Canada is to develop an agreement that would eventually serve as the foundation for a worldwide treaty negotiated through the World Trade Organization [WTO], whose membership is 130 countries strong...

In many countries—particularly developing countries beyond the OECD—the treatment of foreign investment remains unpredictable...these are countries that represent the emerging markets in which our export-oriented Canadian companies will increasingly need to be able to confidently invest and expand if they are to continue to grow and create jobs here at home.[15]

Mr. Marchi's words can only reinforce developing countries' fears that the industrially-advanced members of the OECD plan to use the MAI to foist the deregulatory agenda on them.

Communications and the MAI

Although the U.S.-Canada Free Trade Agreement (FTA), the North American Free Trade Agreement (NAFTA) and the WTO contained sections dealing with telecommunications, they included terms and conditions which limited the application of the more sweeping deregulatory provisions contained in the body of these agreements. Negotiators inserted these terms and conditions deliberately, in order to limit the incursions of foreign communications companies on their respective domestic markets.

Unless similar reservations are included in the pending Multilateral Agreement on Investment, the MAI could have a profound impact on telecommunications. Without such reservations, the agreement's general terms and conditions, designed to prevent governments from imposing performance requirements on companies, will apply to telecommunications.

If pressed on this issue, our negotiators and government politicians may refer to a draft list of reservations filed with the OECD on Nov. 18, 1997. This list includes reservations which apply to telecommunications. At first glance, these reservations appear to provide comprehensive protection in relation to a range of issues at the core of our telecommunications industry. But it must be emphasized that this draft list constitutes Canada's opening negotiating position. As such, it is little more than a wish list. Our negotiators will negotiate down from there.

To date, discussions at the MAI negotiating table have remained fairly abstract. Little detailed work has been done at the working group level. The negotiators have yet to agree on an approach to deal with either telecommunications or culture. Before these negotiations are concluded, however, the U.S. can be expected to exert enormous pressure on the participants to liberalize access to their economies. In this context, verbal assurances from Canada's negotiators and government politicians that all is well and that nothing harmful to Canada will be signed should be taken with a grain of salt.

It should be remembered that the Mulroney government gave Canadians similar assurances in the run-up to the FTA. Mulroney insisted that Canada would walk away from those negotiations unless it achieved guaranteed access to the American market. When the U.S. threatened to walk away from the table, however, our trade negotiators quickly dropped this demand.

The U.S. government can be expected to exert enormous pressure on Canadian negotiators to accept a version of the MAI that meets the objectives of American corporations. The danger is that such an agreement would prevent our elected representatives from compelling these corporations to abide by the conditions contained in the legislation governing our communications sector or from implementing new provisions to deal with new technologies and services as our industrial, social and cultural needs change.

Lest it be believed that these concerns are far fetched, Canadian officials have already acknowledged[16] that the terms of the MAI will force Ottawa to abandon limits on foreign investment contained the regulations which apply to our telecommunications sector.[17]

There are similar problems with the MAI and its potential impact on our cultural industries, including printing, newspapers, broadcasting, multimedia, and audio-visual-related activities, as well as other cultural and Canadian content-related activity. The MAI would dismantle existing policies, regulations, programs and initiatives relating to investment, production and distribution of cultural products and services. It would prevent the introduction of new policies and programs as new, advanced technologies and media are introduced (e.g., the Internet). It would undermine initiatives designed to enhance cultural and linguistic diversity and practices. And it would weaken the protections Canada enjoys under existing agreements such as NAFTA and GATS.

Government politicians and trade negotiators in Canada dismiss such concerns, pointing out that efforts have been made to include reservations which protect Canadian culture. As a result, the WTO's provisions have been restricted to telecommunications and computer-generated information services and broadcasting. Film and television are not part of the agreement.

The problem is that distinctions between telecommunications and culture are increasingly difficult to sustain, given the convergence between "cultural industries" on the one hand and telecommunications and computer services on the other. As media and telecommunications conglomerates such as British Telecom/NewsCorp International, Unitel/Rogers/Maclean-Hunter, WorldCom-MCI and Time Warner/U.S. West offer computer, telecommunications, Internet, video-on-demand and other services over their networks, it will be increasingly difficult to draw a line between the cultural sector and telecommunications. This is the significance of the comment made by Disney chair Michael Eisner, cited at the beginning of this chapter. In other words, Canadian culture may in fact be profoundly affected by the MAI, even if a broad cultural exemption is achieved.

In their single-minded devotion to gaining access to the international market in telecommunications services for Canadian companies, Canada's trade negotiators are ignoring the fact that they are simultaneously creating unprecedented rights for foreign communications companies to operate— without social control— here in Canada. If they are successful, they will expose Canadian companies to the threat of direct competition from transnational giants like AT&T and British Telecom, and open the way to an all-out war for market share which can only lead to further degradation of service quality and job loss in the sector.

CORPORATIONS GAIN UNPRECEDENTED POLITICAL RIGHTS UNDER THE MAI

The text of the MAI grants corporations the same status and political rights as the countries which are party to the agreement. So, under the MAI, transnational companies will be able to bring suits against governments in the courts of host countries *and* in international arbitration panels. Decisions related to the application of telecommunications policy have always been the jurisdiction of the CRTC, subject to review by the federal Cabinet and Canada's courts. Under the terms of the MAI, however, transnational communications companies dissatisfied with the treatment they receive at the hands of the CRTC will be free to take their issues to binding international tribunals which will have the power to determine whether the CRTC has abided by the terms of the MAI. Decisions there will be based on the text of the MAI, not on Canadian law, and "awards for damages would be 'binding' and enforced 'as if it were a final judgment of [the country's domestic] courts.'"[18]

PERFORMANCE REQUIREMENTS OUTLAWED UNDER THE MAI

Flying in the face of terms contained in Canadian legislation, the MAI will eliminate governments' ability to require foreign corporations to meet economic, social and environmental standards. The terms of the draft agreement establish a comprehensive ban on governments' use of performance requirements.

NAFTA already prohibits governments from requiring foreign companies to use domestic labour or resources. The MAI extends this restriction on governments' powers, eliminating performance requirements related to the establishment, acquisition, expansion, or management of investments, the setting of export quotas, or the linking of performance requirements to subsidies. In addition, it severely constrains governments' ability to place conditions on companies when purchasing the goods and services they provide.[19]

In Canada, the licensing process for communications systems and services and the development of new technologies and services have traditionally included performance requirements as conditions of providing service. Depending on governments' priorities, these could include specific levels of job creation, provision of service to rural areas, promotion of Canadian content, or the provision of funding for research and development.

In the past, successful applicants have been required to meet such conditions on a continuing basis. But the terms of the MAI could eliminate governments' use of these and other mechanisms designed to ensure that service is provided on a universal, affordable basis. In addition, they could rule out the requirement that providers contribute to the development of the domestic industry. Finally, they could do away with governments' use of industrial policies to promote domestic research and development, employment, production of content, and the pursuit of a host of cultural and social policy objectives.

The MAI's Rollback and Standstill Clauses

The MAI is designed to make it impossible for governments to pass laws that conflict with the deregulatory purpose of the agreement. Once governments have signed the MAI, they are committed to reducing or eliminating—rolling back—any legislation that does not conform to the MAI's purpose. By signing on, governments undertake not to pass any new legislation that conflicts with the terms of the agreement. This is the standstill provision of the agreement, which will prevent future Canadian governments from intervening in the telecommunications or other sectors if such intervention conflicts with the purposes of the MAI.

Elimination of Protective Measures Under the MAI

The MAI contains terms and conditions that severely constrain governments' ability to expropriate property or to take actions that are "tantamount" to expropriation. This vague term includes any government action that limits the use or value of an investment. The imprecise nature of the term leaves it wide open to interpretation, making it conceivable that government taxation, for instance, could be treated as "creeping expropriation" for which compensation can be demanded.

NATIONAL/PROVINCIAL TREATMENT

The MAI includes provisions which could limit aspects of state and provincial law and regulations which constitute barriers to the liberalization of telecommunications. In the case of Canada, Saskatchewan's government-owned telephone company is currently exempted from certain aspects of federal liberalization. Such exemptions could be declared illegal under the MAI.

SCENARIO FOR THE FUTURE

As Canada's communications industry is increasingly deregulated, we will be offered a range of technologies, networks and methodologies—local loops, wireless, satellite, narrowband, wideband and digital—by which it will be possible to access a range of content services. Given the nature of these technologies, the absence of regulatory barriers will make it possible for transnational companies to provide such services from anywhere in the world.

In other words, the terms and conditions included in the MAI could mean that the telecommunications and broadcasting services Canadians depend on could be provided by foreign multinational companies operating beyond the ability of our governments to control. The impact of such change on the Canadian industry will cause widespread loss of jobs, the diversion of telecommunications traffic to other countries, the siphoning of revenues from services provided to Canadians into the coffers of enormous multinational conglomerates, and the end of social, cultural and economic contributions and performance requirements on companies operating in the

Canadian marketplace—all of which are currently required by the various *Acts* governing Canadian communications.

CONCLUSION

For the past 15 years, Canada's federal government has promoted the liberalization of the communications industry and encouraged competition on terms favourable to Canadian companies, all the while ignoring the anti-social consequences of its actions. Now it appears that our national leaders are plunging forward with this ideologically-driven approach at the level of international trade negotiations, apparently unaware of the devastating consequences that the pursuit of such policies could have on the Canadian industry, Canadian content, and Canadians' social, cultural and economic needs and rights.

There is a pressing need for a national debate on the economic and social effects that competition and liberalization have had on the communications sector, and how it has affected a range of social policy issues such as Canadian culture and content, the extension of services to unserved and underserved areas, carriers' universal service obligations, and the affordability of basic telecommunications service.

In that context, there should be a pause for sober reflection and open discussion of the ramifications of such changes before further moves to liberalize Canadian communications are undertaken domestically or the international arena via the Multilateral Agreement on Investment.

To that end, Canada should show leadership by stepping away from the MAI negotiating table before it is too late. Canadians must decide their own social, cultural and industrial priorities in the area of communications, rather than letting foreign corporations set these priorities for us.

ENDNOTES

1 Pp. 1-5 of *Telecommunications Labor-Management Relations One Decade After the AT&T Divestiture*, a paper presented by Jeffrey Keefe, Institute of Management and Labor Relations, Rutgers University, and Karen Boroff, Stillman School of Business, Seton Hall University, at the conference on International Developments in Workplace Innovation: Implications for Canadian Competitiveness, Park Plaza Hotel, Toronto, June, 1994.

2 *The Continentalization of Canadian Telecommunication Policy: Reorganizing Consent and Increasing Resistance, Vanda Rideout, 1997 unpublished Ph.D. thesis, Carleton University, Ottawa.*

3 Industry Canada. Preparing Canada for a Digital World, Final Report of the Information Highway Advisory Council, September, 1997.

4 *Broadcasting Act*, 1991.

5 *Radiocommunication Act*, 1985.

6 Melnyk, Max, *Inappropriateness of Spectrum Auctioning in a Canadian Context*, Public Interest Advocacy Centre, 1988, pp. 24-25.

7 *Telecommunications Act*, 1993.

8 *Report on Telecommunications*, the Globe and Mail, September 7, 1997, C1.

9 "Internet driving high-tech, report says", Globe & Mail, February 26, 1997, B9.

10 *Trade Agreements on Telecommunications: Regulatory Implications - The Changing Role of Government in an Era of Telecom Deregulation*, Report of the Fifth Regulatory Colloquium, December, 1995, ITU, Geneva, p. 13.

11 ITU. World Telecommunications Development Report. 1996/97, February 1997, Geneva.

12 Gerald Sussman, *Communication, Technology, and Politics in the Information Age*, Sage, 1997, p. 245.

13 *Canadian Communications Network Letter*, May 16, 1994.

14 "Telecom pact widens access to the world", Globe and Mail, Monday, February 17, 1997, B-1, and News Release, Industry Canada, "Canada Welcomes Telecom Deal", February 17, 1997.

15 Notes for an address by the Honourable Sergio Marchi, Minister for International Trade, to the Centre for Trade Policy and Law, Ottawa, Ontario, February 13, 1998

16 "Treaty seen as ending telecom restrictions," The Globe and Mail, Report on Business, May 29, 1997.

17 *Canadian Telecommunications Common Carrier Ownership and Control Regulations*, P.C. 1994-1772, October 25, 1994.

18 *MAI: The Multilateral Agreement on Investment and the Threat to Canadian Sovereignty*, Tony Clarke and Maude Barlow, Stoddart 1997, p. 41

19 Ibid., p. 36-37

Note:

The authors would like to acknowledge the assistance of Max Melnyski in the preparation of this essay.

THE MAI AND THE PROVINCES

by Ian Robinson

INTRODUCTION[1]

This paper explores how the Multilateral Agreement on Investment, or MAI, currently being negotiated in Paris by the 29 members states of the Organization for Economic Cooperation and Development (OECD)[2], will affect the character of Canadian federalism. In particular, it focuses on how the MAI will affect provincial government bargaining power vis-à-vis transnational corporate investors, and how it will constrain the policies and policy instruments that provincial governments may, under international law, employ in order to promote the economic development and social welfare of the people who elect them.

At this point, it seems unlikely that many Canadians have even heard of the MAI,[3] although there has been a recent increase in the agreement's public profile, with the December 1997 release of the Report of the Sub-Committee of the Standing Committee on Foreign Affairs and International Trade.[4] Details will follow below, but in a nutshell, the MAI aims to broaden and deepen the foreign investor property rights first recognized and protected in the investment chapters of the Canada-U.S. Free Trade Agreement (1988), NAFTA (1993), and Uruguay Round of the General Agreement on Tariffs and Trade (GATT) (1994).[5] It is widely understood that, if and when it is signed and implemented, poorer countries wishing improved access to rich country markets and capital will be "strongly encouraged" to submit to the MAI's disciplines. These earlier "neoliberal"[6] trade agreements had important implications for Canada's provincial governments, and the character of Canadian federalism.[7] An MAI that goes beyond them, will, necessarily, have more powerful effects of the same sort.

It is odd that politicians should be contemplating an agreement like the MAI while the Southeast Asian financial and currency meltdown dominates the headlines. Many questions relating to the causes and meaning of that crisis are hotly contested. But one thing on which neoliberals and their critics seem able to agree is that a critical part of the problem is the extraordinary volume of foreign capital that flowed in and out of these economies, and the extraordinary speed at which changes in the direction of those flows occurred. The volume and velocity of international capital movements, even without an MAI, overwhelmed the regulatory capacities of these states.[8] In other words, a critical contributor to the crisis—though certainly not the only one—was the unprecedented volume and pace of international capital mobility.[9]

And one thing that every serious analyst of the MAI can agree on is that, for reasons that will be explained below, it will significantly increase the volume and velocity of international capital mobility. Moreover, it will do this without addressing in any way the problem of its regulation at the national or the supranational level. Indeed, the MAI will reduce existing forms of state regulation which either impede that mobility or attempt to cope with its consequences. Simply put, if implemented, the MAI will pour gasoline on the flames of the Southeast Asian crisis, a crisis whose ramifications continue to unfold and will without question extend to North America in the form of (at a minimum) dramatically increased trade deficits with that region.

It is understandable that transnational corporations (TNCs) want as much protection for their property as they can get, and that as they become more transnational, they want stronger international protections. They take a narrowly self-interested and short-term view, driven by the shareholders and the stock markets to which publicly traded firms are primarily accountable. But why would governments—which should be concerned with the broad public interest over the longer haul—wish to add further fuel to an already over-heated global economy by implementing something like the MAI? This is a question that Canada's provincial governments should be putting to the federal government, even if the MAI had no direct implications for their own powers and jurisdiction. But it seems very likely that the MAI, if implemented in anything like the form taken in its most recent draft, will help to set in motion changes whose cumulative affect over time will be to substantially alter the character of Canadian federalism.

That, too, is—or should be—a cause for concern.

* * *

The Canadian version of federalism has long been more robust than most, characterized by strong provincial governments that have been genuinely sovereign within the fields of exclusive provincial jurisdiction demarcated by the constitution, and have often taken the lead in pioneering new economic instruments and social policies.[10] The MAI will cut deeply into areas hitherto regarded—by convention and by judicial interpretation—as exclusive provincial jurisdiction. It will do this in two basic ways. First, by unilaterally imposing new legal restrictions on a range of provincial policy instruments and policies in areas such as natural resource and environmental management, provincial public enterprises, regional development programs, health care programs, and the like.[11] Second, by increasing the opportunity costs associated with the use of many provincial instruments (e.g., taxes) which are not formally restricted under the agreement, but which will be more expensive to use—in terms of foregone private investment—because the MAI increases international capital mobility.

While often ignored in discussions, which focus exclusively on trade and constitutional law, a substantial loss of regulatory and policy-making powers on the ground, due to changes in market power of governments relative to major private investors, may well have the larger impact on the way that federalism really works.[12]

The MAI's legal restrictions, its impact on the balance of bargaining power between provincial governments and TNCs, and the process by which these changes were imposed on the provinces—by unilateral federal action, under the rubric of the federal power to make international treaties—will together push Canada a considerable way towards the kind of "residual federalism" that has prevailed in the United States since the critical New Deal decisions of 1937.[13]

In the U.S., in the vast majority of policy fields, state governments have the right to legislate and regulate—even within the policy fields assigned to them in the constitution—only insofar as they do not come into conflict with federal laws and regulation.[14] Federalism has not worked like this in 20th century Canada. Here, provincial governments have been sovereign—meaning, the supreme political authority in the nation—in a number of important policy fields assigned exclusively to them in the section of the constitution dealing with the division of powers between the federal and provincial governments.

Such a change amounts to a *de facto* amendment to the Canadian constitution. However, in contrast to Meech Lake, the federal government will not have to win the support of all 10 provinces for the proposed amendments; indeed, it claims the right to make the laws which will bring about these changes with no more than the occasional consultation with the provinces. Still less will there be anything resembling the Charlottetown Accord referendum process, in which the federal government and other MAI supporters would be required to make their case directly to the people and submit to the results of a popular referendum.

Both the substantive changes in the character of Canadian federalism that the MAI will help to promote, and the process by which these changes will have been made, are thus deeply problematic. Canada's form of federalism has a great deal to recommend it, particularly to those who place a high priority on diversity, democracy, and social justice—in short, to progressives (as I shall employ that term). It should not so be modified in such important ways with so little real debate, let alone influence, from the provinces and the people of Canada.

In keeping with the distinction between legal powers and economic bargaining power, this chapter is divided into two parts. The first identifies the ways in which the MAI will intensify market constraints on provincial governments' economic bargaining power vis-à-vis private investors—its most important contribution to reducing the economic power of provincial governments. The second part examines the ways in which the MAI is likely to affect the policies that Canada's provincial governments are permitted under international law to adopt, and the policy instruments that they are entitled to employ in their efforts to realize their policy goals.

MARKET CONSTRAINTS

Even if the MAI provisions did not apply to provincial governments, it would have important impacts on their bargaining power with private corporate investors. The two main avenues by which such effects will be felt are (a) increasing international capital mobility, and (b) deregulating the economy at the national level, thereby increasing competitive pressures (the so-called "race to the bottom") among subnational governments.[15] The MAI promotes the deregulation of the national market economy by eliminating or weakening regulations that are inconsistent with broadly defined concepts of "discrimination" against foreign investors, and of "expropriation" of investors' property. The MAI will promote international capital mobility by (i) protecting foreign investor private property rights abroad more effectively, thereby reducing the risks posed by foreign government regulation or expropriation; and (ii) by reducing barriers to foreign investment, such as public enterprises with monopoly powers, restrictions on foreign ownership levels, performance requirements that would-be investors must meet, subsidies restricted to domestic producers, and so on.[16]

1. *Capital Mobility and Corporate Power*

By substantially increasing international capital mobility, the MAI will significantly increase the bargaining power of private investors (in most cases, the TNCs that are best equipped to take advantage of these new opportunities) vis-à-vis immobile governments and unions. In a mixed economy, democratic governments must persuade private owners to invest a sufficient share of the economic resources that they control to make possible productivity growth, low unemployment, and the other economic desiderata. Private sector investors cannot guarantee good economic performance, but by refusing to invest they can guarantee bad performance.

The only other private interest possessing anything approaching this kind of economic power is organized labour. But workers must organize and act collectively in order to exercise such power, which makes them highly visible and vulnerable to government restrictions on the right to strike. By contrast, private investors need not organize in order to withhold, withdraw, or transfer their investments. Independent action on the part of numerous investors who believe that the government is insufficiently pro-business is sufficient to put great pressure on governments to change their policies.[17] Thus, even where private investors are constrained to invest (or not) within a single national economy, they possess unparalleled power to influence government economic policy, simply by virtue of their privileged position as the principal source of investment capital in a capitalist economy.[18]

The power of private investors is further increased if they are able to move their investments freely from one country to another.[19] As long as private wealth holders are constrained to invest (or consume) within their country of origin, high consumption taxes can create strong incentives to re-invest profits in domestic businesses, even if government economic and social policies are not regarded as particularly congenial to business interests.[20]

However, this tax instrument becomes less effective as international capital mobility increases. Merely pointing to the existence of an increasingly attractive exit option substantially increases the leverage of private investors vis-à-vis governments seeking to maintain and increase investment. It becomes riskier to introduce new regulations or taxes that might impact negatively on corporate bottom lines. Consequently, such taxes—and any others, such as corporate taxes or progressive income taxes, which impact disproportionately on corporate profits, or on the wealthy who invest in and govern them—cannot be raised as much as would otherwise be desirable. As a result, taxes on other economic actors must be raised, or cuts in government spending made, if budget deficits are to be kept from rising.[21]

At the same time that governments' capacity to cope with the costs of restructuring are reduced by these kinds of changes, unions find their collective bargaining power with employers reduced for the same reasons. As a result, the labour movement becomes less effective as a mechanism for redistributing income and stabilizing economic inequalities, other things being equal. The predictable result is growing poverty and economic inequality, even in periods when the economy seems to be performing well in terms of aggregate measures such as gross national product (GNP).[22]

The more "liberal" wing of the neoliberal camp calls upon governments to intervene to reduce inequalities and to create new job retraining and compensation programs for the victims of restructuring. They do not seem to recognize that the international capital mobility that they so assiduously promote is a growing impediment to the kinds of initiatives that they recommend. Thus do neoliberal policies that promote international capital mobility increase the need while simultaneously diminishing the capacity. At least the hard-bitten "devil take the hindmost" wing of the neoliberal camp is clear-sighted. They recognize that theirs is a prescription for a return to social Darwinism, and openly defend that position.

Capital mobility can increase for many reasons—not the least being the computer, the fax, and the Internet—that have nothing to do with national policies of market deregulation. But the impacts of these technological changes on state bargaining power could be reduced or neutralized by international agreements among states designed to prevent TNCs from using their increased international mobility to play governments off against one another. For example, there could be enforceable international agreements committing all governments to keeping basic worker rights and minimum labour and environmental standards out of international competition. But in the neoliberal era, governments have not only failed to negotiate such agreements; they have gone in the opposite direction, negotiating international deals that require them to dismantle national and subnational regulatory regimes that could have been used to maintain greater democratic control over TNCs.[23]

The MAI and other international economic integration agreements inspired by neoliberal ideas (e.g., NAFTA, WTO) thus kill two birds with one stone. They increase international capital mobility beyond the levels that would have resulted simply from technological change. Simultaneously, they remove or curtail many of the policy instruments by which national and subnational governments might have defended—or even extended—their bargaining power vis-à-vis TNCs in response to (and in spite of) this market trend. Thus, national government bargaining power is reduced much more than is necessary or, in my view, desirable by the scissors action embodied in these agreements. The MAI, because its key provisions on private investor rights are likely to be stronger than those found in the WTO, and because they will have much broader application than NAFTA, will result in a substantial shift in this direction.

2. *National-Level Deregulation and Sub-National Government Competition*

National-level deregulation opens up subnational governments to much more competition with one another than would otherwise be the case.[24] As long as the national government is using its superior bargaining power to set certain limits on how corporations and other investors may act within a particular country, subnational governments are not exposed to the full force of interstate competition for private investment. This is not to say that they are fully sheltered.[25] Other things being equal, increased international capital mobility would have had some negative impacts on provincial bargaining power, even in the context of a strong national or international investment regulation regime. But when national governments simultaneously do things designed to increase international capital mobility and reduce their efforts and capacities to regulate TNCs, then the negative effects on subnational governments' bargaining power are increased substantially.

Consider, for example, the three NAFTA countries. It is much easier for TNCs to play off 10 provincial, 50 U.S. state, and 31 Mexican state governments against one another than it is to play the three national governments off against each other.[26] Ninety-one state and provincial governments amount to a competitive market in which any one government is a TNC condition-taker; three national governments are an oligopoly, retaining the power to impose some conditions on TNC investment, although this is also diminished by international competition for investment among nation-states.

Now consider that—even before other countries are pressured to join the deal[27]—the MAI will encompass 29 signatories. The number of subnational units competing for private investment will number in the several hundreds.

Still assuming, for the sake of simplicity, that the MAI has no direct legal effect on provincial governments and the policy instruments available to them, we can conclude that the MAI will likely have substantial negative impacts on provincial government bargaining power with TNCs, domestic and foreign alike. This conclusion will hold *a fortiori* for the much more numerous municipal governments. It will hold more strongly still for both provincial and municipal governments, if the MAI has direct legal application to these subnational governments. For then, like the federal government, they will lose access to policy instruments that they might have used in efforts to re-establish a more favourable balance of power in such bargaining relations.

B. *Legal Restrictions*

If the MAI is signed, we can be reasonably sure that it will have the kinds of effects outlined in the previous section; the details will only affect the scale of those effects. But to assess the question of legal impacts on provincial governments, we need a more precise analysis. This is made difficult by the fact that some of the most important questions about the scope of the MAI remain hotly contested and, as yet, unresolved. Moreover, even if we had a complete final text to analyze, the meaning of many key provisions would still await interpretation by international dispute resolution panels and courts.

Further, if negotiators or interpreters create an MAI that reaches deeply into areas of exclusive provincial jurisdiction, the Supreme Court of Canada might find these provisions *ultra vires*—that is, beyond the constitutional power of the federal government to enforce through legislation.[28] In that case, the MAI might have little or no impact on provincial government legal powers, even though its potential impact—had the court ruled otherwise—would have been substantial.

Faced with these kinds of uncertainties, we cannot proceed without making some assumptions. This analysis assumes that the Canadian courts do not find the aspects of the MAI that affect provincial jurisdiction *ultra vires*.[29] It further assumes that as-yet-unresolved questions in the MAI negotiations are decided in favour of the position that has the greater impact on provincial jurisdiction.

In making these assumptions, I am not predicting that these are the most likely outcomes, a difficult matter to assess. These assumptions instead define the parameters of a *plausible* worst-case scenario, from the standpoint of those who would like to see provincial jurisdiction remain intact. The word "plausible" is important here. A nightmare scenario, based on extreme assumptions that are highly unlikely to be realized, is not very interesting. What we need to know is how bad things could get, based on a scenario that is quite possible, though perhaps not most likely. This will help us to decide what kinds of resources to devote, and what kinds of risks to take, in efforts to prevent the plausible worst-case scenario from becoming a reality.[30]

The discussion in this section will be divided into three parts. The first will examine how and to what degree the MAI's provisions will apply to provincial governments. The second part will then explore the meaning and impact of two components of the MAI which will affect many provincial government policies and instruments: the National Treatment principle, and the requirement of full market value compensation for "expropriation." Finally, the third part will examine other MAI provisions that will have important, though probably more localized impacts on provincial economic development and social policies. This last section could be very long indeed, but it will only explore a few of the most important provisions of this type.

1. APPLICATION TO PROVINCIAL GOVERNMENT MEASURES

NAFTA included an "extent of obligations" clause (Article 105) which required the federal governments of each country (often referred to as the "Parties" to the agreement) to "ensure that all necessary measures are taken in order to give effect to the provisions of this Agreement, including their observance, except as otherwise provided in this Agreement, by state and provincial governments." The phrase "all necessary measures" was novel, and its precise meaning remains unclear.[31] However, it is widely assumed that this language obligates the federal government to bring provincial governments into conformity with the obligations in the agreement, or face fines intended to compensate the Parties (or the private investors) harmed by the non-compliance of one or more provincial governments. Certainly, the OECD is quite explicit that the MAI "aims to cover "measures" taken at all levels of government: central, federal, state, provincial and local. "Measures" will include laws, regulations and administrative practices."[32]

NAFTA's investment chapter explicitly permitted states or

provinces to "grandfather" some types of existing inconsistent measures by listing them as "Annex I reservations" within two years after the date the agreement entered into force.[33] Provincial measures listed in this Annex could not be made more restrictive in the future—this is known as "standstill" in the trade jargon—and if a future government made them less restrictive in the future, a subsequent government could not even return them to the *status quo ante*.

NAFTA also exempted all local government measures from the application of that chapter's provisions.[34] However, NAFTA applied to all provincial—and, by extension, municipal[35]—government measures unless otherwise explicitly exempted or reserved.[36] The only exceptions to this rule were the labour and environmental "side agreements" to NAFTA. In stark contrast to the main text, the side-deals bent over backwards to avoid the appearance of treading on provincial government jurisdiction without express provincial government consent. Their application to each province's laws and regulations was made contingent (among other things) upon the voluntary opt-in of that particular province.[37]

It seems likely that the same type of "extent of obligations clause" and the same approach to provincial government reservations will be adopted in the MAI, but we cannot be sure. The most recent MAI draft text (October 6, 1997)[38] contains no "extent of obligations" clause. The reason for the omission appears to be that the governments most concerned respecting the constitutional rights of subnational governments—Canada and the United States, owing to their federal systems—have decided, as a matter of bargaining strategy, not to put their demands on these matters on the table until other issues have been resolved.[39] Most of the European Union states are unitary rather than federal, and from their perspective, subnational government exceptions and reservations mean that federal states take on lesser obligations than unitary states.[40] Understandably, then, they tend to press for the narrowest possible exemptions and reservations.[41]

Section IX of the MAI draft text deals with reservations. It creates an Annex A which appears modelled on NAFTA's Annex I.

That is, all existing nonconforming measures may be reserved, subject to "standstill," in this annex against challenges based on the National Treatment and Most Favoured Nation Principles.[42] It is widely understood—though it is nowhere made explicit in the present text—that this option extends to subnational as well as national governments. Certainly, that is the position of the U.S. government. Singer, et.al., tell us that "U.S. negotiators have stated that they are prepared to follow the NAFTA precedent and reserve or 'grandfather' all existing state laws."[43]

However, this "general" reservation approach is relatively forgiving, and the European Union countries do not like it.[44] The question is whether the U.S. will prevail in this contest. If it does not, the most likely alternative is a requirement that all existing non-conforming measures to be covered by the Annex A be individually specified—the original approach in NAFTA's Article 1108. The same article in NAFTA explicitly exempted municipal governments from all the four types of obligation found there, but there is no such exemption in the MAI to date.[45]

2. General Provisions

Two elements of the MAI are so potentially far-reaching and will have such profound effects on provincial governments that it makes no sense to discuss them in relation to any particular provincial government function or policy. These are the definition of "discrimination" associated with the National Treatment principle, and the definition of "expropriation."

a. National Treatment

The National Treatment principle was a key component of the first General Agreement on Tariffs and Trade (GATT), signed in 1947. A measure is inconsistent with this principle if it discriminates in favour of national producers, as against foreign exporters. Two important points need to be made on this topic.

First, recent GATT panels have broadened the meaning of National Treatment to mean "equal competitive opportunity" (ECO).[46] On this reading, a government regulation can apply the same rule to nationals and non-nationals and still be discriminatory if the rule has the *effect* of placing foreign exporters or investors at a competitive disadvantage, even if this effect was quite unintended.[47] This approach greatly broadens the potential for finding regulations discriminatory. It also increases uncertainty, since it is impossible to anticipate all the possible fact situations that might render a particular measure discriminatory in effect, even though it is not discriminatory in application or intent. Language reflecting this interpretation was included in the text of a trade agreement for the first time in NAFTA's Financial Services chapter.[48] The latest MAI draft text does not include explicit language of the sort found in NAFTA, but it is nonetheless widely assumed among the negotiators that the ECO interpretation will apply.[49]

The second concern has to do with the meaning of National Treatment when applied to subnational governments. Suppose that a province has licensing requirements that distinguish between provincial and out-of-province residents, giving certain advantages to the former. Under National Treatment, is that province required to give foreign investors the same benefits that it gives to its residents, or only the same benefits that it gives to other Canadian nationals? The latter interpretation permits continued provincial diversity, but the former would put provinces in the untenable position of giving all foreign investors advantages denied to out-of-province Canadian investors. Provinces would then almost certainly feel compelled to extend those benefits to all Canadian investors, rendering all residence-based measures affecting foreign investors ineffective.

Singer, et.al., note that the European Union (EU) has argued for an even more restrictive interpretation—known as "uniform national treatment"—which requires the standardization of all subnational government measures whenever inter-state diversity imposes extra costs on foreign investors.[50] In effect, simply because two provincial measures on a particular kind of investment differ from one another, they are treated by definition as discriminatory.[51]

This last interpretation would obviate one of the basic purposes of a federal system, which is to permit inter-provincial variation, in response to differences in provincial economic circumstances or provincial public priorities. This conception of National Treatment would push federal systems to behave as though they were unitary states in all matters of concern to foreign investors. It does not appear that it will be adopted in the MAI, but the EU has stated that it will settle for nothing less than treatment as good as that accorded to in-province residents, the second strongest position.[52] As already noted, that alone would be enough to undermine the effectiveness of provincial residence-based policy instruments. Moreover, the uniform national treatment interpretation points the way to the future. Each successive round of neoliberal trade and capital agreements—and often, dispute resolution panel decisions between rounds—pushes the envelope, and this is clearly the direction in which it will be pushed.

Finally, even if this stronger version of National Treatment is never included in an international treaty, it may not need to be in order to have equivalent effect, depending upon what the provinces negotiate under the auspices of the Agreement on Internal Trade (AIT). Prof. Bryan Schwartz of the University of Manitoba School of Law has argued that the National Treatment provisions of the AIT and NAFTA could interactively create a "chain reaction" in which "AIT provides that a province must eliminate a barrier to residents of other provinces" and "NAFTA states that if a province extends a certain favourable treatment to someone from another province, it must extent that same treatment to U.S. nationals."

The AIT provision in this chain reaction scenario is a hypothetical situation. It will be very important to keep it that way by resisting the application of the National Treatment principle to provincial measures that discriminate on the basis of the province of residence in cases under the AIT—at least, where such discrimination is an important part of what makes this policy instrument effective, and where the policy objective is deemed more important than marginal increments in the free movement of factors within the Canadian economic union.[53]

b. Expropriation

Even where a provincial government measure is not discriminatory under the above definition, it can still be inconsistent with the MAI if it substantially reduces the value of an investment. The term "expropriation" is not defined in the MAI, but it is clear from the language of the key clause that its meaning is very broad: "A Contracting Party shall not expropriate or nationalize, *directly or indirectly,* an investment in its territory of an investor of another Contacting Party, *or take any measure or measures having equivalent effect (hereinafter referred to as 'expropriation')* except" where four conditions are met [my emphasis].[54] This language is very similar to that of NAFTA, but that does not mean that its meaning is clear, because these provisions have not as yet been litigated, and key terms go undefined in both agreements. What is "indirect" expropriation, exactly? What kind of measure is not expropriation but has an equivalent effect? We aren't told. It is worth briefly considering the range of possible meanings.

Expropriation has always had a very limited meaning in the Canadian common law, and this approach has not been altered in any fundamental way by the Charter of Rights and Freedoms. Unless otherwise specified by statute, only real property could be expropriated; and only the complete "taking" of that property and the "transfer of the value of use, title or benefit to public authority" would count as expropriation. This means that a change in land use regulations or zoning laws could not be considered expropriation under Canadian common law.[55]

The U.S. courts decided that the Fifth Amendment's command that private property shall not "be taken for public use, without just compensation" extends to such "regulatory takings," though not every form of regulation that reduced the prior value of a privately owned asset could be considered such a taking. The precise boundary between those regulations which can and cannot be considered expropriation—and the rationale for drawing the boundary there—remains unclear. There is, however, broad agreement that a regulation must "substantially" reduce the value of the asset if it is to be considered expropriation.[56]

NAFTA's concept of expropriation was evidently much closer to that of the U.S. than to the Canadian conception, and this will likely be true of the MAI, as well. However, it is worth noting that, in their report to the Western Governors' Association, Singer, et.al., argue that "MAI proposals may empower international arbitration tribunals to set lesser standards than those used by American courts for determining when the burden of regulation becomes a taking or 'expropriation'."[57] That serious, mainstream U.S. legal analysts think the MAI might go beyond what many (this author included) would regard as the overly protective property rights doctrines of the U.S. courts is a sobering thought.

One source of their concern is MAI language suggesting that "measures having equivalent effect" to expropriation will include "creeping expropriation" via tax measures. This would mark a significant step beyond NAFTA.[58] Tax measures are generally excluded from the ambit of the MAI (though the National Treatment principle will generally apply). However, the agreement's provisions on expropriation have been carved out of that exclusion—that is, they will apply to taxation—and the language that elaborates on this point is quite striking.[59] Article 2(c) indicates that "expropriation may be constituted even by measures applying generally (e.g., to all taxpayers)," though the text goes on to reassure us that this is less likely than more specific taxes (e.g., perhaps, corporate taxation?).

A tax measure would not be expropriatory "if it was in force and was transparent when the investment was undertaken." By implication, if it was not, then it could be. The best protection against a challenge to a tax measure is probably set out in Article 2(b): whether the measure is "generally within the bounds of internationally recognized tax policies and practices." The MAI provisions on taxation begin to look as though they contemplate the same kind of downward racheting effect that applies to reserved nonconforming regulations.

The MAI would apply this new concept of expropriation—whatever it turns out to mean—much more broadly than NAFTA, not only because many more countries will be signatories, but also because two important aspects of the MAI are more comprehensive than in NAFTA. We can express this as the answers that each agreement gives to two questions. First, what types of state policies or policy instruments may be treated as expropriation? Second, what types of foreign assets may be protected against expropriation?

On the first point, the MAI will apply to all "advantages" granted by government. As Appleton notes, this concept is very broad, encompassing "any government subsidy, concession or incentive." NAFTA excluded "subsidies or grants provided by a Party or a state enterprise, including government-supported loans, guarantees, and insurance" from the application of the National Treatment and Most Favored Nation principles.[60] The implication, Appleton suggests, is that "provincial and municipal government subsidies that discriminate on the basis of residency or that require local residency could be maintained under NAFTA, but may be prohibited by the MAI."

On the second point, Appleton notes that, "Under the MAI, the term 'investment' encompasses every kind of asset owned or controlled, directly or indirectly, by an investor." NAFTA defined "investment" very broadly, but not as broadly as this. It set out a long list of different types of investment, on the understanding that what was not on the list was not covered. The list did not include intellectual property or rights granted by such laws, such as licenses.[61]

Worker rights, labour standards, occupational health and safety rules, and consumer regulations are primarily a provincial responsibility in Canada, while environmental regulation is shared between the two orders of government. Thus, provincial governments may well be challenged by foreign corporations to compensate them for the costs associated with any attempt to strengthen regulations in any and all of these fields, even if they were referenced in their present form. This could happen even if all of their competitors—including Canadian investors—were subject to exactly the same change in the regulation.

New provincial tax measures that affect the value of private investor assets—including any kind of charge or burden that can be construed as a tax—may be vulnerable, as well. It is impossible to know how far these new restrictions will go, but the direction in which they are moving is very clear.

If this kind of rule had been operating in the 1950s and 1960s, Saskatchewan might well have found it impossibly expensive to create the provincial health care system that became the model for the national Medicare program.[62] And if Saskatchewan had not showed that it could be done, would Canada have a public, single-payer health insurance system today? Probably not. The same could be said of public auto insurance in Manitoba. The federal government would have been faced with major compensation claims from foreign-owned insurance companies already engaged in these businesses. It would presumably have found some way to either stop the provinces or to make them pay for these compensation costs. The same concern applies to foreign-owned private day care centres operating in Canada, and any number of other public policies that a majority of Canadians—or just a majority of British Columbians or Quebecers—might wish to create.

3. OTHER CONSTRAINTS ON PROVINCIAL SOCIAL POLICY

Wouldn't most or all of the provincial social policies and programs that might be hobbled by foreign investor expropriation claims be protected by the federal government's requested reservation regarding social services? This reservation replicates the language of the federal government's NAFTA reservation in this area:

Canada reserves the right to adopt or maintain any measure with respect to the provision of public law enforcement and correctional services, and the following services *to the extent that* they are *social services established or maintained for a public purpose*: income security or insurance, social security or insurance, social welfare, public education, public training, health, and child care [emphasis added].[63]

However, even though this is primarily an area of provincial jurisdiction, the current proposed reservation states that it applies only to federal government measures. In NAFTA, by contrast, nothing stated that the reservation applied only to the federal level, and the clear implication of that silence (given that the entire agreement applied to provincial governments unless explicitly exempted) was that it applied to provincial measures, as well. The federal government promises to add provincial government measures to the reservation at a later stage in the bargaining process. So it is probably a mistake to make to much of this omission, though we may wonder what purpose is served by excluding provinces at the outset, when will surely be obvious to all parties that they will have to be included later.

However, important problems will remain, after provincial measures are added to the reservation, because flaws in the NAFTA formulation replicated in the MAI became evident shortly after NAFTA was signed. Most important is the fact that, as indicated by the addition of italics in the quote, only public law enforcement and correctional services are fully protected by this language. All the other services are protected only to the extent that they are "social services established or maintained for a public purpose." The meaning of this proviso can only be understood if we have clear definitions of "social services" and "public purpose." No such definitions were provided in NAFTA, and they are not found in the most recent draft of the MAI, either. The U.S. and Canada disagree on the meaning of both of these key terms.[64] As a result, they also differ on the scope of their social service reservations, and so on the degree to which existing provincial and state government measures of these sorts are exempted from the agreement's provisions.

Based on these differences in interpretation, the federal Ministry of International Trade told provincial governments that they need not list any specific measures in the social services sector in Annex I; they were all covered in the sectoral reservation in Annex II. Meanwhile, the United States Trade Representative (USTR), the responsible party within the U.S. bureaucracy, told state governments that they should reserve measures in this sector, on the ground that any type of social service that was provided by both the private and the public sectors should not be considered a "social" service within the meaning of the Annex II reservation.[65] These differences caused great confusion and no little protest from state and provincial governments.[66] This mobilization of subnational governments precipitated a formal letter of agreement, signed on April 1, 1996, by the governments of Canada, the United States, and Mexico, confirming that all reservable provincial and state laws and regulations (except financial services) in effect on January 1, 1994 are fully protected under NAFTA.[67]

Provincial and state governments alike were pleased with this resolution, which "solved" the problem in the case of NAFTA in a way that gave their measures more security than would otherwise have been the case. However, this resolution does nothing to prevent the same problems arising in the MAI context. At the very least, definitions of these key concepts will have to be included in subsequent drafts of the MAI, and when they are, they will need to be closely scrutinized. If the definitions favoured by the USTR are adopted, then the language of the Canadian reservation—even after it is applied to all provincial measures—will be rendered wholly inadequate. Many provincial and state governments would likely prefer the kind of general reservation of subnational government laws that resolved the NAFTA crisis.

4. OTHER CONSTRAINTS ON PROVINCIAL ECONOMIC DEVELOPMENT POLICY

Beyond the far-reaching concepts of National Treatment and expropriation, the MAI provisions that could have the most constraining effect on provincial governments' capacity to promote provincial economic development are restrictions on: (i) monopolies and state enterprises, (ii) performance requirements, and (iii) government incentives, including tax incentives. From the power perspective employed here, these instruments can be understood as a hierarchy of approaches for increasing state bargaining power with ever more mobile corporations, foreign or domestic. Public enterprises, now used much more extensively by provincial governments than by the federal government, are the strongest approach.

Even the unexercised option of creating a public enterprise says to private corporate actors that they can and will be replaced if they do not cooperate on the government's terms. The granting of private monopolies is the next strongest instrument, since it effectively excludes all but one private corporation from operating in that particular market—the same practical result as the creation of a public enterprise for all but one of the private actors in that market. Performance requirements are weaker than the first two instruments, as they do not involve any threat of excluding most or all private investors. However, in contrast with incentives, they are regulatory commands: if a corporation wishes to invest, it must agree to do X and Y. Incentives are simply offers, and as such, can be turned down by investors: if you'll X and Y, they we'll give you Z; but if you don't want Z, you can still do business here. What does the MAI do to each of these important provincial policy instruments?

The MAI draft text on *public enterprises and monopolies* is one of the least settled in the entire document. Some delegations do not want the MAI to apply to public or state enterprises at all. Others want nothing more than a clause preventing governments from escaping their general MAI obligations (National Treatment and Most Favoured Nations) by delegating authority to public enterprises. If the latter group prevails, public enterprises may not be able to favour local or provincial businesses through their procurement policies or their pricing systems as part of a scheme for regional or provincial economic development.[68] There appears to be general agreement that these restrictions should apply to monopolies (whether private or public). However, there is still debate over whether these restrictions should apply to subnational as well as national monopolies.[69]

Like the provisions on expropriation, the restrictions on the use of *performance requirements and incentives* in NAFTA and the MAI apply even where there is no discrimination among investors of a sort that would violate the National Treatment or the Most Favored Nation principles. Moreover, these restrictions apply not only to foreign investors from the signatory countries, but also to domestic investors and foreign investors from non-signatory countries.[70] Like NAFTA, the MAI has a section that allows exceptions to the restrictions on two of the listed types of performance requirements if governments can show that they are "necessary to protect human, animal or plant life or health," or "necessary for the conservation of living or non-living exhaustible natural resources."[71] The implication is that the other types are not permitted even when such compelling reasons as these can be given.

The MAI's restrictions go beyond the NAFTA in several important respects. NAFTA listed seven types of prohibited performance requirements. First, because of the agreement's broader definition of "investment," already discussed, assets created by provincial licenses and permits will be covered; it was not clear that they were covered under NAFTA. Second, while NAFTA exempted a variety of performance requirements when they were a part of government or state enterprise procurement programs, the MAI text at present contains no such exemptions. Finally, to the eight types of performance requirements prohibited (under most conditions) by NAFTA, the MAI adds five more.[72] It is impossible to assess the importance of these additional restrictions without a systematic exploration of the use of such requirements by provincial governments, something that is far beyond the means of this author. One might have hoped, however, that the government of Canada would attempt to gauge the importance of such measures before acceding to such restrictions.

Turning finally to *investment incentives*, NAFTA explicitly exempted "subsidies or grants...including government-supported loans, guarantees and insurance" from the application of National Treatment and Most Favoured Nation principles.[73] The MAI draft text indicates that some delegations believe that no specific provisions on this topic are required, on the ground that the general principles of the Agreement apply to all such measures without any explicit statement to that effect. Many other negotiators, however, want such explicitness and differ over their nature and scope. The compromise text developed by the latter group would explicitly apply the National Treatment (NT) and Most Favoured Nation (MFN) principles to all such incentives. Either way, the MAI goes beyond NAFTA in restricting the use of these important provincial policy instruments.[74]

CONCLUSIONS

Under any likely scenario, the MAI will reduce both the economic bargaining power and the policies and policy instruments legally available to provincial governments, relative to the previous milestone on the road to residual federalism, NAFTA. The more controversial questions are how great that reduction will be, by which route most of it will take place, what provincial governments can do to minimize this effect, and whether all this is good or bad for Canadians. The plausible worst-case scenario examined here suggests that the negative impact on provincial government powers could be very substantial. Regardless of specific legal provisions, the general thrust of the agreement seems likely to have a major impact on the economic bargaining power of subnational governments vis-à-vis transnational corporate investors. It is quite possible that these effects will be more important, ultimately, than the legal restrictions that have been the focus of the latter half of this paper.

Nonetheless, these legal restrictions could also have a very substantial impact on real provincial government powers to realize the priorities and aspirations of their citizens. Much will depend on the degree to which—and the conditions under which—the MAI's strictures are applied to subnational governments. We can be quite sure that the MAI will apply more directly and more completely to provincial polices and instruments than does NAFTA. What remains less clear are questions relating to how key concepts such as the National Treatment principle and expropriation will be defined and then interpreted.

What we do know here is that the dispute resolution panels that will be charged with resolving many of the interpretative disputes will be populated by experts with a strong professional and ideological commitment to expanding the meaning of these concepts in a market-liberalizing direction. Conversely, these panelists have a strong predilection—backed in this case by the canons of international law[75]—to interpret narrowly and restrictively all exceptions, exemptions and reservations in such agreements. In the plausible worst-case scenario, where the resolution of all of these issues turns against provincial governments, the legal restrictions in the MAI will combine with the impacts of increased capital mobility in a powerful one-two punch that will rapidly press Canada's provinces towards the "residual federalism" model that prevails in the United States.

Such changes will not likely happen all at once, and they will not appear very pronounced at the beginning, owing to the grandfathering of many existing non-conforming measures. Their effects will be felt cumulatively, as their downward-racheting logic steadily pushes national and subnational regulation and taxation toward what some have termed the "low road" model of corporate and national competitiveness. These arguments have been made often, and are familiar to most.

Much less noticed than such pressures on worker rights and environmental standards are the equally powerful pressures that neoliberal trade and capital agreements seem likely to exert on the character of Canadian federalism. Major changes along both of the two roads to residual federalism—declining provincial economic bargaining power and increasing legal restrictions on provincial government policies and policy instruments—can occur without any formal constitutional amendment. This is obvious in the case of the first, non-legal route. But it is important to recognize that it is equally true of the path to residual federalism that flows through the legal restrictions in these international agreements. All that is required for this to take place is that provincial governments and other actors with standing refrain from challenging the federal government's right to impose such legal restrictions on provincial governments through international treaties; or, if they do challenge, that they lose.[76]

It is worth underscoring that there are precedents for such change in the history of Canadian federalism. The most important expansion of federal power in Canadian history—in the first quarter-century after World War II—also took place without constitutional amendment or landmark Supreme Court decisions. It was made possible by a dramatic expansion of the federal "spending power." Since the early 1980s, that power has been contracting rapidly, but the analysis here suggests that—barring a successful provincial constitutional challenge, or other provincial strategies for fighting back—the decline in the federal spending power could be more than compensated for by a dramatic expansion of the *de facto* federal treaty power since 1988.[77]

That would be tragic for Canada, and for the progressive vision of Canada. Most of the progressive policy innovations in this country were pioneered by CCF, NDP, or Quebec governments at the provincial level, and then generalized to the national level when their viability and attractiveness was demonstrated. Everyone knows the story of how Canada got its single-payer public health care system. But parallel stories could be told for lesser-known but still important innovations in pension plans (beginning in Quebec), workers' compensation laws, approaches to the enforcement of occupational health and safety regulations, environmental protection initiatives, and doubtless many more.

In times of great uncertainty and rapid change, nations need to be less dogmatic and more experimental in order to devise the best methods for realizing public goals under complex and tightening constraints. As Pierre Trudeau observed 30 years ago, federalism is a great system of government for promoting this kind of innovation and experimentation.[78]

The foregoing argument holds whether one hopes for the vindication of the neoliberal experiments of a Premier Klein or the social democratic experiments of Premier Clark. But it holds *a fortiori* for those in the latter camp, in an era where federal politics remains preoccupied by constitutional formalism, and the never-ending saga of national unity. The federal Ministry of International Trade seems capable of advancing the neoliberal agenda in the midst of all this through its participation in one neoliberal trade and capital deal after another. But federal ministries to which we might look for a different kind of leadership seem paralyzed by the budget-cutting priorities of the Ministry of Finance.[79]

In such a political context, provincial governments will likely continue to be our best hope for progressive innovations in economic and social policy. They will also be more viable electorally, at least in some parts of the country, than the NDP is likely to be at the federal level. Progressive provincial governments will thus have to be the principal government defenders of the gains that Canadians have already achieved against neoliberals operating at the national level.

The analysis offered here makes it easy to see why proponents of the neoliberal world view would like to see trade and other international agreements used to weaken provincial governments. It also explains why some provincial governments do not complain much about the erosion of their own powers.

Finally, it should make it very clear why progressives should take very seriously the task of defending provincial governments' real capacity for progressive policy innovation against the kinds of threats identified in this paper.

What can and ought to be done in their defense? We could devise long lists of changes to the MAI based on the above discussion, with a view to making the MAI safer for Canadian federalism, democracy, and global economic stability. Or we could point to the list of 17 major recommendations advanced by the Standing Committee on Foreign Affairs and International Trade, many of which would be improvements on the *status quo*.[80] But if we were living in a world where such amendments had a reasonable chance of going through, why not simply call for the termination of all negotiations on increasing the international property rights of corporations, and the beginnings of serious negotiations on constructing a global social dimension?[81]

The reality is this: the trade officials of the federal government of Canada are now among the leading exponents of the neoliberal model of globalization. They miss no opportunity to advance this agenda. The rest of the government is either indifferent, preoccupied with other matters (national unity, budget cuts), intimidated by the complexity of agreements such as the MAI, or demoralized by the apparent invincibility of the neoliberal policy juggernaut. At present, the people who decide federal trade policy and strategy, on MAI and in other respects, have no interest in the kinds of amendments to MAI, let alone the agenda of alternative international agreements, that the progressive social movements in Canada and beyond have been demanding since NAFTA, if not before.

The "true believers" who lead Canada's trade negotiations will make concessions to the demands of the critics, the infidels, and the great unwashed only if public opinion and provincial government pressure are strong enough to extract them, through the agency of their political masters. Even then, Canadian negotiators in Paris cannot be expected to pursue what they will regard as concessions to ill-informed populism with any enthusiasm. These considerations underscore the importance of a strategy that focuses on public education. Such a strategy should put an emphasis on the following three messages:

1. *"No more capital mobility without social responsibility."* This directs attention to the pressing need to develop an adequate international social dimension agreeing to any new measures to further increase the volume and velocity of international capital mobility. And it directs attention to one of the MAI's most important consequences—its contribution to increasing international capital mobility.
2. *"Charlottetown II: No more amendments to Canada's economic constitution without express popular consent."* The French, the Danes, and the Irish held referendums on the Maastricht Treaty, because they recognized that this agreement involved fundamental changes in the real workings of their political economies, even though it did not require formal constitutional amendments.[82] The MAI is the same for us. This demand would focus the minds of federal politicians if it began to garner popular support. And most people are quite predisposed to the notion of being given a vote on matters of fundamental importance to their lives.[83]
3. *"No taking of provincial sovereignty without express provincial consent."* This highlights the central concern of this paper. NAFTA's provisions on government procurement was premised on this principle. Provinces were not covered by the procurement provisions unless they explicitly opted in, "on a voluntary and reciprocal basis," and then only with respect to whatever aspects of their procurement they chose to list in an Annex.[84]

Endnotes

1 Thanks to Matt Sanger and Andrew Jackson for encouraging me to participate in this project, and for their comments on an earlier draft. Thanks also to the government officials with whom I have spoken. My education in these complex matters continues; I have been saved from a number of errors. Any that remain are mine alone.

2 Until 1993, the OECD was exclusively a rich countries' club. In that year, Mexico was admitted to membership as a reward for signing NAFTA. Since then South Korea has also been honored with inclusion.

3 The complete MAI text may be found on various web sites. On is the MAI-NOT! Campaign, run out of Carleton University. It's address is: http://mai.flora.org/. For information on the campaign against MAI in the United States, visit the Public Citizen web page at: www.citizen.org/pctrade. For OECD documents relating to the MAI, go to: http://www.oecd.org/daf/cmis/mai/mai.htm.

4 The full text of the Sub-Committee's report may be obtained on the web, at the following site: www.parl.gc.ca/36/1/parlbus/commbus/house/sint/reports/sintrp01.

5 I have argued that these investment chapters were the most novel and important features of these earlier agreements as well. See (Robinson 1993b, Robinson 1994).

6 "Neoliberal" economic policies are economic policies driven by the beliefs that (a) market deregulation is generally the best means of increasing allocative efficiency, (b) increased efficiency is the best way to promote aggregate economic growth, and (c) maximizing economic growth (as opposed to, say, meeting the basic needs of all or minimizing poverty or reducing economic inequality) ought to be the principal goal of economic policy. These beliefs receive most of their intellectual justification from the dominant—if not quite hegemonic—neoclassical strand of academic economics. However, they receive most of their political support from large transnational corporations and those paid to advance their interests. There are some important tensions between theoretically-driven neoclassical policy prescriptions and the interest-driven policies preferred by politicians who generally operate under the neoliberal banner, but it is not our business to explore these here. On the current state of professional economics, see (Heilbroner & Millberg 1995).

7 I discussed these implications in (Robinson 1993a, Robinson 1995c).

8 This was conceded, in effect, by no less a bastion of neoliberal orthodoxy than the IMF, when it allowed that the Chilean model of regulating capital flows might well be a model for the rest of the world (Sanger 1998, Uchitelle 1998). For many years, the IMF had been one of the most powerful voices against such regulation. In keeping with that orthodoxy, Canadian trade officials did their best to ensure that no such regulation would be permitted in the Canada-Chile bilateral trade deal, based on a NAFTA template, that they negotiated in 1995-96. For other mainstream analyses, see (Sachs 1997, Sanger 1997, Uchitelle 1997). Particularly interesting is (Rodrik 1997). For

perspectives critical of neoliberal assumptions, see (Milberg & Elmslie 1997) and the work cited therein.

9 In a very interesting working paper, John Gerard Ruggie provides a useful overview. The ratio of (the value of) foreign exchange transactions to actual trade in goods and services is now 60:1 and rising. And the share of annual trade (imports plus exports) as a proportion of gross domestic product of a group of 15 OECD countries increased from roughly 45 percent in the 1960s to 65 percent twenty years later. At the same time, Ruggie points out, the global organization of production and exchange of goods and services has shifted from "external markets" to "administrative hierarchies." It is estimated that over one third of world trade—and a far higher share of U.S. and Canadian trade—is intra-firm, meaning that it takes place among different national subsidiaries (or otherwise related parties) of the same transnational corporations (Ruggie 1997). On the web at: wwwc.cc.columbe.edu/sec/dlc/ciao/wps/ruj01/

10 For this author's account of the evolution of Canadian federalism, an account that supports the current division of powers between federal and provincial governments on a number of grounds, see (Simeon & Robinson 1990).

11 The details of the MAI's implications for these and many other fields would take far more space than is available here. The reader is referred to the anthology on MAI, edited by Matthew Sanger and Andrew Jackson, which should be forthcoming soon from James Lorimer Press.

12 Tom Courchene made a parallel point about the importance of real economic power, as opposed to formal legal powers, when he argued that federal cutbacks in transfers to the provinces would result in the decline of the federal "spending power," and with it, a substantial increase in provincial government power in the Canadian federal system, even though there had been no formal statutory or constitutional changes (Courchene 1992).

While Courchene's focus on economic power, rather than legal powers, is sound, his conclusion that Canadian federalism is decentralizing as a result of changes of this sort is flawed in two ways. First, he failed to note the growth of the federal "treaty power," with all of the consequences that will be outlined in this paper. The dramatically expanded use of this treaty power development is centralizing for two reasons: it allows the federal government unilaterally to restrict what provincial governments can do, something that the federal spending power could never do; and the negative impacts of the neoliberal trade and capital agreements on the power of governments vis-à-vis large corporations is greater for provincial than for the federal government, for reasons that will be explained shortly. The second basic problem with Courchene's conclusion is that he construed the loss of federal power associated with federal cuts as an increase in provincial power, as though the power relationship engendered by conditional transfers was zero-sum in character. But this was never the case, protestations from Quebec notwithstanding. If it had been, provincial governments would not have taken the federal money. Federal transfers, even when accompanied by general conditions, were essentially enabling. They gave provincial governments resources which mos if not all of those governments would have found more difficult to raise themselves. This money enabled them to undertake projects (such as national health care) that their electorates very much wanted. The loss of those transfers has been disempowering, not only for the federal government, but for provincial governments as well.

13 I elaborate the concept of "residual federalism" in (Robinson 1995c).

14 On the evolution of U.S. federalism, and the erosion of the constitutional powers of state governments in the New Deal era, see (Kelly et al. 1983, 501-22).

15 Even if Canada refused to sign the MAI, these downward market pressures would increase substantially if the other 28 OECD countries did sign the MAI. This is because federal and provincial governments in Canada would still have to compete against the countries signing the agreement for scarce private investment. However, without the legal restrictions found in MAI, it would certainly be easier for one or both orders of Canadian government to moderate these market pressures by creating public enterprises or encouraging (through tax and other preferences) the formation of non-profit enterprises with a strong commitment to serving specific communities.

16 The most important legal restrictions on government regulation and expropriation in the MAI are the provisions and definitions just discussed. The most important tools in the MAI for reducing barriers to foreign investment—other than risk per se—are the rules restricting the use of performance requirements, taxes and subsidies favouring domestic producers, public corporations, and government approved monopolies.

17 See (Offe & Weisenthal 1980).

18 See (Lindblom 1982).

19 The same dynamic is present within nations, and is particularly evident in federal systems, where there may be considerable subnational government competition for private investment. Examples of the competitive bidding down of taxes and standards can be found in both Canada (e.g., the rapid diminution death duties following their transfer from the federal to provincial governments) and the United States. However, the U.S. is the closer parallel to an international system for two reasons. First, in contrast to most federal systems, there was no formal equalization system, transferring resources from richer to poorer states. This made the struggle to attract private investment more intense. Second, the greater number of U.S. states also made cooperation among states more difficult. See (Elmslie & Milberg 1996).

20 See (Przeworski & Wallerstein 1994).

21 For estimates of the scale of the losses incurred by the Canadian government as a result of cuts in corporate income tax since the early 1970s, motivated in part by the intensifying international competition for investment, see (Wolfe 1985).

22 This outcome is most pronounced in the countries where neoliberal policies have gone furthest: the USA, the UK, and New Zealand. Canada leads the second tier and the current government appears to aspire to join the first three in the top tier. See (McFate et al. 1995, Mishel & Bernstein 1994).

23 For discussions of what such an international social dimension might look like, see (Robinson 1993b, Robinson 1995d, Rothstein 1993). For a recent effort to assess the progressive potential and the limitations of such institu-

tions, see (Common Frontiers & Group 1996).

24 Paul Krugman, in a well known essay, has argued that governments do not compete with one another in the way that firms do. As a result, he argues, the discourse of international competition is misleading and dangerous (Krugman 1997). He makes some valid points against some versions of this argument, but his arguments do not touch the point made here, which hinges on the competition among states for scarce private investment.

25 The classic Canadian case of inter-state competition in an era when international capital mobility was much more limited is the inheritance tax, which was rapidly bid down to zero after authority over the tax was transferred from the federal to provincial governments.

26 This point holds *a fortiori* for local governments. See (Peterson 1981).

27 The explicit strategy of the United States and the other rich countries currently negotiating the MAI is to get much stronger language on investor rights against governments than would have been possible in the GATT forum, where the concerns and interests of large, poor countries such as China, India, Indonesia and Brazil weigh more heavily. These countries resisted many of the goals of the richer countries during the Uruguay Round of the GATT (1986-1994), with the result that the WTO Investment chapter is very weak, relative to both NAFTA and the MAI. The governments of the rich countries hope that once they have agreed on the MAI, they can pressure or entice the large, poor countries into accepting its terms by offering them credit and investment on more favourable terms if they are willing to sign. The markets alone will ensure that this is the case. Other carrots and sticks—e.g., IMF conditions attached to bail-outs in the current crisis—may also be deployed to this end.

28 The landmark *Labour Conventions Case* of 1937 came to just such a result. It determined that ratification of an International Labour Organization convention relating to worker rights did not give the federal government the right to implement this agreement, given that these matters fall under exclusive provincial jurisdiction. See the discussion of Treaties in (Hogg 1985, 241-56).

29 For an exploration of some of the issues that the courts would have to confront—and the leading cases associated with these issues—see (Robinson 1993a) and the references therein.

30 The scale of the resources and risks devoted to this end will, in turn, affect the probability that this scenario actually prevails. If the level of opposition is a major factor affecting this probability, then there could even be an inverse relationship between how bad the plausible worst case scenario is and the probability that this scenario will be realized. But such considerations take us beyond the ambit of this analysis into the Heisenbergian world of the interaction effects between social science and social reality.

31 Does "all necessary measures" include launching a constitutional challenge to assert federal jurisdiction where necessary? Quite possibly, though not everyone agrees. Could it require that the federal government pass along whatever fines it pays with a view to making the provincial polluter pay for the privilege of violating NAFTA rules? Quite possibly. Even if it doesn't, the federal government might well choose to do this in the hope of reducing

future liabilities arising from provincial noncompliance.

32 See (OECD 1997). The Brief is available on the OECD's web site: www.oecd.org/publications.

33 NAFTA, Article 1108.1(a)(ii). This exemption applied to the Most Favored Nation and National Treatment principles (Articles 1102 and 1103), and to Articles 1106 (performance requirements) and 1107 (requirements relating to the nationality of senior management and boards of directors) of the chapter. However, it did not apply to Article 1109 (restrictions on transfers of capital in or out of the country), or to Article 1110 (expropriation and compensation), or to Section B of the chapter, which laid out the new investor-state dispute mechanism that investors could use to enforce the new property rights provided in the chapter.

34 NAFTA, Article 1108.1(a)(iii).

35 Under Canadian constitutional law, municipalities and city governments are creatures of provincial jurisdiction. Thus, in applying to all provincial measures not explicitly exempted, the NAFTA automatically applies to all municipal measures of the same kind.

36 In the technical language of international treaty law, an "exception" applies to all signatories to a treaty and is contained in the text of that treaty. Reservations apply only to the country or countries making them, and are generally found outside of the main text, in an annex to the treaty or in its "instruments of ratification." See (Appleton 1997).

37 The reason for the radical difference between the treatment of subnational sovereignty in the main text of NAFTA, as opposed to the side-deals, is discussed in (Robinson 1993a, 201-4).

38 Unless otherwise indicated, all references in this paper are to this October 6, 1997 draft MAI text.

39 In keeping with this negotiating strategy, Canada's preliminary list of specific reservations includes no provincial government measures. The introduction to the document states that "The application of the MAI to measures under the jurisdiction of the Canadian provinces depends upon a satisfactory overall balance of the rights and obligations in the MAI." In other words, if Canada doesn't get enough concessions in other areas, it will refuse to apply the agreement's obligations to the matters falling under provincial jurisdiction, but if it does get what it deems to be sufficient concessions, then it will accept MAI obligations that extend to the provinces. See (Canada 1997). What role do provincial governments play in the making of judgements concerning the satisfactoriness of the overall balance of rights and obligations? The federal government keeps them informed about the overall state of play of negotiations through regular meetings, and provincial representatives are welcome to express their views on the matter. That's it.

40 Germany is a federal state, of course, but its federalism works very differently from that in Canada and the United States. The German Länder have worked out an arrangement with the federal government—one that involves much more power in shaping the federal government's negotiating objectives in trade deals than in either Canada or the United States. With that power, they seem content to leave questions of their jurisdiction to one side. See (Hrbek 1991).

41 My understanding of strategic dynamics has benefitted from conversations with provincial government officials who wish to remain anonymous, and from *Inside U.S. Trade* and its successors.

42 Other obligations may conceivably be added to these two principles, but the list may not be expanded. It is important to understand that MAI, like NAFTA, contains many obligations other than these two principles—notably, the prohibition on expropriation without full-market value compensation. Reserving existing measures, by whatever means, will not protect them from challenges based on obligations that are not listed in the MAI Section IX on reservations. Thus, without a full specification of the list of obligations against which reservations may be made, it is very hard to evaluate the scope and effectiveness of the MAI's reservations provisions. See (Appleton 1997) for further elabouration of this point.

43 See (Singer et al. 1997, 9).

44 A "general" reservation is a statement to the effect that all existing nonconforming measures are protected. This means that governments do not have to produce a detailed list of all possibly non-conforming measures within a fixed and usually short time period—an onerous burden, particularly for smaller governments. The specific list approach was originally contemplated by NAFTA Article 1108. However, the two year deadline proved unrealistic for a number of reasons. A number of Canadian provinces (notably British Columbia), the Canadian Health Coalition, and U.S. states (notably Oregon) pressed for a general reservation, and eventually they prevailed. See (Coalition 1996). On the different types of reservations, see (Appleton 1997).

45 For more detail, see (Appleton 1998).

46 See (GATT 1990).

47 For example, the Canadian government has recently complained that a U.S. state tax incentive to promote "microbreweries" is a violation of National Treatment, because Canadian breweries are too large to qualify for the benefit. This example comes from (Singer et al. 1997, 7).

48 See NAFTA Articles 1405.5, 1405.6, and 1405.7.

49 This point is based on discussions with provincial government officials, who are in turn relaying what they have learned in briefings by federal negotiators.

50 Another term sometimes used for the same concept is "full market access." See (Singer et al. 1997, 7 n. 14); which cites Working Group A, in *OECD Documents*, p. 119; and European Commission, *Report on United States Barriers to Trade and Investment—1994* (Brussels, April 1994), p. 9.

51 The intuition behind this concept seems to be a concern with fairness between federal and unitary states, rather than non-discrimination among foreign and domestic investors. It is not obvious that market fragmentation puts foreign investors at a competitive disadvantage vis-a-vis domestic investors who must also deal with the same inter-state variations. However, it may be that US investors coming to most European countries face much simpler regulatory regimes than EU investors coming to the United States. Thus, other things being equal, investing in the EU may be less expensive to investors than investing in the US. This concern really only makes sense

from a corporate perspective. Governments want to promote increased private investment, and are therefore pleased if the costs facing investors are lower at home than abroad. Corporations seeking to increase their international mobility, on the other hand, want to reduce the costs of off-shore investment.

52 The statement regarding the EU's bottom line comes from a provincial trade official. See also the MAI (October 6, 1997) Draft Text, Annex, Country Specific Proposals for Draft Texts, "Subnational Measures" [169], which indicates that one party to the negotiations wants foreign investors to be treated as well as provincial investors in cases where those investors are treated better than out-of-province national investors.

53 See (Schwartz 1997).

54 MAI (October 6, 1997) Draft Text, Section IV, "Investment Protection," Subsection on "Expropriation and Compensation," Article 2.1. The four conditions, all of which must be met, are: "(a) for a purpose which is in the public interest, (b) on a non-discriminatory basis, (c) in accordance with due process of law, and (d) accompanied by payment of prompt, adequate and effective compensation."

55 See (Lindgren & Clark n.d.). The leading cases cited by these authors are *Manitoba Fisheries Limited v. R.* (1978), 6 W.W.R. 496 (S.C.C.); and *The Queen in Right of British Columbia v. Tener et.al.* (1985) 17 D.L.R. (4th) 1 (S.C.C.).

56 See (Gunther 1985, 475-87).

57 (Singer et al. 1997, 15).

58 NAFTA Article 2103 on Taxation, Section 6, did apply the Investment chapter's expropriation provisions to tax measures. And the expropriation provisions (Article 1110) did make mention of "measures tantamount to expropriation." However, there was no language in NAFTA suggesting that this provision might stretch nearly as far as that found in the MAI, as discussed below.

59 MAI (October 6, 1997) Draft Text, Part VIII, Taxation, Section 2.

60 NAFTA Article 1108.7(b).

61 All Appleton quotes from (Appleton 1997, 5-6).

62 This counterfactual claim depends upon how much of the health insurance industry in Saskatchewan at that time was foreign-owned, and I have not checked into this. It may not have been a lot. However, we can be quite sure that, under NAFTA, GATT and—if it is signed—MAI, foreign insurers will come to play a larger role in the Canadian market. Thus, over time, in an international regime that maximizes capital mobility, the compensation barriers to the creation of future public services, whether some form of insurance or daycare, will grow.

63 The NAFTA social services reservation is found in Annex II at II-C-9. For the Canada's preliminary request for reservations under MAI, see (Canada 1997).

64 See (Appleton 1997, 12-13), (CHC 1996).

65 See (Inside NAFTA 1995a).

66 The state of Oregon played an important role on the U.S. side of the border. See (Inside NAFTA 1995b).

67 See (CHC 1996).

68 MAI (October 6, 1997) Draft Text, Section III, "Treatment of Investors and Investments," Subsection on "Monopolies/State Enterprises/Concessions," Sub-subsection "[B. Article on [state enterprises] [entities with which a Government has a specific relationship."]

69 MAI (October 6, 1997) Draft Text, Section III, "Treatment of Investors and Investments," Section on "Monopolies/State Enterprises/Concessions," "A. Article on Monopolies," Paragraph 3.

70 The rationale for this extra inclusivity is that otherwise, denying governments access to these policy instruments might encourage them to work more with domestic investors or non-signatory nation foreign investors.

71 MAI (October 6, 1997) Draft Text, Section III, Subsection on "Performance Requirements," Article 4(b) and 4(c). The NAFTA equivalent is Article 1106.6.

72 The five new items are requirements pertaining to (a) the location of world or regional corporate headquarters; (b) the achievement of a given level or value of production, investment, sales, employment, or research and development in its territory; (c) the hiring of a minimum level of nationals, (d) the establishment of joint ventures, and (e) the achievement of a minimum level of local equity participation. See MAI (October 6, 1997) Draft Text, Section III, Subsection on "Performance Requirements," Article 1 (g), (i), (j), (k), and (l). Items (i), (j), and (l) remain bracketed, meaning that they remain disputed, but notes to the text indicate that a large majority agreed to (k) and (l) at the April 1997 Negotiating Group meeting.

73 NAFTA, Article 1108.7(b).

74 MAI (October 6, 1997) Draft Text, Section III, Subsection on "Investment Incentives." The hardliners also want a commitment to negotiate additional MAI disciplines within three years after the signature of the MAI, negotiations that would aim to distinguish between "good" and "bad" incentives, and to resolve questions of whether existing incentives should be subject to "standstill" and "rollback."

75 See (Appleton 1997).

76 At one point, Ontario's NDP Premier Bob Rae stated publicly that his government would request an Ontario Court of Appeal ruling on the constitutionality of various elements of NAFTA. But in the end, the Ontario government did not submit this request. The reason for this change of heart was never given publicly.

77 These points are developed in much greater detail in (Simeon & Robinson 1990).

78 See (Trudeau 1968).

79 See (Barlow & Campbell 1995) for one useful account contemporary federal political dynamics, with a particular focus on the Liberal Party's embrace of neoliberal ideas.

80 See endnote 4, supra.

81 This is the position adopted by the NDP Minority Report, relegated to an Appendix of the Report on the MAI by the Sub-Committee of the Standing Committee on Foreign Affairs and International Trade.

82 On the Maastricht referendum campaigns, see (Criddle 1993, Economist

1996, Franklin et al. 1995, Geyer & Ayres 1995).

83 For a more elaborate defense of the use of the referendum in this kind of context, see (Robinson 1995a).

84 NAFTA, Articles 1001.1(a) and (c)(iii) and Article 1024.3.

BIBLIOGRAPHY

Appleton, Barry. 1997. "Legal Memo Re.: Reservations to the Proposed Multilateral Agreement on Investment." Pp. 24 pp. . Prepared for The Council of Canadians.

Appleton, Barry. 1998. "Municipalities and the MAI." Pp. 12 pp. . Appleton & Associates International Lawyers.

Barlow, Maude, and Bruce Campbell. 1995. *Straight Through the Heart: How the Liberals Abandoned the Just Society*. Harper Collins.

Canada. 1997. "CANADA: DRAFT RESERVATIONS (DAFFE/MAI/RES(97)." . OECD.

CHC. 1996. "The Canadian Health Coalition's Intervention on NAFTA." . Canadian Health Coalition.

Common Frontiers, and Latin American Working Group. 1996. "Social Charters: Perspectives from the Americas." . LAWG Letter.

Courchene, Thomas. 1992. "Global Competitiveness and the Canadian Federation." in *Rearrangements: The Courchene Papers*. Mosaic Press.

Criddle, Byron. 1993. "The French Referendum on the Maastricht Treaty." *Parliamentary Affairs* 46(April).

Economist. 1996. "Denmark: Not So Fast." *The Economist* (August 31):43-44.

Elmslie, B., and W. Milberg. 1996. "Free Trade and Social Dumping: Lessons from the Regulation of U.S. Interstate Commerce." *Challenge* (May-June).

Franklin, Mark, Cees Van Der Eijk, and Michael Marsh. 1995. "Referndum Outcomes and Trust in Government." *West European Politics* 18(July).

GATT. 1990. "United States—Section 337, Report of the Panel (16.1.89)." *World Trade Materials* (January):51-53.

Geyer, Robert, and Jeffrey M. Ayres. 1995. "Rethinking Conventional Wisdom: Political Opposition to Integration in Denmark and Canada." *Journal of Commonwealth Studies* 33(3 (November)):377-399.

Gunther, Gerald. 1985. *Constitutional Law*, Eleventh Ed. ed. The Foundation Press, Inc.

Heilbroner, Robert, and William Millberg. 1995. *The Crisis of Vision in Modern Economic Thought*. Cambridge University Press.

Hogg, Peter W. 1985. *Constitutional Law of Canada*, Second Edition ed. Carswell Company, Ltd.

Hrbek, Rudolf. 1991. "German Federalism and the Challenge of European Integration." Pp. 84-102 in *German Federalism Today*, edited by Charlie Jeffrey, and Peter Savigear. University of Leicester Press.

Inside NAFTA. 1995a. "Draft USTR Guidelines for U.S. States' NAFTA Service Reservations: Guidelines for NAFTA's Non-Conforming State Measures." *Inside NAFTA* (November 29).

Inside NAFTA. 1995b. "Oregon Seeks Extension of NAFTA Deadline for Services Reservations." *Inside NAFTA* (December 27):3-5.

Kelly, Alfred H., Winfred A. Harbison, and Herman Belz. 1983. *The American Constitution: Its Origins and Development*, Sixth Edition ed. W.W. Norton & Co.

Krugman, Paul. 1997. "Competitiveness: A Dangerous Obsession." Pp. 3-23 in *Pop Internationalism*, edited by Paul Krugman. The MIT Press.

Lindblom, C.E. 1982. "The Market As Prison." Pp. 3-11 in *The Political Economy: Readings in Poltics and Economics of American Public Policy*, edited by Thomas Ferguson, and Joel Rogers. M.E. Sharpe.

Lindgren, Richard D., and Karen Clark. n.d. "Property Rights vs. Land Use Regulation: Debunking the Myth of 'Expropriation Without Compensation'." . Canadian Environmental Law Association.

McFate, Katherine, Roger Lawson, and William Julius Wilson (eds.). 1995. *Poverty, Inequality, and the Future of Social Policy: Western States in the New World Order*. Russell Sage Foundation.

Milberg, William, and Bruce Elmslie. 1997. "Free Trade and International Labor Standards: Harder Than You Think." *New Labor Forum* 1(Fall):69-80.

Mishel, Lawrence, and Jared Bernstein. 1994. *The State of Working America, 1994-95*. M.E. Sharpe.

OECD. 1997. "OECD Policy Brief: MAI: The Multilateral Agreement on Investment." . OECD.

Offe, Claus, and Helmut Weisenthal. 1980. "Two Logics of Collective Action." Pp. 67-115 in *Political Power and Social Theory*, edited by Maurice Zeitlin. JAI Press.

Peterson, Paul E. 1981. *City Limits*. University of Chicago Press.

Przeworski, Adam, and Michael Wallerstein. 1994. "Democratic Captialism at the Crossroads." Pp. 335-48 in *The Political Economy: Readings in the Politics and Economics of American Public Policy*, edited by Thomas Ferguson, and Joel Rogers. M.E. Sharpe.

Robinson, Ian. 1993a. "The NAFTA, the Side-Deals, and Canadian Federalism: Constitutional Reform By Other Means?" Pp. 193-227 in *Canada: The States of the Federation, 1993*, edited by Ronald L. Watts, and Douglas Brown, M. Institute of Intergovernmental Relations, Queen's University.

Robinson, Ian. 1993b. *North American Trade As If Democracy Mattered: What's Wrong with NAFTA and What Are the Alternatives?* Canadian Centre for Policy Alternatives and International Labor Rights Education and Research Fund.

Robinson, Ian. 1994. "How Will the NAFTA Affect Worker Rights in North America?" Pp. 105-31 in *Regional Integration and Industrial Relations in North America*, edited by Maria Lorena Cook, and Harry C. Katz. Institute of Collective Bargaining, NYSSILR, Cornell University.

Robinson, Ian. 1995a. "Democratic Critiques of the Institutions and Processes of Neoliberal Economic Integration: An Assessment." *Cahiers de recherche sociologique* 24:161-184.

Robinson, Ian. 1995b. "Globalization and Democracy." *Dissent* (Summer):373-380.

Robinson, Ian. 1995c. "Globalization, Trade Policy and Canadian Federalism." Pp. 234-69 in *New Trends in Canadian Federalism*, edited by Francois

Rocher, and Miriam Smith. Broadview Press.

Robinson, Ian. 1995d. "The NAFTA Labour Accord in Canada: Experience, Prospects, and Alternatives - Symposium on NAFTA at Age One: A Blueprint for Hemispheric Integration?" *Connecticut Journal of International Law* 10(2 (Spring)):475-531.

Rodrik, Dani. 1997. "Has International Economic Integration Gone Too Far?" . Institute for International Economics.

Rothstein, Richard. 1993. "Setting the Standard: International Labor Rights and U.S. Trade Policy." . Economic Policy Institute, Washinton, D.C.

Ruggie, John Gerard. 1997. "Globalization and the Embedded Liberalism Compromise: The End of an Era?" . Max Planck Institute for the Study of Societies.

Sachs, Jeffrey d. 1997. "The Wrong Medicine for Asia." *New York Times*, November 3.

Sanger, David E. 1997. "Analysis: Asian Crisis May Take a Painful Step." *New York Times*, December 29.

Sanger, David E. 1998. " I.M.F. Reports Plan Backfired, Worsening Indonesia Woes." *New York Times*, January 14.

Schwartz, Bryan. 1997. "How Possible Increases in the Scope of the AIT Might Affect the Health and Social Services Sectors."

Simeon, Richard, and Ian Robinson. 1990. *State, Society and the Development of Canadian Federalism*. University of Toronto Press.

Singer, Thomas, Paul Orbuch, and Robert Stumberg. 1997. "Multilateral Agreement on Investment: Potential Effects on State and Local Government." Pp. 39 pp. . Western Governors' Association.

Trudeau, Pierre E. 1968. *Federalism and the French Canadians*. Macmillan of Canada.

Uchitelle, Louis. 1997. "Borrowing Asia's Troubles." *New York Times*, December 28.

Uchitelle, Louis. 1998. "I.M.F. May Be a Bit Closer to Endorsing Lending Curbs." *New York Times*, February 3.

Wolfe, David. 1985. "The Politics of Deficits." Pp. 11-62 in *The Politics of Economic Policy*, edited by Bruce Doern. University of Toronto Press.

THE MAI AND FOREIGN DIRECT INVESTMENT

by Andrew Jackson

CANADA AND GLOBAL INVESTMENT

Foreign Direct Investment (FDI) is conventionally defined as at least 10% equity ownership in a foreign company and usually represents an investment in one company by another through the establishment of an affiliate, a subsidiary, or through a strategic longer-term investment. FDI by Transnational Corporations (TNCs) has been a key driving force of "globalization" since the early 1980s. FDI flows have (with the exception of a lull, 1988-92) grown much more rapidly than either world output or world trade, and the accumulated stock of global FDI doubled as a share of world GDP (to almost 10%) between 1982 and 1994.

Foreign production by affiliates of TNCs now exceeds global exports, and this production is concentrated in the hands of relatively few companies. The top 100 TNCs control more than one-fifth of global foreign assets.[1] FDI flows have grown alongside even more spectacular flows of short-term investment capital between countries.

"Traditional" FDI in resource industries and in foreign affiliates established to serve protected national markets has continued to be important. Alongside it has grown FDI in foreign manufacturing affiliates which export, either independently or as participants in integrated global production networks, and FDI in service industries which had once been relatively insulated from international competitive pressures.

The surge in global FDI has been driven by a number of forces, including reduced transportation and communications costs, which have facilitated corporate strategies to realize economies of scale and scope by allocating production and other tasks to different geographical locales as part of a global competitive strategy.

Corporations could not, however, have "outgrown" national boundaries if states had not made this possible. The most important driving force of FDI has been the significant and conscious lowering of investment "barriers" by governments which have increasingly accepted the arguments of neo-classical economists and TNCs themselves that global efficiency and global growth are best promoted through "free" flows of capital. Governments in OECD countries now maintain only limited, selective controls on inward FDI and virtually no controls on outward FDI. For their part, developing country governments—while often still hostile to full-blown deregulation—have increasingly sought to attract FDI inflows.

As is well-known, Canadian economic development from the days of the National Policy to at least the 1970s was centrally driven by inflows of foreign direct and indirect investment. Foreign direct ownership has long been at very high levels in the key resource industries—forestry, mining, energy—and Canada industrialized in large part by inducing U.S. corporations to establish branch plants in order to access the protected domestic market. Attracting new foreign investment was very much a central part of Canadian economic policy through the 1950s and 1960s, though some sectors of the economy—notably transportation, communications, finance and culture—were and still remain reserved for Canadian enterprises to a significant degree.

In the late 1960s and early 1970s, the Watkins and Gray Reports underpinned a growing view that inward FDI should be regulated so that Canadians, as opposed to foreign shareholders, could capture a higher share of natural resource profits, and so that "active" interventionist industrial policies could be implemented to restructure the dependent "branch plant" manufacturing sector.

Foreign ownership was widely seen as a key cause of relative industrial backwardness, as manifested in low levels of research and development, productivity, and innovative capacity, particularly compared to the U.S.

For a brief period, the policy agenda was driven by the belief that "dependent development"—development driven by foreign, mainly U.S., corporations was responsible for key weaknesses of the Canadian economy in terms of industrial structure, chronic balance of payments problems, weak growth, and increasing unemployment.

The Foreign Investment Review Agency (FIRA) was created by the Trudeau government in 1974 to screen foreign investment, and many FIRA approvals included negotiation of performance requirements to ensure that takeovers brought significant benefits to Canadians. At the GATT in the 1970s, Canada opposed the extension of multilateral trade rules to cover investment issues, and the National Energy Policy was introduced with the express intent of repatriating ownership and control of a key sector in order to advance Canadian economic development. However, in the early 1980s, proposals to move to a full-blown, state-led industrial policy were rejected by a majority of the Liberal Cabinet, and foreign investment review operated in a policy vacuum.[2]

In 1985, the newly elected Mulroney government passed the Investment Canada Act, which mandated Investment Canada to *promote* inward FDI. Screening of foreign acquisitions remained, but the criterion for approval was changed to one of "net" benefit for Canadians. Benefits are judged relative to the impact of an investment on employment, productivity, technological development, Canada's ability to compete in world markets, and upon internal competition.

In principle, Investment Canada can require an investor to transfer technology to Canada, to create jobs, to carry out research and development, and to continue to operate or expand production facilities in Canada. In practice, Investment Canada approvals have been more or less automatic, and very few have been withdrawn because of the imposition of unpalatable conditions. The Free Trade Agreement, followed by NAFTA, prohibited the imposition of trade-related performance requirements on investors and confined foreign investment review to large acquisitions by U.S. investors (with the exception of the cultural sector.) The WTO TRIMS agreement also prohibited the imposition of trade-related performance requirements.

From at least the mid-1980s, the view of the federal government has been that the long-run competitiveness of Canada is best promoted through liberalization of inbound FDI, and no controls have been contemplated on outward FDI. The overall thrust of policy has been to promote Canada as a site for production by TNCs of goods and services for global markets, and this goal is seen as best achieved by getting the macro-economic "fundamentals" right, and by pursuing a non-interventionist innovation policy.[3]

Government support for research and development, training and other activities has not been conditioned by foreign ownership, so industrial and other policies have, to the extent that they have been pursued, been indifferent to the issue of foreign ownership. The government has, however, rightly continued to insist that recipients of subsidies can be obliged to locate production and jobs in Canada. The government has accepted the position of Canadian TNCs that outward FDI is needed to maintain their global competitiveness by providing market access and economies of scale.[4] No controls on outward FDI have been contemplated, and tax rules, which are the obvious instrument of potential control, have, if anything, favoured outward FDI. For example, Canadian life insurance companies—major foreign investors—pay no Canadian corporate tax on foreign-source income.

In the 1990s, there has been remarkably little policy or political debate over the costs and benefits of FDI. Certainly, the debates of the 1970s over foreign ownership have, in large part, been superseded by the dismantling of the old "branch plant" economy. In the 1980s and 1990s, particularly after the passage of the FTA, U.S. manufacturing multinationals operating in Canada restructured their Canadian operations through some combination of plant closures and new investments, so that the Canadian affiliates which remain have been largely reoriented to higher-scale production of a narrower range of products for the continental rather than the domestic market. This was, indeed, an intended objective of the FTA and NAFTA. Meanwhile, many Canadian-based companies have expanded their operations into the U.S. and throughout the world.

In a world economy dominated by transnational corporations, the relative weight of foreign and Canadian-owned transnationals in the Canadian economy has not been seen as a question of pressing interest, and many on the left have shifted from economic nationalism and defense of Canadian ownership to the view of former U.S. Labor Secretary Robert Reich that national ownership makes little or no practical difference to actual corporate behavior in today's global economy. This means that rather little attention has been paid to the changing nature of foreign investment flows in the 1980s and 1990s, and to their implications for Canadian economic development and employment. The purpose of this paper is to provide a broad overview of recent trends, and to raise some critical questions regarding the dominant assumption that "free" flows of capital ultimately benefit all Canadians.

The prevailing policy orthodoxy was clearly spelled out by International Trade Minister Sergio Marchi in his testimony to the House of Commons Committee investigating the MAI (Nov. 4, 1997). The Minister began by making the fundamentally important point that public policy should be judged by its contribution to employment and living standards: *"This initiative is very much about establishing rules to ensure that international investment and trade continue to translate into jobs and prosperity for Canadians at home."*

He went on to argue that facilitating capital mobility—i.e., inward and outward FDI—promotes jobs and prosperity by enhancing *"Canada's ability to compete in world markets."* Inward FDI, it was argued, creates jobs and builds a more productive economy by providing access to new technology and to research and development. Meanwhile, outward FDI—i.e., foreign investment by Canadian companies—was viewed as positive because it gives access to new markets and makes firms more competitive, which *"ultimately creates new jobs at home"*.

Strikingly, business representatives testifying before the same committee clearly acknowledged that their key concern was not barriers to entry of foreign capital into Canada—which are few, and generally enjoy business support where they do exist—but rather, barriers to Canadian FDI abroad. The Business Council on National Issues (BCNI) underscored the importance of breaking down foreign barriers to investment in service industries, while the Chamber of Commerce argued that "the real value of the MAI for Canada will be an outward-looking one."

Critical Views of FDI

The view that international capital mobility is beneficial, that both inward and outward FDI flows promote efficiency, competitiveness and growth, and that national controls on capital flows are damaging, outmoded and destructive is frequently stated. But it rests on many untested assumptions, and is certainly open to question. The International Labour Organization recently noted that: *"(the) positive view of the role of FDI is to some extent supported by recent empirical evidence...but it is important to point out that applied economic research on the subject is beset by methodological and data problems"*.[5]

The ILO notes that research by both the Organization for Economic Cooperation and Development (OECD) and the International Monetary Fund (IMF) has identified both positive and negative effects. On the positive side, FDI inflows can lead to a more productive economy and to greater employment by providing access to capital, technology, skills and markets. On the negative side, inflows can lead to less competitive domestic markets, and to the redirection of profits to foreign shareholders.

While outward FDI and trade are often complementary, in the sense that they lead to trade within the firm, FDI outflows may lead to job losses if foreign production replaces domestic exports. Both the IMF and the OECD have, in fact, reached much more balanced conclusions than the dominant wisdom suggests, particularly regarding the benefits of outward FDI.

Particular controversy has surrounded the issue of the impact of outward FDI on jobs at home. A recent paper by Martin Feldstein for the U.S. National Bureau of Economic Research found that FDI financed by cross-border flows of capital does indeed shift resources between countries. If U.S. companies invest more in other countries than foreign companies do in the U.S. (excluding retained earnings and funds borrowed in the host country), then investment in the U.S. is reduced by the amount of the net capital outflow.[6]

The United Nations agency, UNCTAD, has recently raised a number of critical questions regarding the benefits of FDI for developing countries. The major point made is that FDI can make a contribution to development, but only if it is part of a coherent overall national development plan:

> *"The quality and quantity of investment can be improved by means of closer linkages with the world economy through trade and capital flows, including FDI. But these external linkages must be complementary to, and not a substitute for, the domestic forces of growth through capital accumulation and technological capacity building. This can be achieved only through a carefully managed and phased integration into the world economy, tailoring the process to the level of economic development in a country and capacity of existing institutions and industries. Such a strategy contrasts sharply with the "big bang" liberalization adopted by some countries in recent years."* [7]

UNCTAD notes that FDI played an important role in export-oriented industrialization in Asia, but argues that the assumed positive impacts of FDI may be very limited in the case of TNCs operating globally-integrated production networks in which developing countries are primarily assigned the limited role of low-wage assembly operations in manufacturing. The UNCTAD report as a whole argues that a "market-driven" globalization process driven by deregulating trade and investment flows has given rise to rising inequality, both between and within countries, to a global shift in income from labour to capital, and ultimately to slower growth.

This paper argues that in Canada the presumed benefits of foreign investment liberalization have proved elusive. It is more than a little ironic that liberalization has been associated with a decline in inward investment, and a major and sustained increase in outward investment. Both inward and outward FDI create their own problems for economic development and job creation, and the overall process of continental corporate restructuring—driven by "free trade" and investment liberalization—has not solved our underlying economic problems.

AN OVERVIEW OF RECENT INVESTMENT TRENDS

As shown in Table 1, Canada has not been a preferred location as global FDI has grown rapidly, since 11.3% of global FDI was invested in Canada in 1980, but this had fallen to just 4.0% by 1996. While partly explained by the recent shift of global FDI to some developing countries—particularly the developing countries of East Asia—the Canadian share of FDI in North America has fallen almost as rapidly, from 39.5% in 1980 to 16.7% in 1996. In short, Canada has been increasingly bypassed in the investment decisions of foreign transnational corporations in the 1980s and 1990s.

Meanwhile, again as shown in Table 1, Canada's share of the world outward FDI stock has remained much steadier, and the Canadian share of North American outward FDI stock increased in the 1980s before falling somewhat in the 1990s. Put another way, Canadian FDI abroad has been growing just as rapidly as American FDI abroad.

TABLE 1

CANADIAN SHARE OF WORLD AND NORTH AMERICAN INWARD AND OUTWARD FDI STOCK

	1980	1985	1990	1996
Inward Stock				
Canada as % World	11.3	8.7	6.5	4.0
Canada as % North American	39.5	25.9	22.2	16.7
Outward Stock				
Canada as % World	4.3	5.9	4.7	3.5
Canada as % North American	9.3	14.0	15.3	12.3

Source: UNCTAD World Investment Report 1997 [Annex Tables]

Table 2 documents the fact that Canadian FDI abroad has grown much more rapidly than FDI in Canada. Indeed, quite remarkably, by 1996 Canadian corporations had invested $171 billion outside Canada, almost as much as the $180 billion of accumulated FDI in Canada. Between 1985 and 1996, Canadian FDI abroad almost trebled, while FDI in Canada doubled.

The same story is true of the relative weight of Canadian FDI in the US and US FDI in Canada. Canadian companies have increased their investments in the U.S. at a significantly more rapid rate than have U.S. companies in Canada. This imbalance is even greater when it is taken into account that a significant part of the growth of foreign and U.S. FDI in Canada has been financed from retained earnings, while Canadian FDI abroad has been financed to a greater extent through capital outflows.

TABLE 2

CANADA'S CHANGING FOREIGN DIRECT INVESTMENT POSITION ($ BILLION)

Year	Accumulated FDI in Canada	Accumulated Canadian FDI Abroad	Canadian FDI as % FDI in Canada	Canadian FDI in US as % US FDI in Canada
1975	38.7	11.1	28.7%	19%
1980	64.7	28.4	43.9%	35%
1985	90.4	60.3	66.7%	62%
1990	130.9	98.4	75.2%	71%
1996	180.4	170.8	94.7%	76%

Source: Statistics Canada Cat. 67-202, Table 3, Table 12

In 1993 through 1996 combined, FDI annual flows into Canada totalled $41.2 billion, while FDI outflows totalled $47.0 billion —a net outflow of $5.8 billion over four years.[8] While significant, this outflow was greatly exceeded by the large net outflow resulting from portfolio investment in equities (i.e., equity investments which carried a less than 10% ownership stake). In the four years, 1993 through 1996, Canadian investors invested a staggering $44.9 billion more in foreign stocks than foreign investors in Canadian stocks. The relatively modest net capital outflow for FDI reflects the fact that there is still a very large accumulated stock of FDI in Canada, and reinvestments are regularly made through retained earnings.

The key point is not that foreign TNCs have bailed out of Canada, but rather that the overall contribution of inward FDI to economic growth and development has become quite modest, and has been outweighed by Canadian FDI abroad. Canada has shifted from being a major recipient of FDI to the position of a relatively minor capital exporter in the global economy. Inward FDI is no longer a major driving source of Canadian economic development, while some Canadian-based transnational corporations have become modestly important players on the global stage.

It is ironic that inward FDI has become steadily less significant, notwithstanding the removal of "barriers" such as FIRA. While it is sometimes argued that this reflects low Canadian growth, growth in the 1980s and 1990s combined has been no slower than in either the U.S. or Europe. The more plausible explanation, even though it is seldom heard, is that imports have replaced inward FDI. With the decline of tariff and non-tariff barriers to trade in both goods and services, many foreign TNCs have likely opted to serve the Canadian market from outside Canada, while restructuring (but not greatly, expanding) their existing Canadian operations in order to serve the continental market.

A Closer Look at FDI in Canada

One might have expected foreign and particularly U.S. ownership of Canadian corporate assets to have increased following the FTA and NAFTA and the removal of other "barriers", but this has not been the case. The U.S. share of the FDI stock in Canada has been stable or slightly falling, moving from 75% of the total in 1985 to 64% in 1990, and to 68% in 1996. (Statistics Canada Cat.67-202.) Further, as shown in Table 3, the foreign and U.S.-controlled share of Canadian corporate assets has increased only marginally since 1988.

Within this framework of overall stability, U.S. control of corporate assets has increased significantly since 1988 in wood and paper (14% to 24%), in chemicals (34% to 43%), and in consumer goods and services (14% to 18%). In these sectors, there have been some large foreign takeovers, and U.S. retail chains such as Wal-Mart have established new operations in Canada. The industrial distribution of FDI has changed somewhat in recent years, with the retail and services share of the total increasing from 7.5% in 1990 to 10% in 1996.

What is strikingly indicated in Table 3 is the fact that the foreign and U.S. share of operating *revenues* has increased much more than the foreign share of *assets*. The foreign share of corporate revenues increased from 25.7% in 1988 to 29.8% in 1995, while the U.S.-controlled share increased from 17.3% to 20.1%. This reflects the fact—detailed in the 1995 CALURA report on corporations—that foreign-owned companies tend to be concentrated in the recently very profitable and expanding export sectors of the economy—auto, aerospace, wood and paper, energy, electrical and electronic equipment—and also tend to be more profitable than Canadian-owned companies. Between 1988 and 1995, almost half (46%) of the overall growth in Canadian corporate revenues took place in the foreign-owned sector, and foreign-controlled firms earned 40% more in revenue per dollar of assets than did Canadian-controlled corporations.[9]

TABLE 3

FOREIGN (US) SHARE OF CANADIAN CORPORATE ASSETS AND REVENUES %

Year	Assets		Operating Revenues	
1988	20.5	(11.0)	25.7	(17.3)
1992	20.8	(10.4)	27.2	(17.5)
1993	20.6	(10.7)	28.1	(18.4)
1994	20.4	(10.8)	28.5	(19.3)
1995	21.0	(11.4)	29.8	(20.1)

Source: Statistics Canada Cat. 61-202, (CALURA)

Since the late 1980s, there has been extensive restructuring and "downsizing" in the Canadian manufacturing and resource sectors, where foreign and particularly U.S. ownership has traditionally been high. About one in five manufacturing plants were closed, and more than one in eight manufacturing jobs were lost over this period.[10] It had been anticipated by many that foreign-owned branch plants would bear the major burden of FTA-driven adjustments, since U.S. transnationals operating in Canada often had the option of shifting production to larger-scale and more efficient U.S. plants. There is little evidence, however, to suggest that U.S.-based TNCs were much more likely to close plants or to lay off workers than Canadian companies in the recession of the late 1980s.[11]

That said, closures were probably somewhat more significant in the foreign-owned sector if account is taken of relative size, since smaller plants (which were more likely to be closed) were and are disproportionately Canadian-owned. In any case, it is certain that many U.S.-based TNCs, with surplus capacity in their North American operations, indeed opted to close or radically scale down the operations of their Canadian branch plants in the late 1980s and early 1990s.

Many plant closures and mass layoffs in Canada could be directly linked to the transfer of production to U.S. parents, as documented by the Canadian Labour Congress in its register of plant closings. Restructuring has also taken more positive forms. There has been significant new investment in Canada by some foreign manufacturing transnationals—perhaps most notably in the automotive assembly, aerospace and electrical machinery sectors—and many Canadian branch plants have been restructured to produce longer product runs for the continental market rather than being closed down.

FDI has traditionally been defended as a means to enhance the technological and innovative capacity of Canadian industry, and foreign TNC affiliates in Canada are more productive than comparable Canadian-owned companies, in some part because of the benefits of imported technology and expertise.[12] There are also examples of foreign TNCs which have invested heavily in research and development through their Canadian affiliates. Pratt and Whitney, a major aerospace manufacturer, is a case in point. However, the evidence shows that TNCs are highly likely to centralize R-and-D expenditures and to transfer technology and expertise to affiliates, rather than to invest directly in innovative capacity.

In recent research which echoes the critiques of the Watkins and Gray Reports of the 1970s, John Britton has found that *"in every technologically intensive industry for which data are available, foreign firms in Canada allocate a substantially smaller fraction of their sales to R-and-D compared with Canadian firms."* [13] The OECD has similarly found that, across all OECD countries *"the R- and-D intensity of foreign affiliates in the entire manufacturing sector (is) lower or at most equal to the average intensity for the entire manufacturing industry."* [14]

Foreign buyouts of innovative Canadian-based firms continue to compound the long-standing Canadian problem of weak innovative capacity. Notwithstanding overall Canadian weakness in terms of investment in research and development and "knowledge-based" production, innovative Canadian firms do exist and prosper, particularly in the communications equipment, aerospace and software sectors. The problem is that such firms—which locate R-and-D in Canada and are the potential driving forces behind the development of future capacity and jobs—are often bought out by foreign TNCs and relegated to a subsidiary role.

Such buy-outs also means that the flow of future profits based upon technological innovation does not flow to Canadian owners. In recent years, leading Canadian "high tech" firms such as Mitel, Connaught Laboratories, Lumonics and Leigh Instruments have been purchased, leading to the transfer of indigenous Canadian technology and arguably to the loss of future jobs and future productive potential. Reflecting on such takeovers, Norcliffe has argued that *"productivity and innovation policies that make Canadian industries competitive with U.S. producers need to be coupled with some mechanism to retain the benefits within Canada."*[15]

"New" FDI is dominated by mergers and acquisitions rather than by "greenfield' investments in production facilities, and entry by acquisitions is almost certain to be much less beneficial than new plant construction.[16] Some academic economists who otherwise favour "free" capital flows view acquisition of innovative domestic companies as a special case which requires some government intervention. For example, John Cantwell argues, in a series of studies sponsored by Industry Canada, that *"government policies to sustain a local technological capability may well have a role and indeed it may be very damaging for a national economy if government leaves the outcome entirely to the market. Left entirely to market forces, technological activity tends to polarize in just a few locations. The impact of such a locational polarization of sophisticated capability may be especially significant in the case of a key sector which provides core technologies used in other sectors, or is highly integrated with the remainder of the economy in other ways."*[17]

Even Richard Lipsey—a major and indeed polemical advocate of the FTA—has argued that some screening and regulation of inward FDI is needed in order to ensure that domestic innovative capacity is retained and expanded:

> *"Many of the issues in which Investment Canada gets involved are of this sort. If the agency gives the right push, Canada might become a world leader. If it gives the wrong push, Canada may*

well disappear with respect to that activity. I cannot, therefore, agree with those of my colleagues who hold the opinion that Investment Canada's role is marginal at best and harmful at worst. Governments throughout the world are engaged in a high stakes strategic game. If we refuse to play, it is at our own risk. A small push by Investment Canada now can, as positive feedback theory shows, have enormous effects five to ten years down the line." [18]

Screening of inward FDI and the imposition of performance requirements is a necessary part of an industrial and economic development policy intended to build Canadian capacity in key sectors. The view that leaving it all to the market and concentrating only on getting the "fundamentals" right has not, in practice, proved to be a sound industrial policy for Canada in the 1980s and 1990s. The evidence clearly shows that, under the FTA and NAFTA and within the general context of deregulation and liberalization, the relative performance of Canadian industry compared to the U.S. has not significantly changed for the better.

Free trade and deregulation of investment flows were meant to lead to a more innovative and productive Canadian economy, not least in the industrial sector which has been most affected. Yet, despite some positive restructuring in the direction of higher value-added exports, the productivity gap between U.S. and Canadian manufacturing has *widened* rather than narrowed. Hourly productivity growth in manufacturing averaged 2.0% per year in Canada from 1989 to 1995, compared to 2.6% in the U.S.; Canada continues to run huge deficits in the trade of advanced industrial goods, particularly machinery and equipment; and external competitiveness in manufacturing in the 1990s, as recently argued by both the Conference Board of Canada and Wood Gundy Economics, has been secured through a fall in the Canadian dollar rather than through an underlying gain in economic efficiency and innovative capacity.

The OECD commented extensively in its 1996 Report on Canada on the very limited shift of the Canadian economy to "knowledge intensive" and "high value-added" manufacturing, adopting a tone of puzzled surprise that the anticipated gains from "structural reform" had not materialized. Those less fixated on "free market" ideology than the OECD might conclude that the central assumption behind the NAFTA and the MAI—that "free" flows of FDI further national economic development—is suspect and unproven. The warnings of UNCTAD that inward FDI may be beneficial but must be controlled as part of a national economic development policy merits much greater attention than it has been given.

CANADIAN DIRECT INVESTMENT ABROAD

As indicated in Tables 1 and 2 above, Canadian FDI abroad has grown extremely rapidly in recent years, with the accumulated stock trebling to $171 billion since 1985. As shown in Table 4, this growth has been accompanied by some important shifts in the distribution of outward FDI. The U.S. has been and remains the most important destination, and sales by Canadian corporate affiliates in the U.S. actually exceed the value of Canadian exports.

Many Canadian resource-based companies, particularly forestry, pulp and paper and food processing companies, as well as leading Canadian manufacturing companies such as Northern Telecom and Magna, operate in the U.S., and the distribution of goods sector investment in the U.S. tends to mirror the distribution of Canadian exports. Currently, Canadian companies have also invested heavily in property development, the retail sector, transportation and other "non-traded" service industries. Canadian companies account for almost 20% of total FDI in the U.S., representing more than 1% of the capital stock of that country.[19]

TABLE 4

Composition of Canadian Foreign Investment Abroad

A] BY INDUSTRY

Year	Resource Based	Machinery Transportation and Equipment	Finance	Service/ Retailing
1985	34%	1%	21%	8%
1990	25%	3%	29%	8%
1996	26%	3%	29%	14%

B] BY AREA

	US	NON OECD
1985	69%	13%
1990	61%	13%
1996	54%	19%

Source: Statistics Canada Cat. 67-202

While still accounting for the majority of Canadian outward FDI, the U.S. share has fallen, reflecting the fact that new outward investment has predominantly been directed to Europe and, to a somewhat lesser extent, to non-OECD developing countries. Part of the increased European share is accounted for by the investments of Canadian media TNCs such as Conrad Black's Hollinger, and by the expansion of Bombardier, Northern Telecom, and other manufacturing companies.

A significant part of the growing outward flow to developing countries has been in the mining sector. Companies such as Alcan, Noranda, Inco, Falconbridge and Placer Dome are significant players in mineral development in countries like Chile and Indonesia.

There has also been a significant growth in Canadian FDI in manufacturing in developing countries. Recently, Canadian companies such as Northern Telecom, Magna and other auto parts producers have established plants in the Mexican border region to produce labour-intensive manufactured goods as part of continentally integrated production chains. Between 1990 and 1993, the number of Canadian-owned manufacturing plants in Mexico increased from

24 to 31, the number of employees in thoses plants increased from 13,000 to 17,000, and the value of production grew from $428 million to $765 million.[20] While the developing country share of outward FDI is still modest at 14%, it has grown at a fast pace, and this underpins much of the current Canadian business interest in the MAI.

In sectoral terms, the distribution of outward FDI has tilted away from resource-based industries—though 26% of the stock is still in such sectors—to finance and the service sector. About 29% of outward FDI is in the finance sector, reflecting major investments by Canadian life insurance companies in the U.S., and high levels of foreign investment by some Canadian banks. Canadian real estate conglomerates such as Olympia and York in the 1980s have been major foreign investors, and the services share of outward FDI has increased from 8% to 14% since 1996. The manufacturing share of outward FDI is modest, and is concentrated in the "high tech" sectors such as aerospace and communications equipment in which Canadian companies are also significant exporters.

Industry Canada research has shown that the outward FDI stock is heavily concentrated in the hands of a small number of Canadian transnational corporations—the top 20 alone control almost half of all foreign assets, and the top 100 control 80%.[21] A simple listing of the top 20 (ranked by sales) conveys a sense of the nature of Canadian FDI abroad. From the financial sector, the top 20 (as of the early 1990s) included the Bank of Nova Scotia, Trilon, and Royal Trust Co. In the services sector, the list included Thomson Corporation, Loblaws, Steinberg, and Canadian Pacific. From the resource sector, the list included Alcan, Inco, Noranda and Abitibi-Price. Finally, in manufacturing, the list included Ford Canada, BCE and Northern Telecom, Seagram, Labatt, Moore Corporation and Bombardier.

The very broad distribution of Canadian FDI abroad reflects a wide variety of underlying reasons for such investment. In non-traded sectors, foreign establishment is required to maintain foreign operations, and thus is not an alternative to domestic exports. Arguably, such investment maintains some headquarters jobs and is thus positive for Canadian economic development, but the fact remains that capital actually transferred outside the country almost certainly has less job-generating impact than an equivalent investment in Canada. Such investments clearly make sense from the point of view of shareholders and generate income for Canadian residents, but the positive employment effects are inherently limited.

In the resource sectors, it can be argued that global operations again secure headquarters employment, particularly of managers and skilled professionals, but expansion of foreign mining, forestry and food-processing operations does carry some danger of displacing Canadian exports. In manufacturing there is a still greater danger of export displacement, since firms can and do consider foreign production as an alternative as well as a complement to domestic production.

Northern Telecom, for example, has consciously shifted manufacturing to lower-labour-cost regions and correspondingly reduced manufacturing employment in Canada. It is argued that corporate competitiveness would not have been sustained if production had been maintained in Canada, but the fact remains that outward FDI has been job-displacing in the same way that imports replace domestic production.

Finally, some outward FDI reflects the fact that other countries limit imports, and require that an affiliate be located if orders are to be obtained. Some recent Bombardier foreign investments likely reflect the fact that many aerospace and urban transportation equipment purchases are effectively conditional on their national content.

There has been remarkably little analysis of the impacts of large and growing FDI outflows on Canadian economic development and employment. Studies sponsored by Industry Canada have outlined how and why outward FDI has become a central part of the competitiveness strategy of firms, and there can be little dispute that such investments generally make sense form the point of view of firm and shareholders. But the implications of significant net capital exports have not been squarely faced up to. While outward FDI can be financed by the reinvestment of earnings earned outside Canada (as well as by borrowing outside Canada) only about one-third of the $47 billion of Canadian FDI abroad in the four years 1993 through 1996 was financed through retained earnings.[22]

It has been argued by Industry Canada that there is little or no relation between FDI outflows and the level of domestic investment, but this is contradicted by the research of Feldstein cited above. Capital exported abroad may well have some positive employment and economic development impacts, but it is highly unlikely that these benefits outweigh the alternative of equivalent capital investment in Canada. Feldstein's key argument is that, at the level of the overall economy as opposed to the level of the individual firm, a dollar invested outside a country is a dollar lost to domestic investment.

It is often argued that outward FDI does not displace exports, since it results in higher trade. Certainly, intra-firm trade has been growing enormously in importance, and now accounts for about half of all Canada-U.S. trade, in large part because of integrated production networks such as those in the auto sector. It is likely that if Bombardier, for example, purchases a subsidiary to produce for the Mexican market, the purchase will result in higher exports from Canada to the U.S. in the form of the Bombardier subsidiary's purchases of capital equipment, services, and so on.

All that said, Industry Canada research has shown that the export generating power of Canadian FDI outside Canada is significantly less than the import generating power of FDI in Canada. A 10% increase in Canadian FDI was found to result in a 4.8% increase in Canadian exports, while a 10% increase in FDI in Canada increases imports by 12.6%.[23] Another study has shown that, notwithstanding the fact that Canadian FDI in the U.S. is now close to the level of U.S. FDI in Canada, intra-firm trade between the two countries takes place mainly among U.S. rather than Canadian TNCs. Of .U.S intra-firm imports from Canada, 82% are U.S. parent imports from their Canadian affiliates, and just 17% are imports by Canadian-owned affiliates from their Canadian parents.[24] The same imbalance is seen in Canada-U.S. services trade. In short, it cannot be assumed that Canadian FDI promotes Canadian exports.

Industry Canada research has also shown that the employment growth of outward-oriented firms between 1986 and 1991 was slower than that of domestically-oriented firms, averaging just 0.7% per year compared to 2.7%. This result arose notwithstanding the fact that sales growth and asset growth were higher for outward-oriented firms.[25] Employment growth for outward-oriented firms was negative in this period in several sectors, including textiles (-3.6%), food products manufacturing (-8.1%), primary metals (-6.5%), and mining (-4.7%.) Meanwhile, returns on assets seem to have been higher for outward-oriented firms.

CONCLUDING COMMENTS

It is often simply asserted by reference to neo-classical economic theory that "free" capital flows promote efficiency, growth and job creation. However, this view—like all neo- classical economic theory—abstracts from specific national circumstances. As UNCTAD has argued, the costs and benefits of FDI must be considered within the framework of the needs and circumstances of national development, and costs and benefits can be differently distributed between capital and labour.

In the case of Canada, investment liberalization in the 1980s and 1990s took place within the context of an economy which had been shaped by the process of dependent development. Foreign ownership was high in the key areas in which Canada had a strong competitive position in external markets—the resource and resource-based manufacturing sector, auto sector, and in large parts of the domestically oriented manufacturing sector. Canadian corporations were a strong force in the resource sector, dominant in finance and most of the service sector, and there was limited indigenous strength in some technologically advanced manufacturing activities. Overall, the Canadian economy was underdeveloped in the critical sense that it lacked a strong core of innovative industrial companies.

The restructuring of Canada's economy through trade and investment liberalization under the GATT, the FTA and NAFTA has resulted in significant change at the corporate level. Within this process, a relatively small number of Canadian transnational corporations have "globalized" their operations and have become important players in some world markets—in resource industries, finance (to a limited degree), in some service industries, and in a handful of advanced industrial sectors such as aerospace and communications equipment. The Canadian affiliates of foreign TNCs have also extensively restructured their operations. In manufacturing, most affiliates now exist as part of continental or even global production chains serving continental and global markets.

Restructuring may have been difficult, but most large Canadian TNCs and their shareholders have clearly benefited from liberalization, in that profitability is high and competitiveness has been maintained in a rapidly changing national and global economy. The official line is that what is good for corporate Canada is good for Canadians, but current reality is less acceptable to Canadian workers and communities. Shifting flows of investment have been intimately related to trade-driven restructuring which has resulted in fewer jobs, particularly in manufacturing, stagnant wages, and increased insecurity.[26]

To be sure, good jobs, particularly for managers and professionals, do exist in the restructured operations of TNCs operating in Canada, but labour market conditions for the majority of workers remain dismal. "Globalization" has broken down the assumed shared interests of corporations and citizens. From the point of view of workers and communities, the impact of liberalized investment is little different from that of liberalized trade: it can and does result in job losses and downward pressures on wages and working conditions.

The dominant policy discourse holds that Canada must attract inward FDI to create jobs, and must accept and even welcome outward FDI since it promotes corporate competitiveness in global markets. However, the reality is that Canada has been losing rather than gaining FDI, and has almost certainly experienced job losses as a result. The reality is that the long-standing problems of the Canadian economy in terms of lack of indigenous innovative capacity have not been resolved, and that the productivity and innovation gap between Canada and other industrial countries has been growing rather than narrowing.

Advocates of "free" capital markets will argue that there is no alternative, and that the only realistic development strategy in today's economy is to attract footloose productive capital by offering what it wants—stable macro-economic conditions, good infrastructure, skilled workers, and "competitive" taxes, wages and labour and social standards.

In honesty, no comprehensive alternative comparable to the interventionist industrial policy prescriptions of the late 1970s and early 1980s has recently been advanced, and past positions clearly need major reconsideration, given the massive restructuring of the economy. At a minimum, however, it can be suggested that there remains a strong case for screening new inward investment to ensure that it contributes to national economic development and job creation, and that more thought should be given to the problem of how to build and maintain sophisticated productive capacity in Canada when investment is allocated by globally-oriented transnational corporations. The current policy of subsidizing R-and-D and training—generally regardless of ownership—is problematic if control of technology and skills can be lost through a foreign acquisition.

The issue of how to build stronger linkages between different sectors of the economy is almost impossible to address if it is simply taken as a given that production networks will be organized by TNCs alone, rather than by some shared decision- making between governments and corporations. Some thought must also be given to the growing problem of capital outflows. To a significant and likely growing degree, Canada has become a loser from global deregulation of investment in the simple sense that more capital for private investment is flowing out than is flowing in. This will be reversed only if some degree of control is imposed, most appropriately through the tax system which could be used to adjust relative returns from foreign and domestic investment.

The central point is that the interests of transnational corporations, be they Canadian or U.S.-controlled, are not the same as those of Canadian workers and citizens. Debate over the MAI could and should open up a much broader debate over the meaning of national economic development in a global economy dominated by transnational capital.

ENDNOTES

1. See United Nations (UNCTAD) World Investment Report, 1997.
2. Alan D. MacPherson. *"Shifts in Canadian Direct Investment Abroad and Foreign Direct Investment in Canada"* in John Britton (ed.) Canada and the Global Economy. McGill — Queen's Press. 1996.
3. See Lorraine Eden. *"Multinationals as Agents of Change: Setting a New Canadian Policy on FDI"*. Industry Canada Discussion Paper. 1994.
4. See Investment Canada Annual Report, 1992-93.
5. See International Labour Organization. *"Recent Reports on Foreign Direct Investment and Implications for Employment and Social Policy"*. November, 1996.
6. Martin Feldstein. *"The Effects of Outbound Foreign Direct Investment on the Domestic Capital Stock"*. National Bureau of Economic Research. Working Paper #4668
7. UNCTAD. Trade and Development Report, 1997. p. vii.
8. Statistics Canada. Canadian Economic Observer. October, 1997. Table 17
9. Statistics Canada Cat. 61-220. CALURA. Corporations. 1995.
10. See Andrew Jackson. *"Impacts of the FTA and NAFTA on Canadian Labour Markets and Labour and Social Standards."* CLC Research Paper #7. 1998.
11. See Ian MacLachlan. *"Organizational Restructuring of US Based Manufacturing Subsidiaries and Plant Closure"* in Britton (Ed) (1996)
12. See Lorraine Eden (Ed). *Multinationals in North America.* University of Calgary Press. 1994.
13. John Britton. *"High Tech Canada"* in Britton (Ed.) P. 260
14. *"Findings of the OECD's Work on Foreign Direct Investment"*. OECD. November 19, 1997

15. Glen Norcliffe. *"Foreign Trade in Goods and Services"* in Britton (Ed.) P. 37
16. Alan D. MacPherson. *"Shifts in Canadian Direct Investment Abroad and Foreign Direct Investment in Canada"* in Britton (Ed.) P. 76
17. John Cantwell. *"The Theory of Technological Competence"* in D. McFetridge (Ed.) *Foreign Investment, Technology and Economic Growth*. University of Calgary Press. 1991.
18. McFetridge (Ed.) P. 382
19. See Industry Canada. *"Canadian Based Multinationals: An Analysis of Activities and Performance"*. Working Paper #2. July, 1994. See also S. Globerman (Ed.) Canadian Based Multinationals. University of Calgary Press 1994.
20. Activities of Foreign Affiliates in OECD Countries. OECD. 1996
21. Canadian Based Multinationals. Industry Canada Working Paper #2, July, 1994.
22. Calculated from Table 25. Statistics Canada Cat. 67-001
23. Canadian Based Multinationals. Industry Canada Working Paper #2. July, 1994. P. 31
24. Lorraine Eden (1994). P. 12
25. Industry Canada (1994). p.37
26. See Jackson (1998)

THE MAI AND DEVELOPING COUNTRIES

by Martin Khor

INTRODUCTION

A Multilateral Agreement on Investment (MAI) is currently being negotiated by the 29 OECD countries. The MAI seeks to radically broaden the freedom of movement and operation of foreign investors and their investments, while severely restricting the rights and powers of states to regulate the entry, establishment and operations of foreign companies and their investments.

Although only member countries of the OECD are negotiating the text of the MAI, it is meant to be a multilateral treaty, as its name implies, and thus open to all countries that can meet its provisions. Indeed, the OECD has made it clear that it considers most barriers to foreign investment to be located in developing countries, where allegedly investors have the greatest need for protection of their rights. The real target of the MAI, therefore, is to put pressure on the developing countries to sign on.

The basic assumptions of the MAI draft text are: 1) that the MAI regime is fair and equitable for all parties; and 2) that the targets of "high standards for liberalization and protection" backed by an effective enforcement mechanism will lead to efficient resource use, job creation, and higher living standards. These are only assumptions that remain to be tested in line with existing knowledge of the investment-development nexus. For example, "high standards" of liberalization in countries where local firms are not yet able to compete with the transnationals could result in a net loss of jobs.

Not yet agreed-to are proposals that the MAI be consistent with environmental protection and sustainable development, and that it provide for observance of internationally recognized core labour standards. These proposals have come from countries where NGOs have pointed out that the MAI provides strong rights for investors while failing to spell out any obligations on their part. All that has been done in that respect by the OECD is to insert a set of voluntary and non-binding Guidelines for Multinational Enterprises.

The MAI's definitions of what constitutes an "investor" and an "investment" are extremely broad. The OECD itself has said that the definitions "go beyond the traditional notion of FDI (direct foreign investment) to cover virtually all tangible and intangible assets." This broad coverage has serious implications, implying the right of foreigners to freely put in and take out funds in all forms (through loans, portfolio investment, FDI, etc.), with potentially serious effects on a country's financial policy, money supply, exchange rate, and balance of payments.

TREATMENT OF INVESTORS

The MAI contains the following agreed text:

> *"Each contracting party shall accord to investors of another contracting party, and to their investments, treatment no less favourable than the treatment it accords (in like circumstances) to its own investors and their investments with respect to the establishment, acquisition, expansion, operation, management, maintenance, use, enjoyment and sale or other disposition of investments."*

This is perhaps the most significant of the MAI's principles, articles and provisions. It is broad in scope: covering both pre- and post-establishment phases; it would forbid de facto as well as de jure discrimination; and, most significantly, it specifies that, while foreign investors cannot be treated less favourably than local investors, they can be treated better.

This article has very serious implications for developing countries, most of whom now have foreign investment agencies that screen investment applications against certain criteria in line with national goals and objectives. Many of these are aimed at protecting local enterprises from stronger foreign enterprises, for monetary and fiscal purposes, but also for social, cultural or political reasons. For example, in an agricultural sector with a predominance of small farms, foreign ownership of land may be prohibited or restricted to protect the resources and livelihood of a large and vulnerable segment of the population.

In many developing countries, the financial sector is also protected because of its crucial economic role, as are the health, educational and media sectors for valid cultural and social reasons.

The rationale is that, partly due to the colonial experience, locals firms and farms have not yet been given an opportunity to develop to a level where they can compete successfully with large foreign enterprises. The development of local enterprise capacity is also important for national development, in terms of upgrading local technology and skills, retention of income within the economy, job creation, and for economic, social and political security. Most governments therefore, while welcoming foreign investments, also take positive measures to promote and assist local enterprises through grants, subsidies, and other "most favoured" initiatives.

The MAI's "national treatment" principle seeks to deny the validity of state policies and actions that aid or protect local enterprises. Such policies are incompatible with the MAI, which would oblige a signing country to "roll them back" or subject them to a "standstill."

Closely allied with the MAI's "national treatment" principle is the "most favoured nation" (MFN) principle, which would prohibit (or at least restrict the ability of) a country from developing more favourable relations with other countries in relation to investment. This could be a drawback to developing countries wishing to establish or maintain closer links with other developing countries at the same stage of development, or in the same regional area.

Thus, an ASEAN country that participates in preferential arrangements for investors and investments within the ASEAN region would have to offer the same terms to investors from other MAI countries, should it join the MAI. The prospects for more special and extensive South-South or regional investment links would clearly be made more difficult.

TRANSPARENCY

The MAI text obliges parties to publish laws, regulations, procedures, administrative rulings and judicial decisions that may affect the operation of the agreement. But no party shall be required to allow access to information on particular investors or investments that would contravene its own laws protecting privacy and confidentiality.

Thus, while corporations are to be given much broader new rights under the MAI, through enforced changes in law in MAI countries, their home governments will not be obliged to provide information about these corporations, on grounds of existing confidentiality laws.

ENTRY, STAY AND WORK

The MAI obliges contracting parties to grant temporary entry, stay and authorization to work to a foreign investor and to key personnel, and to permit such investors to employ anyone of their choice, regardless of nationality.

Many developing countries restrict the number and functions of foreign staff that a foreign investor can bring in, and also specify that local citizens should occupy certain senior managerial positions. The aim of these policies is to guard against a predominance of foreign personnel, particularly in joint-venture operations, and ensure job opportunities for local managers and professionals. The MAI would prevent or severely restrict governments from maintaining these policies.

PERFORMANCE REQUIREMENTS

The MAI prohibits contracting parties from imposing performance requirements on foreign investors. Such investors must not be required, for example, to locate its headquarters in the party's territory, purchase locally-made goods or services, achieve a given level of domestic content, to hire a given number of nationals, to establish a joint venture, to transfer technology to local enterprises, or to achieve a minimum level of local equity participation.

Many developing countries have regulations or policies obliging foreign investors to follow many or most of the performance requirements that are banned by the MAI. These requirements are felt necessary to ensure that foreign investors help host countries fulfill their national goals, such as upgrading technology, stimulating local economies, creating jobs for local citizens, and earning or saving foreign exchange so as to enhance the balance of payments. Without these policies, desired development might not take place or be sustainable.

The removal of the right of governments to impose these requirements would deprive host countries of key economic instruments to pursue macroeconomic and industrial policies and development strategies.

The prohibition against requiring joint ventures and minimum local equity participation is also very significant. This implies that foreign firms (whether or not from MAI countries) must be allowed 100% equity ownership. Many countries now have limits on the equity participation of foreign firms, designed to increase local ownership, prevent foreign monopolization, and retain more profits and revenues within the country—objectives that are seen to be important to maintain social and economic stability.

The MAI's prohibition of such performance requirements could thus have serious adverse effects on a host country's ability to reach development goals, and on the attainment or preservation of economic, social and political stability.

PRIVATIZATION

The MAI does not oblige member countries to privatize any of their public institutions or services, but, once a state does decide to privatize a publicly-owned enterprise, then the treaty's national treatment comes into play and foreign investors must be given the same rights as those within the country to acquire government-held assets.

For developing countries, this article also has serious implications. Many countries are in the process of privatizing public enterprises of various kinds, and have a policy of giving preference to local investors—or reserving a certain percentage of shares for them. This policy is needed to maintain significant local participation in what are often key social or economic sectors.

The MAI would therefore make it difficult, perhaps even impossible, for governments to retain any control over privatized enterprises. Since privatization is often a socially or politically controversial activity, the sale of a lot of the "family silver" to foreigners could generate discontent and discord among the population.

INVESTMENT PROTECTION

The MAI seeks to protect investors from all conceivable threats. It stipulates that they must be accorded "fair and equitable treatment and full and constant protection and security," that their investments must not be expropriated or nationalized, that they be free to move their investments into and out of a host country "without delay," and that, in the event that their investments are adversely affected in some way, they must be compensated (again, without delay) to an amount "equivalent to fair market value," plus interest. Failing such compensation, the investor can sue the host government and have the case decided by a three-person international tribunal.

These provisions give maximum protection to foreign investors, a situation that puts the host country on the defensive in its use of measures or policies that may cause the foreign investor to feel aggrieved.

The definition of expropriation is very broad, going far beyond the usual meaning of a direct government takeover to include any government action that the investor might construe as damaging his investment—even tax increases.

The section on transfers is most significant for developing countries, since it obliges them to have the most liberal policy on capital inflows and outflows. Many developing countries feel it is necessary to have some limit or control on foreign inflows, as well as on fund repatriation, in order to prevent balance-of-payments or foreign exchange crises. The MAI would prohibit such policies, and would even apply retroactively to investments made prior to a host country's joining the MAI.

Dispute settlement

In addition to providing for the arbitration of disputes between member countries, the MAI sets forth a dispute settlement process in which an investor can sue a host country for damages and have the case heard by an international tribunal whose juudgment will be final and binding.

The MAI thus gives sweeping new rights to corporations and investors. With the MAI obligations being so many and so broad, they could result in a developing host country facing a long series of expensive legal cases filed by foreign companies. That possibility alone would put the host country very much on the defensive in its dealings with foreign firms, for fear of the costs of tribunal cases. The big corporations would have their power very much strengthened, with the power of host governments being correspondingly weakened.

FINAL PROVISIONS AND CONCLUSION

Among the significant "final provisions" are those pertaining to accession, amendment and withdrawal.

The MAI will be open to accession by any state that is willing to abide by its terms and obligations. Amendments could only be made if ratified by all member countries. And a country could withdraw from the MAI after five years, on six months' notice, but all the provisions of the agreement would continue to apply for another 15 years.

Clearly, whether or not to join the MAI will be a difficult choice for developing countries. Each country will have to conduct a detailed study of the agreement and all its articles to weigh the pros and cons of participating. It will be one of the toughest and most important decisions they are likely to make for many years. Such a thorough study of its likely effects on a developing country's economy and society is essential if the probable benefits and costs are to be accurately assessed.

THE MAI AND THE WORLD ECONOMY

by Gregory Albo and Chris Roberts

Introduction

A dizzying array of new international institutions have emerged to forge a new international economic order: the powerful World Trade Organization (WTO) has replaced the General Agreement on Tariffs and Trade (GATT); the North American Free Trade Agreement (NAFTA), the European Union (EU), and the Asian Pacific Economic Cooperation group (APEC) mark the formation of new regions of accumulation; and Western hemispheric and even trans-Atlantic free trade loom on the horizon.

The current efforts to construct a liberalized world economy, at times coordinated and at others ad hoc, stand in a long line of such efforts that can be traced back to the early period of merchant capitalism. The arguments of neo-liberals in favour of globalization date back to Adam Smith, who argued that mutual exchange between countries allows an international specialization in the division of labour in areas of comparative advantage that raises the general welfare of both (although a range of dubious assumptions, including full employment and perfect competition, are necessary for the results to hold). The neo-liberal thinkers who dominate the World Bank continue to assert that "the liberalization of trade and investment laws around the world has contributed to an enormous increase in the volume of world trade and foreign direct and portfolio investment, whose impact on the welfare of participants has been considerable and for the better."[1]

The case for free trade has been for a reduction in tariffs to reallocate factors of production to more 'efficient' uses within a national economic space. The internationalization of economic activity is also defended today in terms of "more efficient" international financial activities. The freeing of currency trading, the lifting of restrictions on capital movements, the proliferation of offshore credit sources, and the deregulation of national banking laws are all defended as adding to 'efficient' global capital allocation and balancing risk in an 'integrated' world economy. The International Monetary Fund's (IMF) policies of liberalization of balance of payments transactions and the Bank of International Settlements' (BIS) defense of international banking and advocacy of lower reserve requirements have been central to the processes of financial internationalization.

Free trade advocates have come to defend the international mobility of investment in production, on the grounds of market 'efficiency,' favouring the global reallocation of production as if the world constituted a *single* market. The investor-protection and national treatment clauses of NAFTA are an example of the neoliberal defense of this side of internationalization.

The Multilateral Agreement on Investment (MAI) is a further effort to liberalize investment in the world economy which expands the investment provisions won in NAFTA and seeks to generalize them to the world economy as a whole through a WTO-like treaty process.[2] The preamble in the draft MAI promises that investor protections "will contribute to the efficient utilization of economic resources, the creation of employment opportunities and the improvement of living standards."[3] In this view, the MAI is an engine of growth which will contribute to the elimination of international economic inequality and raise incomes.

The MAI proposes to protect not just foreign direct investment (FDI), but also financial internationalization in an all-encompassing definition of investment as "every kind of asset owned or controlled, directly or indirectly, by an investor," including intellectual property rights, a range of legal claims, and seemingly all private property forms.[4] FDI has usually been differentiated from short-term capital flows and defined as the internationalization of capital via transnational corporations (TNCs) investing in new plants or engaging in merger and acquisitions outside their home country.

TNCs are increasingly active in the internationalization of services, from financial services to producer and marketing services. In other words, TNCs are national firms operating across national boundaries.

Portfolio capital may be invested for the long-term in acquisition of foreign securities (without control over the management of the company), although the structure of secondary markets and the strategies of institutional investors have certainly made them less so. Financial flows internationalizing production also take the form of direct investment diversifying production sites of a common process across national boundaries and linking different processes in production networks that span several countries.

Internationalization of production has been a response to stagnant output and cost conditions in the corporate search for a 'spatial fix' to increase profits. The volatility due to international costs, currency and interest rate movements has provided further impetus to diversify production sites. This aspect of internationalization, it needs to be stressed, has not produced a global production system outside of national states and indifferent to local production conditions.

There are distinct geographical and temporal limits to the mobility of fixed capital. Foreign investment in productive activity is internalized within the host country, in linkages to the rest of the economy, and to the constellation of political power, even as it redefines national political autonomy and shifts a larger portion of economic activity outward.

In this essay, we note that the expansion of the capitalist world system has seen successive phases of liberalization and integration, contraction and disintegration. It is necessary, in assessing liberalization measures like the MAI, to avoid "confusing the effects of continuing stagnation in the world capitalist economy with the auguries of a transformation of the global capitalist order."[5]

Alongside 'cooperation and growing interdependence' between countries, we also see the 'chaos' and 'sources of tensions between the leading capitalist powers' that Magdoff warned about.

Contrary to the claims made for globalization, the internationalization of capitalism has frequently brought periods in which inequality and instability have increased rather than lessened. Indeed, as more resources have been thrown into export-oriented economic strategies by all countries adopting trade liberalization at the same time that domestic demand is being curtailed, the world economy is more and more reproducing conditions of 'competitive austerity'. The neo-liberal project of globalization cemented in the MAI contributes to an unstable and polarizing world economy and impedes democratic capacities to establish alternative distributional systems that support egalitarian economic outcomes.

1. National Economies in a World System

Capitalism is inherently an expansionary productive system. Social and political institutions, not least military force, have been crucial to providing the labour force, resources and organized coercion necessary for this expansion within nation-states.[6] The expansion of trade and the export of capital across boundaries, under the state system, is a logical extension of the internal expansion within states.[7]

The institutionalized regimes of the world economy structure the flows of capital and commodities connecting national spaces, of value formation, combining the development of national economies within an evolving international division of labour.

The international expansion of capital, whether via trade, portfolio investment, or foreign direct investment, has always occurred within the patterns and structures established by international regimes, which historically have been organized under the leadership of a hegemonic political power and encompass trade, the international monetary system, the international credit system (including a loan enforcement and repayment regime), and the security regime.[8] The evolution of these regimes establish distinct phases of world order, which facilitate and constrain the national and international expansion of capital in different ways.

In any given period, the construction of a trade and investment regime faces the task of orchestrating the expansion of national capitalisms growing at different rates and occupying different niches within the world economy. The world economy does not consist of spontaneously complementary national economies. Rather, the world economy amounts to 'a world configuration' between different national economies within a historically and geographically variable international division of labour). As Lipietz points out, globalization as a process of universalizing capitalist exchange relations has not effaced the problem of world order:
"...the world economy has not (yet?) developed beyond this implicit level of organization. No institutional form regulating world demand has been possible. No supra-national authority to control money supply has been created. The complementarities and antagonisms that exist between national economies remain unstable, constituting little more than partial and random *configurations*."[9]

The integration of national sites of production into the world of circulation always produces tensions and potential contradictions, setting up tensions between national modes of economic regulation and the international conjuncture.

Investment capital itself embodies this tension between the local and the global. As a stock of capital, investment must be rooted in local production relations to produce a surplus; as a flow, investment capital seeks to overcome all fixed relations and barriers to its circulation and realization. National and international investment regimes, from local zoning restrictions to national foreign investment review agencies and international agreements on investment measures, link local accumulation with the world of capital circulation.

The relationship between the international regime and national economic development has had different consequences for democratic capacities to pursue egalitarian goals at different times. The struggle to *constrain* (and even to disengage from) the market and impose social priorities on its workings has historically been most effective at the national level, primarily because the political and institutional means to control capital have been developed most strongly at the level of the nation-state.

Capitalist development has always required the visible hand of the state to counteract its crisis tendencies, and labour movements and other groups have historically organized at this level to attempt to contain, and even reverse, what Polanyi identified as the tendency of the self-regulating capitalist market to 'disembed' the economy from the social protections of non-market relations.[10] In reaction to the fact that capital has always been better able to command social space, labour movements seeking to constrain market processes and counteract competition have directed their energies at trying to 'anchor' capital within national and local spaces.[11]

Democratic struggles over egalitarian objectives to direct economic activity where it is needed or to redistribute income, have benefited from international regimes that regulate and constrain trade and capital mobility, permitting the imposition of social and political controls on the market. Liberal international regimes, conversely, have historically weakened domestic constraints on the market to serve domestic welfare goals. During historical phases in which the international regimes facilitating the world expansion of capital undermine the national regulation of capitalism, the effects have often been stagnation, increasing polarization, and insecurity.

The key question raised by the MAI is whether, in the context of a liberalizing international financial and trading order, the expansion of FDI in the 1980s and 1990s is a force for growth, stability and growing equality in the world economy, or whether it promises to do little to rectify mounting imbalances and instability. What is the relation between the growth and liberalization of international investment (globalization) and the dismal state of the world economy today (stagnation, polarization and instability)?

Globalization in Historical Perspective

The present period of liberalized portfolio and direct investment flows is commonly compared with the period between 1870 and 1913, which also witnessed the growth of large-scale international flows of both short-term and long-term (primarily portfolio) capital.[12] During this period, the world economy reached levels of openness unmatched until the 1970s; trade and output grew steadily, though somewhat more slowly than portfolio capital flows, which also outstripped FDI growth.[13] In the quarter-century after 1880, however, with the spread of tariff barriers among the late-industrializing economies of North America and beyond, FDI began to take on added importance. Technological advances in transportation, communications and storage promoted the internationalization of production, as did the transformation of business organization, which permitted firms to develop greater coordination and efficiency over an expanded scale. In the industrialized and industrializing world, a substantial proportion of FDI went into manufacturing; in the Third World, primary production was the principal outlet for direct investment flows from abroad (Canada, of course, being a case of both).

The period spanning the late 19th and early 20th centuries saw many states that today belong to the advanced industrialized world successfully 'catch-up' to the leading capitalist economies, and it is therefore pointed to as evidence of the "convergence effects" of a regime of free trade and capital flows. However, the context and nature of economic development in the earlier period was very different from the laissez-faire environment of today.

In the late 19th century, late-follower countries everywhere contended with the challenge of capital shortages, imported technology, and infant industries which necessitated a role for barriers to trade and state involvement in the development process.[14] Despite free flows of capital and trade among a number of regions, the world economy could still be characterized as strongly protectionist; FDI and portfolio investment assisting the industrialization of late-followers after 1880 increasingly needed to jump tariff walls, as the example of U.S. companies entering into Canada suggests.

Unlike the present, the context for expansion at the turn of the century was one of active state involvement in the mobilization and allocation of capital required for the large-scale infrastructural projects of industrialization. Moreover, in the colonial possessions of the South, where the pattern was more consistently liberalized trade with the imperial powers, de-industrialization and declining shares of world manufacturing resulted. If the world economy is considered as a whole, global investment flows prior to World War I did not produce international convergence. Rather, the period is remembered as marking an historical divide between the industrialized world and the non-industrialized world—the classic 'age of imperialism'—from which time world inequalities widened considerably.[15]

The international monetary regime increasingly adopted after 1880—the classical "gold standard" under British hegemony—was as much a barrier to employment and income equality as a force for stable growth. Under the inflexible rules of the gold standard, the imperative of balancing international accounts displaced the objectives of employment and stable incomes. By forcing deficit countries to adjust via deflation, the gold standard placed the burden of external adjustment on working-class incomes and the unemployed, the social consequences of which were only offset by large-scale migration from Europe to the New World.

In the wake of World War I, the reconstructed gold exchange standard was more clearly a destabilizing force in the world economy. Amidst the trade dislocations of post-war reconstruction and the global imbalances of the 1920s, the return to gold forced deflationary adjustment onto the weaker economies. The 'beggar-thy-neighbour' tariff spiral was the result—and not the cause—of the structural imbalances in the world economy. With world economic collapse, adherence to gold impeded reflation and spread deflationary pressures around the world. Only with a break from the gold standard, the imposition of exchange controls, and the shift to divergent development strategies and managed trade were states

TABLE 1

INDICATORS OF ECONOMIC PERFORMANCE IN THE G7 COUNTRIES
UNDER VARIOUS INTERNATIONAL MONETARY REGIMES

	Gold Standard		Bretton Woods				Floating Rates	
	1881-1913		1946-58		1959-1970		1974-1989	
Indicator	Mean	Variation	Mean	Variation	Mean	Variation	Mean	Variat.
Real Growth Per Capita	1.5	2.5	4.3	0.5	4.5	0.4	2.2	1.1
Inflation	1.0	3.4	3.9	1.5	3.9	0.5	7.2	0.5
Real Long-te term Interest Rate	3.5	0.7	2.0	2.0	2.7	0.4	2.7	1.6
Change in Real Exchange Rate	0.9	0.9	5.8	1.5	2.0	1.0	8.2	0.8

Source: UNCTAD, Trade and Development Report, 1997, p.79.

able to take steps to expand and cope with the high unemployment and social crisis of the Great Depression.[16]

The Bretton Woods System

Capitalist expansion in the post-war period mainly took the form of a deepening of national markets. To be sure, trade expanded internationally (mostly conducted within the industrialized core), as did flows of FDI, from an initially low level. In particular, American investment abroad grew rapidly. On the whole, however, investment was largely confined to national spaces, and growth was centred around the deepening of national markets.[17] While foreign investment grew at a rapid pace, faster than output or trade, among the industrialized economies it remained a minor share of GNP.

The international regime provided a framework supportive of the unprecedented growth of the post-war boom, partly through default from the collapse of trade in the inter-war period and the needs of reconstruction, and partly through restrictions on the mobility of short-term capital flows and currency trading from countries facing large debts and minimal foreign exchange reserves.

The institutional framework established at the 1944 Bretton Woods conference was designed with the memory of the instabilities and inflexibilities of the inter-war system in mind, and was meant to achieve a system of international integration permitting flexible adjustment that would not come at the expense of employment and welfare goals.

The Bretton Woods institutions established the foundations for a new world economic regime, reconstructed under American political and economic hegemony, and committed to the reconstruction of the European and Japanese economies within the capitalist world, the restoration of currency convertibility, and the formation of a free trading world order in which trade and international capital flows would be subordinate to domestic job growth programs and welfare programs. The deflationary bias of the gold standard was replaced by the flexible and expansionary regime of national currencies pegged to the American dollar, which was in turn exchangeable for gold.

Over the post-war period, the liberalization of the flow of goods interacted virtuously with growth, employment, and rising incomes: both trade and output expanded at unprecedented rates, and the world economy moved from an initially low level of international openness towards a more open trading environment at a faster pace than prior to World War I.[18] Approximately 80% of all tariffs were eliminated in less than 15 years after the establishment of GATT, and colonial markets were opened up to the penetration of foreign, especially American, capital.[19] Despite the commitment to, and growth of, a liberal world economy, however, world trade remained fragmented, uneven, and subject to controls. Most of the socialist bloc remained disengaged, and Japan and other capitalist economies retained controls over the creation and flow of credit in the interests of national industrial strategies. Capital controls and planned credit allocation systems kept finance centred on national spaces, subordinated to the imperatives of reconstruction and domestic-economy-centred growth, and permitting fiscal and monetary policy to be utilized to support domestic welfare goals.[20]

Moreover, private international lending took a back-seat to official lending from the World Bank and the other international financial institutions channelling direct investment to the developing world. Only by the end of the 1960s did private international lending regain its pre-war importance.[21] FDI grew steadily and substantially, especially U.S. TNCs, but this activity remained small relative to output and was often subject to government screening and monitoring.

As world economic integration proceeded, however, the contradiction between growing trade imbalances and the international monetary system helped undermine the post-war institutional order. The reconstruction of the devastated economies of Europe and Asia, and world liquidity, relied on the United States running persistent balance of payment deficits, financed by the export of American currency.

In the 1960s and 1970s, unregulated capital markets made possible speculative attacks on weak currencies that helped undermine thc Bretton Woods system. The integration and rapid reconstruction of the European economies and the return to convertibility of the European currencies set the stage for sharpened international competition in the form of a 'non-American challenge' as European states and firms, in particular, used their growing dollar reserves to purchase foreign assets as well as invest in new plants.

A corresponding accelerated expansion of direct investment from American TNCs followed, reproducing the imperialist rivalry of the early part of the century.[22] With the offshore accumulation of U.S. dollars, American banks began to pressure for deregulation in order to compete in Eurocurrency markets, setting in train pressures for the competitive deregulation of financial markets.[23] Speculative flows soon created accumulated pressures on the system of fixed exchange rates, sparking the United States to suspend parity with gold in 1971, a process that eventually broke the fixed exchange rate regime and ended the Bretton Woods system by 1973.

After Bretton Woods

The demise of the Bretton Woods system ushered in a period of economic internationalization of trade, financial flows and currency and banking deregulation, equally a period of stagnation, mounting instability, and growing income inequality. Intensified international restructuring and a dramatic growth of the world stock of FDI have coincided with a significant slowdown in growth. Output growth across the OECD after 1974 fell to an annual average of 2.9% for the years 1973-1989, having averaged 4.8% between 1960 and 1973.[24]

Similarly, after the stock of business capital grew at an annual average of 5.3% between 1965 and 1973, it fell to 3.2% yearly growth in 1982, and manufacturing accumulation especially has fallen off.[25] The 1980s expansion failed to restore private invest-

TABLE 2

GROWTH OF REAL GDP, 1966-95
(PERCENTAGES, ANNUAL AVERAGES)

	1966-73	1974-80	1981-90	1991-93	1994	1995
World total	5.1	3.4	3.2	1.2	2.9	2.8
OECD countries	4.8	2.9	3.1	1.2	2.9	2.4
Transition countries	7.0	5.1	1.8	-12.5	-8.4	-2.5
Eastern and Central Europe	6.9	6.1	2.1	-9.0	-7.5	-0.7
Former Soviet Union	7.1	1.1	1.0	-15.5	-12.6	-4.0
Developing countries	6.9	5.0	3.3	4.6	4.6	4.9
East Asia	7.9	6.8	7.6	8.7	9.3	9.2
China	8.5	6.3	9.9	12.3	12.2	10.2
South Asia	3.7	4.0	5.7	3.2	4.7	5.5
Sub-Saharan Africa	4.7	3.4	1.7	0.6	2.2	3.8
Latin America/Caribbean	6.4	4.8	1.7	3.2	3.9	0.9
Middle East/North Africa	8.5	4.7	0.2	3.4	0.3	2.5

Source: ILO, World Employment 1996/97, p. 3.

ment to post-war 'Golden Age' rates, despite the apparent restoration of favourable conditions for investment and profits in the 1980s.[26]

Amidst slower growth, the liberalization of financial markets and the growth of enormous pools of highly-mobile short-term financial capital, uncoupled from output, trade and productive investment, have been a major force behind the destabilization of the international monetary system. In the 1990s, the world's financial markets are integrated on an unprecedented scale; short-term capital movements have grown to the point where turnover in currency markets now dwarfs the value of trade, or for that matter, the combined official reserves of the world's governments. In the 1990s, daily foreign exchange trading is estimated at over US$1 trillion, 50 times the value of daily trade volumes, with no sign that the pace of growth is likely to slacken.[27]

Relative stagnation in manufacturing has sparked a shift of capital out of long-term productive investment and into financial speculation, encouraged by the adoption of floating exchange rates and the removal of capital controls which had separated national financial markets. Financial liberalization has been permitted by the same technological developments—computer and information technology networks—that have enabled the global coordination of production and distribution by transnational corporations. However, the movement in the direction of liberalization is not a consequence of technology, but was driven by states.

TABLE 3

CROSS-BORDER TRANSACTIONS IN BONDS AND EQUITIES, 1975-1996
(PERCENTAGE OF GDP)

	1975	1980	1985	1989	1990	1991	1992	1993	1994	1995	1996
United States	4	9	35	101	89	96	107	129	131	135	164
Japan	2	8	62	156	119	92	72	78	60	65	84
Germany	5	7	33	66	57	55	85	171	159	172	200
France	..	5	21	52	54	79	122	187	201	180	227
Italy	1	1	4	18	27	60	92	192	207	253	468
Canada	3	10	27	55	64	81	113	153	212	194	258

Source: Bank for International Settlements, Annual Report, 1997, p. 79.

The shift to floating exchange rates, together with the liberalization of capital movements, has created the opportunity for speculative activity, bringing with it exchange rate volatility and an uncoupling of currency values and output and trade performance. A quarter of a century after the end of fixed exchange rates, the vast majority of short-term capital movements are unrelated to the state of production and trade in individual economies, and currency values offer little or no indication of the balance of trade or current account.[28]

The fact that the American dollar has remained the international currency standard despite stagnant productivity, chronic trade deficits and a massive world surplus of dollars is a particularly glaring example of this.

This development has made a mockery of neo-liberal assurances that moving from a system of fixed exchange rates to a floating system would result in greater national policy autonomy. The deregulation and international integration of national financial markets has increased the ability of capital to constrain domestic monetary policy. Speculative short-term capital movements have forced governments to direct energies towards stabilizing the external balance. This stabilization increasingly comes, as in the gold standard period, in the form of the competitive austerity of deflation and cuts in working class living standards.

Ad hoc attempts to coordinate exchange rate policy among the G-7 have ensued. Indeed, emergency world economic summitry to battle payments crises is a constant feature of the world configuration today, though the currency crises in Italy and the U.K. in 1992, in Mexico in 1994, and East Asia in 1997-98 underline the volatility generated by unregulated short-term capital movements.

Despite fears of a revival of protectionism amidst a stagnant world economy, the international trade regime continues to be liberalized; a proliferation of bilateral, regional and multilateral trade liberalization agreements now pursue the 'deep integration' of national economies through the removal of non-tariff barriers and the harmonization of trade-related legislation.[29] The GATT rounds have moved beyond trade in manufactures, to provisions around agriculture, intellectual property and trade-related investment measures (TRIMs).

Under the stewardship of the WTO, which replaced the GATT in January 1995, service-sector activity has become the focus of trade liberalization efforts, as trade in services has doubled over the last 10 years to reach US$1 trillion per annum, representing over 20% of total trade.[30] Most recently, the Uruguay Round concluded under the WTO with an agreement committing member states to liberalize their markets in financial services, an astounding leap of faith amidst the currency turmoil, banking crises and debt problems plaguing all zones of the world.[31]

TABLE 4

IMPORTS AND EXPORTS OF GOODS, 1970-1993
(PERCENTAGE OF GDP)

	Imports of Goods					Exports of Goods				
	1970	1980	1985	1990	1993	1970	1980	1985	1990	1993
United States	4.0	9.2	8.9	9.3	9.5	4.2	7.9	5.1	6.7	6.8
Japan	9.3	13.3	9.6	7.9	5.7	9.5	12.2	13.1	9.8	8.6
Germany	16.2	22.9	25.3	22.2	17.9	18.5	23.6	29.4	25.9	19.9
France	13.2	20.2	20.4	19.4	16.0	12.4	16.7	18.5	17.5	16.4
Italy	13.9	21.8	20.8	16.2	14.6	12.3	17.4	18.5	15.5	17.1
United Kingdom	17.4	21.9	23.7	22.9	22.4	15.5	21.2	21.9	18.8	18.2
Canada	15.3	21.8	21.7	20.2	23.6	19.0	23.8	24.5	20.8	24.5
OECD Average	21.1	26.9	27.6	25.1	23.0	17.7	22.8	26.0	23.5	23.4

Source: OECD, OECD Economies at a Glance: Structural Indicators (Paris: OECD, 1996), p. 63.

Since the mid-1980s and the slowdown in world output growth, foreign direct investment has replaced trade as the principal form of international capitalist expansion. Global sales of foreign affiliates since 1987 have climbed faster than exports, as the extension of production facilities to foreign markets has allowed the exploitation of economies of scale unavailable from the continued penetration of markets through exports.[32] Between 1982 and 1994, the world's stock of FDI increased by a factor of four, doubling its share of world GDP to 9%, and growing twice as fast as gross fixed capital formation between 1986 and 1995.[33] Much of the growth of FDI has taken the form of cross-border mergers and acquisitions, rather than new investment.

Alongside this concentration and centralization of FDI, the share of intra-firm trade in total trade flows has also risen, while the internationalization of services, and especially business and financial services, has driven much of the growth of FDI. An ever-growing share of output, trade and investment is organized by TNCs, as integrated international production links national economies more closely.

TABLE 5

VALUE OF THE GROSS PRODUCT OF FOREIGN AFFILIATES AND THEIR SHARE IN GDP BY REGION (BILLIONS OF DOLLARS AND PERCENTAGE)

	Gross Product of Foreign Affiliates			Gross Product of Foreign Affiliates as percentage of GDP		
Region	1982	1990	1994	1982	1990	1994
World	553	1 383	1 557	5.2	6.7	6.0
Developed Countries	403	1 098	1 099	5.1	6.7	5.4
Western Europe	179	607	610	6.0	8.7	7.9
European Union	164	570	568	5.7	8.6	7.7
Other Western Europe	15	37	43	9.9	10.7	11.0
North America	177	407	392	5.1	6.7	5.2
Other Developed Countries	47	84	97	3.4	2.4	1.9
Developing Countries	150	283	445	6.0	7.0	9.1
Africa	15	28	32	4.4	7.4	8.8
Latin America/Caribbean	59	101	162	7.6	9.3	10.3
Asia	74	151	248	5.6	5.9	8.6
West Asia	30	39	36	6.7	4.0	6.7
South, East & South-East Asia	44	112	211	5.0	7.0	9.0
Central and Eastern Europe	0.1	2.3	12.6	0.1	1.1	2.3

Source: UNCTAD, World Investment Report 1997, p. 267.

TABLE 6

INWARD AND OUTWARD FDI STOCK BY REGION, 1980-1995
(PERCENTAGE OF GROSS DOMESTIC PRODUCT)

Region	1980	1985	1990	1995
World				
inward	4.6	6.4	8.3	10.1
outward	4.9	5.9	8.1	9.9
Developed Countries				
inward	4.8	6.0	8.3	9.1
outward	6.5	7.5	9.8	11.5
Developing Countries				
inward	4.3	8.1	8.7	15.4
outward	0.5	1.0	1.8	4.5

Source: UNCTAD, World Investment Report 1997, annex table B.6

TABLE 7

INWARD AND OUTWARD FDI FLOWS
AS A PERCENTAGE OF GROSS FIXED CAPITAL FORMATION,
BY REGION AND ECONOMY, 1985-1995 (PERCENTAGE)

Region/economy	1985-1990 (annual average)	1991	1992	1993	1994	1995
World						
inward	5.4	3.1	3.3	4.4	4.5	5.2
outward	6	3.9	3.8	4.8	4.7	5.6
Developed Countries						
inward	5.5	3.2	3.2	3.7	3.5	4.4
outward	8	5.3	4.8	5.4	5.1	6.3
Developing Countries						
inward	8	4.4	5.1	6.6	8	8.2
outward	3.5	0.9	2.2	3.1	3.6	4

Source: UNCTAD, World Investment Report 1997, annex table B.5.

TABLE 8

CROSS-BORDER MERGER AND ACQUISITION PURCHASES, 1990-1996
(MILLIONS OF DOLLARS)

Region	1990	1991	1992	1993	1994	1995	1996
World	159 959	85 279	121 894	162 344	196 367	237 184	274 611
Developed countries	152 201	79 900	99 168	134 895	163 010	212 084	239 139
European Union	90 967	50 537	50 017	74 770	75 333	98 725	114 316
North America	26 234	15 690	26 361	44 655	52 042	80 386	87 496
Developing countries	7 548	5 199	22 319	26 858	32 365	24 464	32 827

Source: UNCTAD, World Investment Report 1997, p. 358.

While most FDI originates in the industrialized countries of the North, in the 1990s a growing share has been directed at the developing world, increasingly in manufacturing and services. The privatization of state industry in the South, and the opening up of national infrastructure to direct foreign involvement has presented opportunities for FDI originating in the North.[34] A number of newly-industrializing economies account for the majority of inward investment; countries traditionally closed to foreign penetration, such as China and India, have grown in importance as sites for foreign direct investment.

The increasing role of transnational corporations in reshaping and integrating production systems on a global basis is behind much of the increase in FDI flows. But control in the form of product ownership (in the form of patents) rather than equity ownership have allowed corporations to control production and marketing (practices that the MAI would enhance). The influence and control of TNCs over the growth and integration of international production and marketing extends beyond what is indicated by FDI indicators and other measures of capital ownership:

> *...by differentiating their machinery, processes, and product, transnational corporations can preserve supply, servicing, and maintenance linkages.... Many of the ventures of transnational corporations therefore no longer include much or all equity: joint ventures, management agreements and service contracts, licensing and franchise arrangements, production-sharing agreements, and subcontracting can all replace equity.*[35]

Profits on foreign direct investments may thus be complemented or substituted for by interest, royalties, management costs, and service charges, so that the scale of TNC influence is underrepresented if FDI figures are considered alone.

The pattern of trade and investment flows is producing regional economic integration in the shape of continental trading blocs. Integration via trade and investment is occurring to its greatest extent between member states of the European Union, and between Canada and the United States. TNCs operating at a European or North American level make use of different national labour markets, capital markets and technological networks to coordinate a continental intra-industry division of labour.[36]

Regionally-operating firms can take advantage of resource and wage differentials between production sites to reshape the intra-firm division of labour. "Firms are increasingly able to divide the production process into different stages and locate them according to comparative advantage—'slicing up the value chain'—thus increasing trade in inputs and semi-finished manufactures."[37] Even within blocs, TNCs are still reliant on home-base support, economically and politically, and competition between nationally-based transnational firms has in many respects intensified.

Despite increasing regional integration, trade and investment flows between blocs remain substantial. Capitalist rivalry via internationalization has by no means disappeared.[38] Capitalist competition is most visibly taking the form of imperialist rivalry at the margins of the world economy—for example, in the struggle for advantage in the newly-integrating regions like Cuba and Iran, in the newly-privatized state sectors of telecommunications and infrastructure in the South, in the often-criminal scramble over the division of assets and markets in the 'transition economies' of Eastern Europe, and in the struggle to pry open East Asian markets to Western buyouts and joint ventures with the aid of IMF adjustment packages.

Competitive Austerity and Economic Instability

Balance of payments equilibrium in capitalist economies crucially depends upon unit labour costs at the prevailing exchange rate. Any country that can combine new techniques with relatively cheap labour will gain competitive advantage and increased production. All countries cannot run a surplus. Trade can turn nasty, as some countries run into balance of payments problems and stagnation.

Trade deficits require financing in the hope that borrowing to get in balance will later generate the surpluses to pay off loans. To do so requires that investments build up competitive capacity and not be used to finance consumption. More importantly, surplus countries must later go into deficit so that foreign exchange may be earned for repayment of loans and interest. This typically depends in deficit countries upon some mixture of devaluation and deflation in an attempt to reduce imports while increasing exports.

These policies, however, raise their own problems. Deflation reduces demand and creates unemployment, while devaluation destabilizes investment although industrial capacity must be developed to meet import substitution and export demands. The more widespread are payments imbalances between countries, the less likely the adjustment process can work for any single country without damaging its economy. The repeated failures of structural adjustment polices for developing countries have all too clearly shown this.

Moreover, there is a competitive incentive for other countries to match devaluation and austerity to avoid large losses. Liberalization of trade and financial flows cannot be justified on the basis of actual remedies, but by the religious faith that capital and exchange markets are always efficient and *in the long run it will all work out.*

Structural imbalances have characterized capitalism for some time now. In the post-war period, the U.S. supplied dollar liquidity to the world through capital exports to finance trade imbalances. This continued until the dollar became unsustainable as the hub currency and Bretton Woods collapsed in the early 1970s.

Since the late 1970s, the IMF and the World Bank have promoted financial liberalization as the mechanism to finance trade adjustments and have used foreign exchange markets to impose market imperatives on national economies. Yet trade imbalances and debt loads have not cleared. Many countries, especially in Africa, have pushed the effort to meet external obligations and to increase exports to desperate levels of poverty and environmental destruction. The Asian economies, which but a few months before they became enveloped in economic crisis were being touted as the model and locomotive of economic advance, now potentially face the same dire consequences.

The lesson that flexible rates had the capacity to destabilize national economies moved the world economy to more managed rates after the Plaza and Louvre Accords of the 1980s. Through the 1990s, fears of inflation and external instability have imposed a quasi-fixed exchange rate system. This is especially so for the U.S., where capital inflows have again raised the value of the U.S. dollar out-of-synch with its trade position: yet currency devaluation (or even the U.S. bringing its trade balance under control) would potentially throw the world economy into enormous turmoil.

Hence adjustment of trade imbalances has increasingly had to fall entirely on what the IMF calls expenditure reductions and more flexible labour markets—austerity and unemployment. The trade imbalances, however, remain and it is becoming quite unclear, even to those favourable to this approach, how they can be corrected and financial obligations be met without politically unpalatable measures.

Regional and national policies for competitiveness through high-technology have everyone trying to export more, while cutting wages and social expenditures, under the discipline of portfolio and direct investment financial flows. This has established an international configuration of intense structural conflict—the interdependence and rivalry of national states, the stagnation and instabilities of the economic system.

Liberalization of international economic activities has neither been smooth nor soundly based. It has occurred in a context of deepening stagnation, redistribution of productive activity from the domestic to the traded sector dominated by TNCs, and the growth of hyper-active international financial markets. Against the one-sided accounts of globalization generated by the World Bank, the International Labour Organization's recent survey of world labour conditions concludes that "the world employment situation remains grim...there has been growing concern over the social exclusion that is breeding."[39] Far from being unique, the recent turmoil in Asia shows just how unstable world capitalism is.

2. Contrasting Perspectives on Globalization of Investment

The imbalances and precariousness of the world economy have kept discussion of reform front and centre. It is notable that further expansion of the world market has been persistently invoked as a solution to both payments imbalances and national income and employment problems. FDI figures prominently in these discussions.

Neo-liberalism, Direct Investment and the MAI

Liberalization of investment flows is defended by neo-liberals on a number of specific grounds, over and above the invocation of the imperatives of globalization. A treaty to protect the gains from open investment flows is being pursued as a necessary institutional support to market processes that are seen as too often subject to capricious actions by states (even if these states are acting through constitutional means and democratic mandates).

The fundamental argument, of course, is that market allocations of investment are inherently efficient and that lifting barriers to investment flows will increase competition, and thus efficiency and innovation. Performance requirements, protections for home industry, incentives and the like that distort the 'efficient' allocation of capital, as much within states as between them, should be dismantled.

Free markets, rather than state planners, allocate resources best via price signals free of the distortions of regulation and screening of foreign investment (or other short-term capital flows). Foreign direct investment, freed from distortions and barriers, allows industrial rationalization so that higher-productivity, more competitive firms will prevail and 'best-practice' technologies spread.

Liberalizing and deepening international capital markets, it is argued, would also be *equalizing* internationally insofar as protected investment flows encourage and permit private lenders in the mature economies of the North, where savings exceed investment opportunities and investments face declining returns, to lend to the savings-constrained economies of the South or the emerging markets of the transition economies of Europe and Asia, just beginning to develop and promising higher returns on investments.[40] Profit incentives would therefore direct flows of portfolio and direct investment from the mature economies of the rich world to newly industrializing states and emerging markets, and thereby contribute to global convergence of incomes through market processes.

These alleged gains from trade and specialization should, in their turn, be *stabilizing* of the world payments system in the long-term. There is an additional, more immediate reason to favour investment liberalization. The debt burden and the instability of short-term financial flows has made it less than prudent for countries, it is argued, to rely on private bank lending for financial requirements.

External financing to support the domestic growth process, and to strengthen long-term economic capacities to innovate and trade, is better in the form of direct investment that lengthens the payments period and, in an open trading system, would earn foreign exchange.

Thus, neo-liberal proponents conclude: "An MAI would provide a better institutional structure with which to reflect the interrelated and complementary nature of investment, trade, services, intellectual property, standards setting, competition policy and related 'domestic' policies, all of which have become key determinants in the international contestability of markets."[41]

The argument for FDI is really the contention that unimpeded market forces offer direct benefits to host countries. TNCs are the source of technical and social progress in a globalized world. This result, of course, depends upon the absence of market failures such as externalities, research and development spread effects, non-monopolistic market structures, linked investments, and so on. All of these types of technological and institutional capacity-building have depended upon industrial policy-making, especially the political capacity to enforce TNC performance requirements and to review and even prohibit market access.

There is even less guarantee that the investment that does take place will be of the type that addresses any kind of social and democratic prioritizing of needs. Only in the idealized view of TNCs, legitimate shepherds of the development process, can the limitations that an MAI imposes be justified.

There are few grounds for claims about the global allocational efficiency of liberalized investment flows. Instead of capital flowing into long-term productive investment in the South, the debt crisis of the early 1980s combined with monetarism and tax cuts in the North to produce capital flight out of long-term lending to the South to finance consumption and the upwards redistribution of wealth in the developed countries of the North. Such misallocation is in fact a more common feature of deregulated markets than neoclassical economists concede, as investors' 'herd instincts' can lead flows to become cumulative rather than stabilizing.

Global capital flows have recently produced disastrous flights of short-term and long-term capital in Mexico and East Asia. These forms of 'investor uncertainty' go far deeper than the risks of 'expropriation' or 'discrimination' that MAI advocates warn. The source of investor uncertainty lies in the asymmetries in the world economy that have massively increased the risk (the rational basis for the irrational growth in hedge markets, and so on) and severed any strict relation between capital flows and allocative efficiency. FDI raises these risks by committing in the long term a significant portion of the payments balance to capital outflows through eventual profit repatriation. Thus, FDI may well add to present destabilizing elements in the world economy.

The second claim that liberalization will be equalizing historically only holds for the advanced industrial countries and fails to explain the persistence of world inequalities.

More recently, the growth of FDI and liberalization of FDI flows have coincided with increasing global inequality, including greater impoverishment of the poorest. According to UNCTAD, the richest 20% of the world's population increased its share of world income from 69% in 1965 to 83% in 1990.[42] Per capita income among the richest quintile averaged 31 times that of the poorest; by 1990 it had reached a factor of 60.

The growing inequality during this period of liberalisization extends to inequalities *between* countries and *within* rich and poor countries, as well. When one considers that 98% of world FDI comes from TNCs based in 23 OECD countries, and is in fact reinvested in this zone, there is good reason to be skeptical about the equalizing tendencies of financial liberalization, including that of the MAI.

The 'deep integration' proposed by MAI investment liberalization is, finally, likely to be destabilizing. The interaction between trade balances, national demand conditions and increasing economies of scale from investment in advanced technologies reinforces patterns of relative economic strength and weakness. The persistent world inequalities stem from this tendency, as "existing

TABLE 9

INCOME INEQUALITY SINCE 1970 BY REGION

Region	Number of Countries	Gini Coefficient in per cent			Ratio of Richest Quintile to Poorest		
		1970-1979	1980-1989	1990-1994	1979-1979	1980-1989	1990-1994
Developed Market-Economy Countries	12	31.60	32.02	32.78	5.59	5.56	6.02
Transition Economies							
Eastern Europe	4	22.34	22.94	27.85	3.09	3.13	4.05
Russian Federation			26.40	30.53			5.08
China			31.51	36.20		4.74	6.10
Developing Countries							
Latin America	10	49.86	51.39		14.46	15.58	
East Asia	7	41.08	40.98		8.29	8.20	
Sub-Saharan Africa	10			44.64			9.52
North Africa	4			38.03			6.57
South Asia	2	31.06	31.73	31.28	4.56	4.71	4.63

Source: UNCTAD, Trade and Development Report, 1997, p. 108.

advantages are reinforced and the resulting spatial distribution of economic activity is likely to exhibit strong divergences, leading to increasing inequalities within and between regions."[43]

The tendency is the reverse for deficit countries which are compelled to adjust by deflating and use their price advantage in a liberal trading environment to export their way to economic advance. But, with slow output growth, global overcapacity and the fact that the richest and largest economy in the world capable of absorbing imports must also begin running a surplus to pay off the largest buildup in sovereign debt ever make this a precarious proposition. The threat to transmit deflation around the world is now an active concern, even among the backers of liberalization.[44]

As under the gold standard, deregulated capital flows and bond rating agencies are the anonymous disciplinary agents enforcing deflationary regulation of economic policy. Investment liberalization encourages the vicious interaction of austerity and polarization: it strengthens the capacity of firms to invest internationally and, through competition to capture investment, to engage in competitive bargaining over taxes and wages (a process well understood by the architects of post-war order capital controls).[45]

This also explains why lower wage countries in the South, with lower labour and environmental standards, are seeking to avoid having their 'competitive advantages' prohibited by the inclusion of labour and environmental standards in the WTO or the MAI. By casting a 'chill' on government reflationary or redistributive interventions, the MAI would further enforce the fiscal austerity and monetary tightening of the past decade around competition for investment. Indeed, as external financing in the form of private financial flows continues to account for a significant proportion of capital formation and to claim a larger portion of payments balances, the liberalization of investment flows will carry potentially greater consequences as national and economies become more and more dependent on an uncertain and competitive international situation. By entrenching investor rights and fully deregulating short-term and long-term flows, the MAI makes the world economy more unstable and uncertain.

Open-Economy Social Democracy

The failures of neo-liberalism have led many to become skeptical of the panacea of globalization. However, confusion around what medium and long-term alternatives there might be to global neo-liberalism is equally pervasive. Just as Keynes observed in 1933, there is a growing feeling today that—

> *...decadent international but individualistic capitalism...is not a success. It is not intelligent, it is not beautiful, it is not just, it is not virtuous—and it doesn't deliver the goods. In short, we dislike it and we are beginning to despise it. But when we wonder what to put in its place, we are extremely perplexed.*[46]

Opposition to neo-liberal globalization is certainly building everywhere. But what might replace it remains an exacting question.

For one strand of left critics, globalization represents a 'world market of opportunities' in which domestic prosperity and international capital mobility are mutually reinforcing. Hirst and Thompson, for example, argue that "free trade, in combination with the management of investment, offers the best prospect for promoting growth through fairer redistribution."[47] Investment regulations such as the UN *Draft Code of Conduct on TNCs*, which epitomize an outdated era in which TNCs were viewed as "exploiters and a threat to national economic autonomy," need to be replaced by a regulatory regime able to realize mutual gains from global capital mobility. Such an accord "would avoid 'beggar-my-neighbour' policies, first by governments in terms of their competitive attempts to attract FDI, and second by firms in their attempts to try to play one country off against another."[48]

In addition to setting out the property rights of TNCs, such an agreement would protect labour rights and working conditions, and "recognize the rights of government to defend certain of their legitimate national functions in respect to the economy— support for R&D, defence considerations, balance of payments issues, etc."[49]

Precisely because the tendency of international investment to exacerbate inequalities within and between regions threatens to undermine growth, Kozul-Wright similarly argues that "the full benefits of international integration require a complementary and robust framework of social agreements and constraints—including strong nation states—to resolve problems generated in production and to manage distributional conflicts."[50]

Above all else, this 'open-economy social democracy' viewpoint is concerned to preserve governance functions that facilitate accumulation within legislative frameworks of minimal social provision. It devotes little attention to strengthening the ability of democratic authorities to constrain capital, a view that they would no doubt charge with anachronistic "hostility" and "antagonism" towards TNCs, as if capitalist agencies had suddenly become merely efficient organizations of social progress apart from the economic stagnation and social inequalities that have been growing.[51]

In this strategy, there is no conception of conflicting interests that involve power and struggle between the objectives of private accumulation and of democratic provision for social need. The revisionist naiveté of such arguments is alarming in a period where capital mobility and threats of capital strikes are regularly being invoked to overturn redistributional policies. The capacity to determine social priorities is being displaced, through trade liberalization in general and investor-protection proposals like the MAI in particular, from democratic deliberation and coordination of economic activities to the ability of the state to supply profit-enhancing inducements to capitalists, national and foreign, to invest and hopefully to then be taxed. But why floors on these inducements should not be eroded by mobile capital—especially as states compete to provide competitive investment locales, if there are no direct constraints placed on capital—is left unexplained. This is ultimately the view that there are forms of 'progressive competitiveness' where social partnerships can be struck between workers and capitalists, national and foreign, that advance a general interest apart from class divisions.

A more common Left critique is far less naive about the obstacles that TNCs pose to social priorities that conflict with the logic of the market, and some of the power issues at stake. An alternative investment treaty to the MAI is needed, it is argued, that protects redistributional goals against the deterioration of public goods and the environment from commodification and social dumping. The alternative, possibly fashioned around the 1974 UN Charter of Economic Rights and Duties of States, would begin by recognizing and protecting the sovereign right of states to regulate investment in the 'national interest'.[52]

Explicitly raising performance requirements for corporations around employment, labour adjustment, and the environment would be complemented by a tighter competition policy that restricted corporate concentration (especially via foreign acquisitions of Canadian companies) and speculative activity. Although often ambiguous on this point, some form of international agreement on capital controls and profit repatriation is also often sought, as for example in the endorsation of the Tobin Tax on currency trading. This perspective is clear, if not always forthright enough about where contemporary social democracy is placed, in the political opposition and mobilization necessary to install these provisions into any multilateral investment agreement.

This critique has a number of limitations, however. Strategically, social forces attempting to rein in capital are better placed to be effective organizing on national and local levels rather than the international level, where the political base to mobilize pressure for constraints on capital are stronger. Politics remain principally national rather than supranational, and, without strong national bases of support, the scope for re-regulating capital at the international level, and forming a wider and necessary internationalist politics, is limited.

In the absence of national and local movements, side agreements on environmental and labour standards contained in international trade deals will remain marginal and weak protection against the imperatives of capitalist competition and economic internationalization, if the NAFTA side-agreements are at all indicative.[53]

International solidarity and pressure for regulation is a crucial and effective part of confronting globalization. But it is most effectively organized as stemming from strong national and local efforts to control and shape market processes. Local communities and nation-states have historically permitted workers the means, through struggle and political mobilization, to impose social and political controls on the logic of capitalist accumulation, thereby improving working conditions and extending some limited measure of democracy into the economic sphere.[54] As Bienefeld has noted,

> *...history has demonstrated the importance of the nation state as the one arena within which it has occasionally been possible to harness and channel the explosive but volatile and potentially de-*

> *structive power of the market...The absence of a plausible global alternative implies that national controls over capital must remain the most important immediate object of struggle.*[55]

International effectiveness is therefore a reflection of the balance of social forces within local and national bases. Only until significant opposition is mounted in a significant number of local and national settings can the balance of power be shifted.[56]

However, allowing capital mobility and international competitiveness to determine the value-formation process, while imposing performance requirements on transnationals and limits on the downward levelling of competition, contains a more basic contradiction. To begin with, the internationalization of production has provided the ammunition for the <u>attack</u> on national controls on capital. With capital mobility preserved, domestic welfare goals such as employment and redistribution can be met only to the extent competitiveness is secured.

Yet floors placed under competition by international agreements will always be at risk in a world of massive inequalities and labour surpluses. Burdened by debt or plagued with faltering competitiveness, it will always be in the interest of some countries to exploit their 'comparative advantage' of surplus labour or lax environmental protection. Insofar as the imperative of competitiveness and rapid export-led growth is preserved, so is the incentive for states to remove restrictions on competition, precisely in the interests of employment and income.

The *threat* of mobility of investment is frequently sufficient to extract concessions from defensive workers and unions, leaving aside the actual capacity of firms to shift production activity. Facilitating the expansion of production on an international scale preserves the external orientation of national economies, maintains the dependence of national economies on private decision-making, and sustains the terrain of operation from which capital can whipsaw governments and labour forces.

3. BEYOND THE MAI

After two decades of freer markets and policies, neo-liberal globalization continues to strip away the limited stabilizing and redistributive structures of state regulation built up over the post-war period, without constructing any stable institutional order in its place. This threatens to reinforce and aggravate the relationship between greater inequality, slower growth, and financial instability. Far from being inevitable or desirable, therefore, global neoliberalism is looking increasingly *unsustainable* economically, socially, and environmentally.

The deep-seated contradictions of the present volatile and polarized world economy point to the need to encompass opposition to the MAI within a broader strategy of confronting globalism. The ability to impose performance requirements on TNCs will be of limited value in reversing the downward pressures of globalization if they must be restricted to measures promoting competitiveness; labour standards enshrined at the international level will be weak if states and firms—and workers themselves—are under constant pressure to ignore them.

Entrenching property and mobility rights for corporations undermines labour and other groups, not by weakening the state, but by diminishing the political space from which to impose democratic priorities on capital. Globalization, even in the shape of the MAI, is not so much a threat to <u>state</u> sovereignty as it is to <u>popular</u> sovereignty in the form of substantive capacities to democratically coordinate economic activities and enforce egalitarian measures. For this reason, the restructuring of the state in response to the internationalization of capital, the problem of envisaging and pursuing a more democratic state is more pressing than ever, if we are to break the impasse of seeking international guarantees for regulatory powers that political éltes and capitalist classes are doing their utmost to rid themselves of.

Expanding the scale of democracy will require reimposing controls on capital, redirecting production, re-establishing the credibility of public ownership, reversing the polarization of work and income, and fashioning institutions and industrial strategies to develop workers' skills and democratic capabilities.

At present, it is difficult to envisage institutions existing at the international level that might be capable of subordinating capitalist power to democratic decision-making apart from strong local and national movements.[57] The construction of these institutions is daunting. Yet market liberalization measures like the MAI that continue to strengthen unaccountable private power have placed the building of democratic institutions adequate to a more egalitarian and sustainable society more firmly on the agenda.

ENDNOTES

1 *World Development Report 1997: The State in a Changing World* (Washington: The Bank, 1997), p. 133.

2 See several of the essays gathered in P. Sauve and D. Schwanen, eds., *Investment Rules for the Global Economy: Enhancing Access to Markets* (Toronto: C.D. Howe Research Institute, 1996).

3 OECD, Negotiating Group on the Multilateral Agreement on Investment, *Multilateral Agreement on Investment: Consolidated Text and Commentary* (Paris: OECD, October 1997), p. 8. Available from http://web.uvic.ca/german/ /hendrik/mai-1097.txt.

4 *Ibid.*, pp. 8-9.

5 D. Gordon, "The Global Economy: New Edifice, or Crumbling Foundations?" *New Left Review*, 168 (1988), p. 25.

6 For a discussion see: G. Arrighi, *The Long Twentieth Century* (London: Verso, 1994), Ch. 1.

7 The organizational history of this process is recounted most famously by business historian A.. Chandler, Jr., *The Visible Hand* (Cambridge, Mass.: Belknap Press, 1977).

8 G. Epstein, "International Financial Integration and Full Employment Monetary Policy," *Review of Political Economy*, 7:2 (1995).

9 A. Lipietz, *Mirages and Miracles* (London: Verso, 1987), p. 41.

10 K. Polanyi, *The Great Transformation* (Boston: Beacon Press, 1957).

11 This point has been made, with different strategic conclusions, in: D. Harvey, "The Geography of Class Power," in L. Panitch and C. Leys, eds., *Socialist Register 1998: The Communist Manifesto Now* (London: Merlin, 1998); and M. Lebowitz, "Trade and Class: Labour Strategies in a World of Strong Capital," *Studies in Political Economy*, 27 (1988). To be sure, in different his-

torical conjunctures the nation-state has mediated and authored the internationalization of capital as well as facilitating domestic accumulation. But, as is argued below, precisely because of its role as steward of the globalization process itself, the state continues to afford strategically the most crucial site for struggles to constrain capital and the centrifugal effects of competition.

12 R. Zevin, "Are World Financial Markets More Open? If So, Why and With What Effects?" in T. Banuri and J.B. Schor, eds., *Financial Openness and National Autonomy* (Oxford: Clarendon Press, 1992); and J. Williamson, "Globalization, Convergence, and History," *Journal of Economic History* 56:2 (1996).

13 R. Kozul-Wright and P. Bairoch, *Globalization Myths: Some Historical Reflections On Integration Industrialization and Growth in the World Economy* (Geneva: UNCTAD Discussion Paper N. 113, March 1996), pp. 5-6, 11.

14 *Ibid.*

15 G. Laxer, *Open For Business* (Don Mills: Oxford University Press, 1989), pp. 42-3; and A. Maddison, *Monitoring the World Economy, 1820-1992* (Paris: OECD, 1995), p. 22.

16 M. Kitson and J. Michie, "Depression and Recovery: Lessons from the Interwar Period," in J. Michie and J. Grieve Smith, eds., *Unemployment in Europe* (London: Academic Press, 1994).

17 Lipetz, *Mirages and Miracles*, p. 39.

18 Armstrong et al., *Capitalism Since 1945*, Ch. 8; and M. Kitson and J. Michie, "Trade and Growth: A Historical Perspective," in J. Michie and J. Grieve Smith, eds., *Managing the Global Economy* (Oxford: Oxford University Press, 1995).

19 P. Giussani, "Empirical Evidence for Trends Towards Globalization," *International Journal of Political Economy*, 26:3 (1996), p. 19.

20 J. Crotty and G. Epstein, "In Defence of Capital Controls," in L. Panitch, (ed.) *Socialist Register 1996: Are There Alternatives?* (London: Merlin, 1996).

21 J. Kregel, "Capital Flows: Globalization of Production and Financing Development," *UNCTAD Review 1994*, p. 24.

22 S. Hymer and R. Rowthorn, "Multinational Corporations and International Oligopoly: The Non-American Challenge," in C. Kindleberger, ed., *The International Corporation* (Cambridge, Mass.: MIT, 1970); and R. Kozul-Wright, "Transnational Corporations and the Nation State," in J. Michie and J. Grieve Smith, eds., *Managing the Global Economy* (Oxford: University Press, 1995), p. 146..

23 E. Helleiner, "Explaining the Globalization of Financial Markets: Bringing States Back In," *Review of International Political Economy* , 2:2 (1995).

24 25. Armstrong, et al., *Capitalism Since 1945*, p. 234.

25 Armstrong, et al., *Capitalism Since 1945*, pp. 237-39.

26 A. Glyn, "The Costs of Stability: The Advanced Capitalist Countries in the 1980s," *New Left Review*, 195 (1992).

27 J. Perraton, D. Goldblatt, D. Held and A. McGrew, "The Globalisation of Economic Activity," *New Political Economy* , 2:2 (1997), p. 265.

28 M. Webber and D. Rigby, *The Golden Age Illusion* (New York: Guilford Press, 1996), p. 31.

29 A. Boltho, "The Return of Free Trade?" *International Affairs*, 72:2 (1996).
30 Perraton, et al., "The Globalisation of Economic Activity," p. 261.
31 H. Scoffield, "Agreement Opens World Financial Services Markets," *Toronto Globe and Mail*, 15 December 1997.
32 UNCTAD, *World Investment Report 1997* (Geneva: UNCTAD, 1997), p. xv; and R. Rowthorn, "Manufacturing in the World Economy," *Economie Appliquée*, tome L, 4 (1997), p. 92.
33 UNCTAD, *World Investment Report 1997*, pp. xv-xvi.
34 See: S. Lall, "TNCs: The New Custodians of Development?" in R. Culpeper, A. Berry and F. Stewart, eds., *Global Development Fifty Years after Bretton Woods* (London: Macmillan Press, 1997).
35 Webber and Rigby, *The Golden Age Illusion*, p. 33.
36 P. Hirst and G. Thompson, *Globalization in Question* (Cambridge: Polity, 1996).
37 Perraton, et al., "The Globalisation of Economic Activity," p. 263.
38. K. van der Pijl, "Neoliberalism versus Planned Interdependence: Concepts of Control and the Struggle for Hegemony," in J.N. Rosenau and H. Tromp, eds., *Interdependence and Conflict in World Politics* (Aldershot: Avebury, 1989).
39 ILO, *World Employment Report 1996/97* (Geneva: ILO, 1997), p. xiii.
40 Kregel, "Capital Flows," p. 27.
41 A. Rugman and M. Gestrin, "A Conceptual Framework for a Multilateral Agreement on Investment," in Sauve and Schaweren, eds., *Investment Rules for the Global Economy*, p. 172.
42 UNCTAD, *Trade and Development Report, 1997*, p. 81.
43. Kozul-Wright adds: "in a world where history is continuously present in the contemporary structures and strategies of firms, where corporate rivalry is inherent in the dynamics of production and competition, and where the spatial distribution of economic activity reflects the complex interdependencies of firms, states, and market exchanges, TNCs are not a neutral conduit for the efficient allocation of capital, technology, and know-how guided by an invisible hand. Equally, the growing importance of FDI, no more than expanding trade flows, does not harbour a global equilibrium path." See: "Transnational Corporations and the Nation State," pp. 138-39.
44. M. Mandel, "The Threat of Deflation," *Business Week*, 10 November 1997; and M. Wolf, "The Threat of Deflation," *Financial Times*, 24 February 1998.
45. J. Crotty, "On Keynes and Capital Flight," *Journal of Economic Literature* 21 (1983); and E. Helleiner, "Explaining the Globalization of Financial Markets."
46 J.M. Keynes, "National Self-Sufficiency," *The Yale Review* (Summer 1933). Reprinted in D. Moggridge, ed., *The Collected Writings of John Maynard Keynes*, Vol. 21 (London: Macmillan, 1982), p. 239.
47 Hirst and Thompson, *Globalization in Question*, p. 52.
48 *Ibid.*, p. 73.
49 *Ibid.*, pp. 73-4.
50 Kozul-Wright, "Transnational Corporations and the Nation State," p. 136.
51 Hirst and Thompson, *Globalization in Question*, p. 73.
52 T. Clarke and M. Barlow, *MAI: The Multilateral Agreement on Investment and the Threat to Canadian Sovereignty* (Toronto: Stoddart, 1997), Ch. 8.

53 S. Silcoff, "Environmental Commission a Disaster, NAFTA Critics Say," *Toronto Globe and Mail*, 29 July 1996.

54 M. Bienefeld, "In Defence of Nationalism as a Trade Union Perspective," in R. Southall, ed., *Trade Unions and the New Industrialisation of the Third World* (London: Zed, 1988), p. 336.

55 *Ibid.*, p. 336.

56 S. Gindin, "Notes on Labour at the End of the Century: Starting Over?" *Monthly Review*, 49:3 (1997).

57 See: L. Panitch, "Globalisation and the State," in R.Miliband and L. Panitch, eds., *Socialist Register 1994: Between Globalism and Nationalism* (London: Merlin, 1994); and Albo, "A World Market of Opportunities?"

NGO STATEMENT ON THE MAI

Endorsed by 565 Organizations in 68 Countries

INTRODUCTION

As a coalition of development, environment, human rights, labour, consumer and women's groups from around the world, with representation in over 70 countries, we consider the draft Multilateral Agreement on Investment (MAI) to be a damaging agreement which should not proceed in its current form, if at all.

There is an obvious need for multilateral regulation of investments in view of the scale of social and environmental disruption created by the increasing mobility of capital. However, the intention of the MAI is not to regulate investments but to regulate governments. As such, the MAI is unacceptable.

MAI negotiations have been conducted without the benefit of participation from non-OECD countries and civil society, including non-governmental organizations representing the interests of workers, consumers, farmers or organizations concerned with the environment, development and human rights.

As a result, the draft MAI is completely unbalanced. It elevates the rights of investors far above those of governments, local communities, citizens, workers, and the environment. The MAI will severely undermine even the meagre progress made towards sustainable development since the Rio Earth Summit in 1992.

The MAI is not only flawed in the eyes of NGOs, but conflicts with international commitments already made by OECD member countries.

The MAI fails to incorporate any of the several relevant international agreements, such as the Rio Declaration; Agenda 21; UN Guidelines for Consumer Protection (1985); the UNCTAD Set of Multilaterally Agreed Principles for the Control of Restrictive Business Practices (1981); the Beijing Declaration on Women; and the HABITAT Global Plan of Action.

The MAI fails to comply with OECD commitments to integrate economic, environmental and social policies (1).

The MAI removes responsibilities on transnational enterprises which were previously agreed by the OECD under the OECD Guidelines for Multilateral Enterprises 1976 (2).

The exclusion of developing countries and countries in transition from the negotiations is inconsistent with OECD policy on development partnerships (3).

Problems with the MAI stem both from the broad restrictions it places on national democratic action, and from its failure to include sufficient new systems of international regulation and accountability.

As the MAI stands, it does not deserve to gain democratic approval in any country. All the groups signing this statement will campaign against its adoption unless changes, including those cited below, are incorporated into the body of the MAI.

SUBSTANTIVE CONCERNS

As drafted, the MAI does not respect the rights of countries—in particular, countries in transition and developing countries—including their need to democratically control investment into their economies.

The level of liberalization contained in the MAI has already been opposed as inappropriate by many developing countries. However, non-OECD countries are under increasing pressure to join.

There are differing investment and development needs of OECD and non-OECD countries. In particular, the potential for economic diversification and development of the developing countries—especially the least developed countries—and countries in transition would be severely undermined by the provisions of the MAI. The standstill principle would cause particular problems for countries in transition, many of which have not yet developed adequate business regulation.

The MAI's withdrawal provision would effectively bind nations to one particular economic development model for 15 years; prevent future governments from revising investment policy to reflect their own assessment of the wisest economic course; and force countries to continue to abide by the agreement even if there is strong evidence that its impact has been destructive.

The MAI contains no binding, enforceable obligations for corporate conduct concerning the environment, labour standards and anti-competitive behaviour. The MAI gives foreign investors exclusive standing under a legally binding agreement to attack legitimate regulations designed to protect the environment, safeguard public health, uphold the rights of employees, and promote fair competition.

Further, citizens, indigenous peoples, local governments and NGOs do not have access to the dispute resolution system, and subsequently can neither hold multinational investors accountable to the communities which host them, nor comment in cases where an investor sues a government.

The MAI will be in conflict with many existing and future international, national and sub-national laws and regulations protecting the environment, natural resources, public health, culture, social welfare and employment laws; will cause many to be repealed; and will deter the adoption of new legislation, or the strengthening of existing ones.

The MAI is explicitly designed to make it easier for investors to move capital, including production facilities, from one country to another, despite evidence that increased capital mobility disproportionately benefits multinational corporations at the expense of most of the world's peoples.

WE CALL ON THE OECD AND NATIONAL GOVERNMENTS TO:

With regard to substantive concerns:

1) Undertake an independent and comprehensive assessment of the social, environmental, and development impact of the MAI with full public participation. The negotiations should be suspended during this assessment.
2) Require multinational investors to observe binding agreements incorporating environment, labour, health, safety and human rights standards to ensure that they do not use the MAI to exploit weak regulatory regimes. Ensure that an enforceable agreement on investor responsibilities takes precedence over any agreement on investor rights.
3) Eliminate the investor state dispute resolution mechanism and put into place democratic and transparent mechanisms which ensure that civil society, including local and indigenous peoples, gain new powers to hold investors to account.
4) While none of the undersigned NGOs object to the rights of investors to be compensated for expropriation by a nation state, there are adequate principles of national law and jurisprudence to protect investors in circumstances such as these. The current MAI exceeds these well-accepted concepts of direct expropriation, and ventures into areas undermining national sovereignty. We therefore request that OECD members eliminate the MAI's expropriation provision so that investors are not granted an absolute right to compensation for expropriation. Governments must ensure that they do not have to pay for the right to set environmental, labour, health and safety standards even if compliance with such regulations imposes significant financial obligations on investors.

With regard to process concerns:

1) Suspend the MAI negotiations and extend the 1998 deadline to allow sufficient time for meaningful public input and participation in all countries.
2) Increase transparency in the negotiations by publicly releasing the draft texts and individual reservations and by scheduling a series of ongoing public meetings and hearings in both member and non-member countries, open to the media, parliamentarians, and the general public.
3) Broaden the active participation of government departments in the official negotiations beyond state, commerce and finance to a broader range of government agencies, ministries and parliamentary committees.
4) Renegotiate the terms of withdrawal to enable countries to more easily and rapidly withdraw from the agreement when they deem it in the interest of their citizens. Developing countries and countries in transition which have not been a party to the negotiations must not be pressured to join the MAI.

Conclusion

The current MAI text is inconsistent with international agreements signed by OECD countries, with existing OECD policies, and with national laws to promote sustainable development. It also fails to take into account important work carried out by investment experts and official bodies such as the UNCTAD "development friendliness" criteria for investmentagreements (4) and other work on investor responsibility.

If the OECD policy statements are to have any meaning, the above provisions must be fully integrated in the MAI with the same legal force as those on economic liberalization.

Given our grave concerns about the MAI and the unrealistically short time frame within which the MAI is being concluded, we look to the OECD and its member governments to fundamentally reconsider both the process and substance of the draft agreement. We call on the OECD to make a specific and detailed written response to our concerns. We also call on the OECD to avoid talking publicly about its consultations with NGOs without also talking about the serious concerns raised at those consultations.

Finally, we will continue our opposition to the MAI unless these demands are met in full.

Endnotes

[1] OECD Ministerial Communique May 1997
[2] OECD Code of Conduct for Multinational Enterprises, Paris 1992
[3] "Shaping the 21st Century: The Contribution of Development Cooperation", OECD 1997.
4 UNCTAD, World Investment Report 1997; UNCTAD Expert Meeting "Development Friendliness Criteria for Investment Frameworks," 1997.

Non-Governmental Organizations supporting this statement include:

Argentina:
- Friends of the Earth Argentina

Australia:
- AID/Watch
- Australia Greens
- Australian Conservation Foundation
- Australian Coalition for Economic Justice
- Australian Health and Development Group
- Australians for Animals
- Children South Australian MAI Community Awareness Campaign Southern Women's Group
- Friends of the Earth Australia
- Mineral Policy Institute
- National Council of Single Mothers and their Children
- Public Health Association
- South Australian MAI Community Awareness Campaign
- Southern Women's Group, Inc.
- TOES Australia Economic Reform
- Urban Ecology Australia
- Women's International and Referral Exchange, Inc.

Austria:
- Alternate and Green Syndicat
- Arbeitsgemeinschaft Entwicklungszusammenarbeit
- Austrian Anti-Nuclear NGO

Basis Initiative Nawi Gruene (BING)
Beirat fuer gesellschafts-, wirtschaffs-und unweltpolitsche
Bitte um Bestatigung unter
Commission Internationale pour la protection des Alpes (CIPRA)
Encounter Center for Active Non-Violence
Friends of the Earth Austria
Gewerkschaftlicher Linksblock (GLB)
Green Party of Austria
Komm Ent
OEIE-Kaernten
Sandwind-Agentur Vorarlberg
Southern Austrian Documentation and Cooperation Centre

Bangladesh:
Friends of the Earth Bangladesh
Ubinig

Belarussia:
Belarussian Division of International Academy of Ecology

Belgium:
Centre de Recherche e d'information des Organisations de Consummateurs
European Environmental Bureau
National Centre for Development Cooperation

Bosnia Herzegovina:
Bosnian Environmental Technologies Association

Brazil:
Assoceatia F.G. Guidotti for Studies and Nature Conservation
Associacao para Projetos de Combate a Fome
Brazillian Institute of Economic and Social Analysis (IBASE)
Fundacao Francisco
Fundacao CEBRAC
Global Forum on Sustainable Food and Nutritional Society
IBASE
Institute for Southern Minas Gerais for Studies and Nature Conservation
NGO World Ideas Network
Rede Dia Mundial da Alimento
Science Club 11th August

Bulgaria:
Centre for Environmental Information & Education
MAR - Bulgaria Youth Alliance for Development
Za Zemiata

Canada:
Albernai Environmental Coalition
Alliance for Public Accountability
Antigonish Coalition for Economic Justice
The Area Clamdiggers Association
B.C. Green Party
Borrowers' Advocate
Calancan Bay Villagers' Support Coalition

Canadian Association for the Study of Adult Education Peace Group
Canadian Catholic Organization for Development & Peace
Canadian Centre for Policy Alternatives
Canadian Consortium for International Social Development
Canadian Council for International Cooperation
Canadian Environmental Law Association
Canadian Environmental Networks
Canadian Institute for Environmental Law and Policy
Canadian Labour Congress
Canadian Parks and Wilderness Society
Canadian Union of Public Employees
Canadian Voice for Women and Peace
Costa Rica Saskatchewan Twinning Project
Council of Canadians
Council of Canadians - B.C. Chapter
Council of Canadians - Cowichan Valley Chapter
Council of Canadians - Mid-Island Vancouver Chapter
Council of Canadians - Montreal Chapter
Distributed Knowledge Project
Earth Rainbow Network
Eco-Materials Group
Enviro Clove
Falls Brook Centre
Federation Nationale des Associations de Consommateurs du Quebec
Friends of Temagami
The GAIA Project
Georgia Strait Alliance
Global Compliance Research Project
Greenpeace Canada
Greenways Committee
Guideposts for a Sustainable Future
The Halifax Initiative, which includes:
- CCIC
- Inter-Church Coalition on Africa
- Oxfam-Canada
- Results-Canada
- Social Justice Committee of Montreal
- Sierra Club of Canada
- Toronto Environmental Alliance
- World Inter-Action Mondiale

Indonesia - Canada Alliance
Inter-Church Committee on Human Rights in Latin America
Island Natural Growers
Lifecycles Project Society
Malaspina Students Union Local 61, Canadian Federation of Students
Manitoba MAI Awareness Coalition
Manitoba Federation of Labour
Manitoba Future Forest Alliance

Montreal Raging Grannies
Nanoose Conversion Campaign
National Action Committee on the Status of Women
The New Democratic Party Opposition
Nipissing Environmental Watch
North Island Students Association
Northwatch
North-South Institute
Nova Scotia Public Interest Research Group
Nova Scotia Voice of Women
Ocean Voice International
Ottawa Local Employment and Trading System
OPIRG - Ottawa
OPIRG - Carleton
Pacific Institute
Polaris Institute
Power River Greenways
The Powell River Regional District
Quality of Life Network
Reach for Unbleached Foundation
Rogers Environmental and Educational Foundation
Saskatchewan Environmental Society
Saskatoon Chapter of Council of Canadians
Sierra Club of Canada
Sierra Youth Coalition
Solution to Pollution
Turtle Island Earth Stewards
West Coast Environmental Law Association
Western Canada Wilderness Committee
The Windsor Arena MAI-Day Coalition
The Windsor Chapter of the Council of Canadians
Women's International League for Peace and Freedom
The World Federalists of Canada
World Interaction Mondiale
University of British Columbia MAI-Not Group
University of Victoria Students' Society

Chile:
Centro de Estudios Uruguayo de Tecnologas Apropriadas
Friends of the Earth Chile

Costa Rica:
Friends of the Earth Costa Rica

Croatia:
Green Osijek
Oasis

Czech Republic:
Institute for Environmental Policy
Hnuti Duha/Friends of the Earth Czech Republic

CURACAO:
Friends of the Earth Curacao
DENMARK:
Friends of the Earth Denmark
EL SALVADOR:
Friends of the Earth El Salvador
EGYPT:
Eco-Peace - Middle East Environmental NGO Forum
ESTONIA:
Tartu Student Nature Protection Group
EUROPE:
AEDENAT
A SEED Europe
Central and Eastern European Bankwatch Network
Climate Network Europe
Women in Development Europe (WIDE)
FINLAND:
Finnish Association for Nature Conservation
Friends of the Earth Finland
FRANCE:
Ecoropa-France
Friends of the Earth France
Helio International
GERMANY:
Alliance 90/the Greens
Friends of the Earth Germany
Germanwatch North-South Initiative
Germanwatch
Heinrich Boll Foundation
Initiative bessere Zukunft
Kairos Europe
Southwind Agency
Urgewald
World Economy, Ecology and Development Association (WEED)
GREECE:
Association of Social and Ecological Intervention
GRENADA:
Friends of the Earth Grenada
HAITI:
Friends of the Earth Haiti
HUNGARY:
Egyetemes Letezes Teremeszetvedelmi Egyesulet (ETK)
For the Danube' Association
Hungarian Traffic Club
National Society of Conservationists
INDIA:
Alliance for Secular and Democratic South Asia

Bombay Environmental Action Group
Consumer Unity & Trust Society (CUTS)
Dahanu Taluka Environmental Welfare Association
International Study for Gandhian Studies
Lokayan
People's Alliance for Implementation of the Law (PAIL)
The Tamilnadu Peoples Forum for Social Development

Indonesia:
Friends of the Earth Indonesia

International:
Association for Sustainability & Equity in the Americas
Forum Environment and Development
Friends of the Earth International (FoEI)
Global Action Plan
Global Help Project
Greenpeace International
Guideposts for a Sustainable Future
ICDA
NABU
Pacific Environment & Resources Center
People-Centered Development Forum
Third World Network
Witness for Peace
Women's International League for Peace and Freedom (WILPF)
Women's Environment & Development Organisation (WEDO)
World Wide Fund for Nature International (WWF-I)
World Information Transfer

Ireland:
An Talamh Glas
Friends of the Earth Ireland

Israel:
Eco-Peace - Middle East Environmental NGO Forum
Shatil

Italy:
Associazone Proiezione Peters
Associazone per la Pace - Pordenone
Campaign Globalizzazione
Centro Nuovo Modello di Sviluppo
Centro Internazionale Crocevia
Cooperativa Itaca- Pordenone
CTM-Movimondo
Fondaziane Internazialelio Basso per i diritti Tribunale Permanente del Popoli
Friends of the Earth Italy
Greenpeace Italy
IDOC International
Mani Tese
Reform the World Bank Campaign
Service Civil International

World Wildlife Fund

JAPAN:

APEC Monitor NGO Network
Baraban Heritage Society
Blue Sky Network
Friends of the Earth Japan
International Peoples Health Council
Institute for Alternative Community Development
Japan Tropical Forest Action Network
Kansai NGO Council
Network Earth Village'
Osaka YMCA
Pacific Asia Resource Center
People's Forum 2001

JORDAN:

Eco-Peace - Middle East Environmental NGO Forum

KENYA:

Eco-News Africa
Economic and Social Policy Initiatives
Environment Liason Centre International
National Council to Combat Desertification

LATVIA:

Association for a Different Europe
Environmental Protection Club

LITHUANIA:

Friends of the Earth Lithuania
Lithuania Green Movement

LUXEMBOURG:

Friends of the Earth Luxembourg

MACEDONIA:

Center for Civic Initiatives
Friends of the Earth Macedonia

MALAYSIA:

Friends of the Earth Malaysia

MAURITANIA:

Maudesco
Small Farmers Movement

MEXICO:

Accion para la Democracia
Accion Ciudadana de Sonora
Accion Estrategica y Pastoral(SPAN)
Alianza Vallesana
Alianza Cuidadana Ambientalista A.C.
Alimentos, Medicinas y Equipos para la Paz A.C.
Asesores para el Avance Social
Campo de Oaxaca
Centro de Estudios del Campo Mexicana
Centro de Estudios Ecumunicos

Centro de Atencion a la Mujer
Centro de Apoyo al Movimiento Popular Oaxaque
Centro de Integral para Promotir es Comunitanos A.C.
Centro de Investigacion y Asesoria Laboral
Centro de Investigacion y Accion de la Mujer, A.C.
Centro de Ecologia y Desarollo
Centro de Estudios Sociales y Ecologicos
Comision Mexicana para la Defensa y Promocion de los Derechos Humanos
Comite de Derechos Humanos de Tabasco
Convergencia Veracruzana
Convergencia de Organismos Civiles por la Democracia, A.C.
Desarrollo, Ambiente y Sociedad
Educacion, Cultura y Ecologia, A.C.
Equipo Pueblo
Escuela de Capacitacion Civica SLP
Espiral
Federacion de Sindicatos Autenticos de Guanajuato
Frente Civico de Sinaloa
Frente Civico de Acapulco
Frente Autentico del Trabajo
Frente por el Derecho a la Alimentacion
Fronteras Comunes
Gabriel Camara (Personal)
Grupo Ecologista del Mayab A.C.
Grupo de los Cien Internacional
Grupos de Estudios Ambientales A.C.
Indicadores Desarrollo y Analisis (IDEA)
International Federation of Human Rights (LIMEDDH-FIODH)
Intersindical Valle de Mexico
Investigacion y Educacion Popular Autogestiva A.C.
Liga Mexicana por la Defensa de los Derechos Humanos, subsidiary of theMovimiento por la Paz con Justicia y Dignidad
Movimiento Cuidadano por la Democracia
Mujeres sin Fronteras A.C.
Mujeres Comprometidas Con Mexico
Mujeres en Accisn Sindical (MAS) A.C.
Nuevo Amanecer Press
Pacto de Grupos Ecologistas
ProNatura Chiapas A.C.
Red Mexicana de Accion Frente al Libre Comercio (RMALC)
Red Yucateca de Organizaciones
Red Nacional de Organizaciones Ecologistas "Pacto de Grupos Ecologistas"
Red Mexicana de Cabildeo por el Desarrollo
Servicios Informativos Procesados A.C.
Servicios Informacion Procesada
Sindicato de Trabajadores de Elevadores Otis

Sindicato Nacional de Trabajadoras de la Industria del Hierro y el Acero
Sindicato Libertad de Trabajadoras de la Confeccion
Sindicato de Trabajadores de la Industria Metalica, Acero, Hierro, Conexos ye Similares
Sindicato de Trabajadores de la Contruccion 1 de Mayo
Sindicato de Trabajadores de la Industria Textil "Belisario Dominguez"
Sindicato de Trabajadores del Inca Rural
Sindicato Unico de Trabajadores de la Secretaria de Pesca
Sociedad Mexicana de Psicologia Social
Trasparencia
UCISV-Vearacruz, Pobladores A.C.
Union de Productores de Vidrio del Estado de Mexico
Union de Cooperativas Independientes
Union de Ejidos del Distrito de Jimenez Chihuahua
Universidad Autonomo Metropolitana

Moldovia:
Biotica Ecological Society

Nepal:
Forum for Protection of Public Interest
SAWTEE, Kathmandu
SEWA Nepal

Netherlands:
Alternatieve Konsumentenbord
ANPED, Netherlands
BothENDS
Corporate Europe Observatory
De Kleine Aard
Friends of the Earth Netherlands
Greenpeace Netherlands
Health Action International
Infocentrum Wageningen
Institute for Cultural Ecology
Naar Een Ander Europa
Netherlands Committee of the IUCN
Tools for Transition, Netherlands
Towards a Different Europe
Women in Europe for a Common Future
Women for Peace International
Women's Party
Working Group for a Feminist Group

New Zealand:
Fair Deal Coalition
Friends of the Earth New Zealand
Women's International League for Peace and Freedom

Nicaragua:
Centre for Information and Advisory Services Health
Grupo Propositivo de Cabildeo

International Peoples Health Council
Regional Committee for Community Health

Nigeria:
Friends of the Earth Nigeria

Norway:
Friends of the Earth Norway
Red Electoral Alliance

Palestine:
Eco-Peace - Middle East Environmental NGO Forum

Pakistan:
Society for Conservation and Protection of Environment (SCOPE)

Philippines:
Alternate Forum for Research in Mindanao (AFRIM), Inc, Philippines
Asian NGO Coalition for Agrarian Reform and Rural Development
Center for Alternative Development
Ecological Society of the Philippines
Institute for Popular Democracy
Lingkod Tao-Kalikasan

Poland:
CEECAP-Poland
Polish Ecological Club

Portugal:
Ambiental para Barlavento

Romania:
Ecosens
Rhodendendron

Russia:
Centre for Environment and Sustainable Development "Eco-Accord"
Eco-Defense
Environmental Education Coordination Center
Green Cross
Green World
KE Association
Socio-Ecological Union
St. Petersburg Society of Naturalists
World Information Service on Energy (WISE)

Slovakia:
Centre for Environmental Public Advocacy
SOSNA, Center for Sustainable Alternatives

Slovenia:
LABECO - Centre for Environmental Research
Institute for Cultural Ecology
The Slovenian Foundation for Sustainable Development
Umanotera

South Africa:
South African Municipal Workers Union

South Korea:
Green Korea United

Sri Lanka:
- Environmental Foundation Ltd.

Sweden:
- Africa Groups of Sweden
- Forests, Trees & People at Department of Rural Development Studies
- Friends of the Earth Sweden
- Swedish Society for Nature Conservation

Switzerland:
- Friends of the Earth Switzerland
- Swiss Interchurch and Cambodia Programme
- Swiss Coalition of Development Organizations
- Women's World Summit Foundation

Thailand:
- Focus on the Global South

United Kingdom:
- Abantu for Development
- Action on Disability and Development
- Catholic Fund for Overseas Development (CAFOD)
- Centre for Complexity and Change
- Christian Ecology Link
- Environmental Investigation Agency
- Friends of the Earth England, Wales and Northern Ireland
- Green Party of England and Wales
- Iona Community
- International Coalition for Development Action
- Lancashire Global Education Centre
- Socialists' Environment and Resources Association
- Third World First
- World Development Movement

United States:
- 4D Manifestations
- 8th Day Centre for Justice
- Alliance for Democracy
- Alternatives in Action!
- Animal Welfare Institute
- Arizona Toxics Information
- Asia Pacific Environmental Exchange
- Association of State Green Parties
- Border Ecology Project
- Boulder Independent Business Alliance
- California Fair Trade Coalition
- Campaign for Labour Rights
- Carolina Interfaith Task Force on Central America
- Centre for Sustainable Systems
- Centre for International Environmental Law (CIEL)
- Centre of Concern
- Centre for Popular Economics
- Chicago Religious Leadership Network of Latin America

Chicago Metropolitan Sanctuary Alliance
Chicago Local of the Democratic Socialists of America
Citizen's Alliance of Santa Barbara
Coalition for Forests
Comboni Missionaries, Justice and Peace Resource Centre
Community Nutrition Institute
Cornell Greens
Cornucopia Network of New Jersey
Cross-Border Network for Justice and Solidarity
Culture's Edge
Cumberland Counties for Peace and Justice
Defenders of Wildlife
Democratic Reform News
Democratic Socialists of America
Development GAP
EarthWINS
Employment Research Association
Epicentre
Fair Trade Coalition of Colorado
Federal Land Action Group
Fifty Years is Enough
Friends of the Earth United States
General Board of Church & Society of the United Methodist Church
Global Exchange
Global Corporate Accountability Issue Group
Greater Kansas City Fair Trade Coalition
Green Table
Green Party of Rhode Island
Ground Work for a Just World
Guatemala News and Information Bureau
Hightower & Associates
Howard County Friends of Central America and the Caribbean
Institute for Agriculture and Trade Policy
Institute Justice Team for Sisters of Mercy of the Americas
Institute for Food and Development Policy
Inter-Hemispheric Resource Centre
Interfaith Centre on Corporate Responsibility
International Law Centre for Human, Economic and Environmental Defense (HEED)
International Forum on Globalization
International Union of Electricians (IUE) Local 1140
International Brotherhood of Teamsters
International Labour Rights Fund
International Study for Gandhian Studies
International Rivers Network
International Peoples Health Council - North America
Jobs with Justice - Portland
Jobs with Justice - Mid-Willamette Valley Chapter

Kansas Farmers Union
Klamath Siskiyou Wildlands Centre
Latin American Energy Response Network
Leadership Council of Sisters, Servants of the Immaculate Heart of Mary
Long Island Progressive Coalition
Maryknoll Education Centre
McKeever Institute of Economic Policy Analysis
Medical Mission Sisters' Alliance for Justice
Midwest Center for Labour Research
Mining Impact Coalition of Wisconsin
Minnesota Fair Trade Coalition
Mountcastle International
National Family Farm Coalition
National Wildlife Federation
National Farmers' Union
National Commission for Economic Conversion & Disarmament
Native Forest Council
Network for Environmental and Economic Responsibility
NETWORK: A National Catholic Social Justice Lobby
Network for Environmental and Economic Responsibility
of the United Church of Christ
New Economic Foundation
New York Student Environmental Action Coalition
New Jersey Citizen Action
New Jersey Work Environment Council
New Jersey State Council of YWCAs
New York Citizen Action
New York State Labour-Religion Coalition
Nicaragua Network
Northern Sanitiam Watershed Council
Pacific Environment & Resources Centre
Pax Christi-Maine
Pax Christi Michigan State Council
Peace Action of San Mateo County California
Peace and Justice Centre of Vermont
Pennsylvania Consumer Action Network
Pennsylvania Fair Trade Campaign
Pesticide Action Network North America
Pittsburgh Labour Action Network for the Americas
Prairie Rural Action
Presbyterian Church
Progressive Review
Project Biodiversity in Public Forests Network
Project South: Institute for the Elimination of Poverty & Genocide
Project Underground
Public Citizen's Global Trade Watch
Pure Food Campaign

RAFI-USA
Rainforest Action Network
Reform Party of Texas
Resource Centre for the Americas
Robert F. Kennedy Memorial Centre for Human Rights
Rural Vermont
San Francisco Labour Council for Latin American Advancement
Sane Distribution
Sierra Club
Sisters of the Holy Cross, Notre Dame
Society for a Clean Environment
Southeast Regional Economic Justice Network
Steering Committee of Association of State Green Parties
Student Environmental Action Network Montana
Sustainable Alternative to the Global Economy (SAGE)
Synapses
Texas Centre for Policy Studies
Texas Fair Trade Campaign
The Edmonds Institute
Tourism Industry Development Council
U.S. Catholic Mission Association
United for a Fair Economy
United Church Board for World Ministries
United Church of Christ
United Labour Council of Redding and Berks County
United Electrical, Radio and Machine Workers of America
University Conversion Project
Upavim Crafts
Values Project
Washington Office on Latin America
Western Ancient Forest Campaign
Wetlands Preserve
Witness for Peace
Woodstock Institute
Workgroup for People's Health & Rights
World Hunger Year
Worldview
WorldWise

Ukraine:

Green Peace of Izmail
Mama-86
National Ecological Centre
Ukrainian Society for Sustainable Development

Uruguay:

World Rainforest Movement

Yugoslavia:

Centre for Non-Violent Conflict Resolution

NDP MINORITY REPORT ON THE MAI

Submission to *The Sub-Committee on International Trade, Trade Disputes and Investment*

The NDP, like many who expressed their opposition to the MAI, is not against a rules-based global economy. We believe in rules, and in the need to regulate economic activity in the public interest. We welcome the prospect of multilateral agreements and global rules that would create a world in which nations are not played off against each other, and in which no unfair advantage is taken of business, labour, the environment or government. Precisely because of this we do not believe in a rules-based global economic regime, such as that which the MAI seeks to establish, which gives special status to the rights of investors.

Granting various forms of binding protection to investors while making workers, environments, societies, and cultures subservient to investor rights, to be protected only by lofty sounding, non-enforceable language in various agreements, is an example of perverse priorities. There is no urgency to protect further the rights of those who are already very powerful. Many of the global corporations who seek to further limit the power of governments to require certain behaviours of them, are already larger and more powerful economic units than many of the governments they would like to further subdue.

What is urgently needed is new forms of global governance that can hold global corporations accountable to the common good in the way that national governments were once able to discipline earlier forms of corporate activity in the interests of society. For instance, we urgently need an enforceable rules-based global economic regime that requires all countries and corporations to adhere to the core labour standards of freedom of association, free collective bargaining, prohibition of forced labour, elimination of child labour exploitation and non-discrimination in the workplace. Those who are content to complete or perfect the enshrining and enforcement of investor rights, while leaving the enforcement of corporate responsibilities and the rights of workers, the environment, and societies for another day, perhaps even another generation, have much to answer for by way of moral reasoning.

The NDP holds, therefore, that the MAI, from a social democratic point of view, is irredeemable, and that no combination of reservations and exemptions can make up for the overall unacceptability of the general provisions of the MAI, and the global corporate agenda of which it is the latest manifestation.

The MAI, by the government's own admission, is an attempt to replicate NAFTA at the level of the OECD, in the hope that the MAI itself can one day be replicated at the level of the WTO. And NAFTA, of course, was a replication of the Canada-U.S. Free Trade Agreement. The strategy of those who have successfully advocated a liberalization of trade, investment and services, and a limitation of the role of government that goes far beyond anything that would have been regarded as possible 15 years ago, has been to start with smaller agreements that become prototypes for larger agreements.

To its everlasting shame, Canada, a country which became one of the best countries in the world by employing the power of government in a positive way to offset the inequity and injustice of the marketplace, has been a major player in the development of such prototypes. This tradition continues with the MAI. Unable to overcome, at the WTO, the objection of developing countries to a liberalized investment discipline that would hamstring the ability of their governments to make sure foreign investment actually helps rather than hinders development, the more powerful countries in the world, urged on by the international investment community, want to be able to present the MAI as an established reality that poorer countries abstain from at their peril.

The most significant and exclusive right the MAI would entrench for investors expands on a feature of NAFTA that enables investors to take governments to a dispute settlement process established by the agreement. Under the existing NAFTA investor-state dispute settlement process, U.S.-based Ethyl Corporation is demanding $350 million compensation from the Canadian government for profits lost due to the banning of the toxic gasoline additive MMT. The NDP finds this feature of NAFTA to be offensive, and therefore cannot condone its extension through the MAI. It gives corporations an inappropriate status, sets up a binding, secretive process that will have not only a legal effect, but also a "chilling" effect, by virtue of which governments may, out of fear of such litigation, refrain from environmental and other legislative actions.

This "chilling" effect is enhanced by the way in which the MAI expands the definition of "expropriation" to go beyond tangible assets such as property or money to include measures "having equivalent economic effect" and for which "payment of prompt, adequate, effective compensation" is required. This expanded definition, combined with a definition of investment that is extremely broad, including investment in its pre-establishment phase, means that a comprehensive range of what are more properly regarded as domestic political choices can become the object of a binding international arbitration.

The binding investor-state arbitration is stunningly illustrative of the bias that exists within the current global corporate agenda. Neither the NAFTA, nor now the MAI, contain provisions by which a trade union could take a government to a binding dispute settlement process for violation of core labour standards. Global agreements on environmental measures to save the planet are to be voluntary. No opportunity is provided, for example, for the Sierra Club to take a government to binding dispute settlement process for violating emission standards or ozone depletion protocols. But for investors, the sky's the limit when it comes to enforceability of their rights. Corporate responsibilities, however, as sometimes set out in various guidelines, will continue to be voluntary.

The aforementioned features of the MAI, when added to other objections that the NDP has about the agreement, such as the uncertainty about the effectiveness of reservations in protecting healthcare, education and social services, the extension of national treatment to "investment incentives," the stigmatization of "performance requirements", and the possibility that the provinces will also be included, give rise to an even greater objection about this affront to the flexibility of democratic decision-making.

The MAI would bind Canada for 20 years. Unlike even the NAFTA, which has a six-month notice period for termination, MAI requires at least a five-year period before notice can be given, followed by the requirement to honour existing obligations to existing foreign investors and companies for another 15 years. This is a feature of the MAI that would bind several Parliaments, and is so anti-democratic on the face of it that the MAI cannot be supported by the New Democratic Party of Canada.

NOTES ON THE FEBRUARY 1998 NEGOTIATING TEXT

This is a quick and by no means definitive comparison of the new (February, 1998) and old (May, 1997) drafts of the MAI. As noted below, there is one additional clause which deserves public attention and scrutiny: a measure to limit "unbound" country-specific exceptions.

* * *

- The very broad definition of investment remains intact; e.g., government concessions and licences and intellectual property are still covered.
- The core principles of national treatment and most favoured nation remain intact.
- There are slight changes re performance requirements. Prohibition of requiring maintenance of a given level of employment has been replaced with a prohibition on requiring employment of a given level of nationals. This seems to mean that foreign investment approval could be conditional on maintenance of jobs. Prohibition of trade-related performance requirments and R-and-D requirements remains. (As in the May draft, it is recognized that countries can require job creation, R-and-D, etc., in return for subsidies.)
- National Treatment and MFN still apply to privatizations, although alternative formulations qualify this obligation and some would allow for share-holding restrictions.
- Provisions re monopolies and state concessions are basically unchanged.
- National Treatment still applies to the granting of investment incentives. It is still envisaged that there should be consultations

over incentives, and perhaps later negotiation of MAI disciplines.

- There is a new section qualifying (or simply clarifying) the impact of the MAI re intellectual property rights. The significance of this new section is difficult to assess at this stage.
- The alternatives already in play re not lowering environmental and labour standards in order to attract an investment are repeated. There is a draft new clause, based on GATT Article XX, providing that environmental measures would be exempt from MAI disciplines, though this is extremely heavily qualified. One delegation (the U.S.?) has proposed much more open-ended language on environmental measures which seems to amount to a carve-out and may be worthy of support. (This is in the Annex to the MAI.)
- Provisions re investment protection remain unchanged; i.e., the MAI could prohibit "unreasonable" measures and governments would still have to pay compensation in the event of expropriation or "measures having equivalent effect."
- The Investor-State dispute settlement mechanism remains intact.
- There are still general exceptions only for public security and (heavily restricted) balance of payments measures.
- Provisions which would allow for "unbound" country-specific exceptions (e.g., the cultural and public services exceptions Marchi has said Canada must have) remain in brackets. Further, *a new bracketed provision IX(c) has been added which provides that future measures should not require a foreign investor to sell or dispose of an asset. This would mean that, even if there was, for example, a health and public services "unbound" exception, we could not take privatized health services back into the public or not-for-profit sector. Even if there was a cultural exemption, a future government could not reverse previous liberalization measures if this required divestiture.*
- The agreement would still remain in place for up to 20 years.
- There is no provision to exempt sub-national levels of government, and one delegation has proposed language to make it clear that all investors should be placed on the same basis as domestic investors by sub-national governments.

LIST OF CONTRIBUTORS

FOREWORD

Bob White is President of the Canadian Labour Congress

THE MAI. WHAT IS IT? WHAT'S WRONG WITH IT

Andrew Jackson is Senior Economist with the Canadian Labour Congress and a Research Associate of the Canadian Centre for Policy Alternatives.

FIGHTING THE MAI

Elizabeth May is Executive Director of the Sierra Club of Canada.

THE MAI AND DISPUTE SETTLEMENT

Steven Shrybman is Executive Director of the West Coast Environmental Law Association.

THE MAI AND FIRST NATIONS

Ovide Mercredi is the former National Chief of the Assembly of First Nations and is currently a visiting professor at the University of Lethbridge.

THE MAI AND LABOUR RIGHTS

Roy Jones is Senior Policy Advisor with TUAC, the Trade Union Advisory Committee to the OECD in Paris. TUAC is a trade union organization which has official consultative status with the OECD.

The MAI and Human Rights

John Foster is Ariel F. Sallows Professor of Human Rights, College of Law, University of Saskatchewan. Former director of OXFAM-Canada. Dr. Foster has extensive experience in human rights, world development and Canadian Foreign Policy.

The MAI and the Environment

Michelle Swenarchuk is Director of International Programs with the Canadian Environmental Law Association.

The MAI and Culture

Gary T. Neil is a consultant working on cultural policy issues with Neil Craig Associates of Toronto.

The MAI and Public and Social Services

Matt Sanger is a Senior Researcher with the Canadian Union of Public Employees in Ottawa.

The MAI and Municipalities

Barry Appleton is a leading international trade lawyer with Appleton and Associates International Lawyers.

The MAI and Telecommunications

Sid Shniad is Research Director of the Telecommunications Workers Union in BC.

Andy Reddick is Director of Research at the Public Interest Advocacy Centre, a not-for-profit organization representing the interests of consumers. (Co-author with Sid Shniad of the chapter on telecommuniations.)

The MAI and the Provinces

Ian Robinson teaches in the Department of Political Science at Reed College in Oregon. He formerly worked in the area of inter-governmental relations for the Ontario Government, and has written widely on the impacts of NAFTA.

The MAI and Foreign Direct Investment

Andrew Jackson is Senior Economist with the Canadian Labour Congress and a Research Associate of the Canadian Centre for Policy Alternatives.

The MAI and Developing Countries

Martin Khor is Director of the Malaysia-based Third World Network.

The MAI and the World Economy

Greg Albo teaches Political Science at York University and has written widely on employment issues in Canada and internationally.

Chris Roberts teaches in the Political Science Department of York University. (Co-author with Greg Albo of The Mai and the World Economy.)